MY

PISCES

HEART

ALSO BY JENNIFER NEAL

Notes on Her Color

MY PISCES HEART

A Black Immigrant's Search for Home
Across Four Continents

JENNIFER NEAL

CATAPULT NEW YORK

MY PISCES HEART

This is a work of nonfiction. However, some names and identifying details of individuals have been changed to protect their privacy, correspondence has been shortened for clarity, and dialogue has been reconstructed from memory.

First Catapult edition: 2024

ISBN: 978-1-64622-184-4

Library of Congress Control Number: 2024941159

Jacket design by Farjana Yasmin
Jacket image of waves © Shutterstock / marukopum;
airplane © Shutterstock / ILYA AKINSHIN
Book design by Laura Berry

Catapult
New York, NY
books.catapult.co

Printed in the United States of America

10 9 8 7 6 5 4 3 2 1

For Warren Neal Jr. (1919–2004),
who gave me the courage to leave

And Brenda Neal (1953–2012),
who gave me a path to return

This is my letter to The World
That never wrote to Me

—EMILY DICKINSON

Contents

PART 3:
NAARM (MELBOURNE), VICTORIA, AUSTRALIA

PART 4:
BERLIN, GERMANY

Preface

WHEN I WAS A YOUNG GIRL, MY FATHER'S CAREER ambitions uprooted and replanted us repeatedly—which meant that, approximately every three years, I could become someone else. I spent my adolescence learning and relearning the necessary art of reinvention, which helped me blend in with different crowds at different schools: goths, refugees, artists, criminals, and bookish outcasts with hearts of solid gold. We were not a military family but a banking one, which, for many millennials forced to endure the global financial crisis and its subsequent apocalyptic hellscape, represents something much more dangerous. For me, it created a problematic relationship between money, self, sacrifice, and stability—which has continued to shape and influence my choices to relocate overseas—from being an English teacher in Japan, to falling in love in Australia, to attending a prestigious art school in Chicago, and finding my long-lost community of creative misanthropes in Berlin. Not to mention the delicious meals, foreign embarrassments, and romantic interludes

that took place in all the in-between places, at indeterminate moments, while I was being imprecise and unsettled all across God's
green Earth.

My transience as a kid gave me the skills needed to turn my
adolescence from a minefield of shame into an exercise in curiosity. Surviving the instability of my youth allowed me to navigate
foreign countries, acclimate to unfamiliar cultures, and learn new
languages that bored new holes into my brain, becoming portals to
other worlds as an adult. As I've grown more confident in applying
those tools, I've overcome encounters with police officers, racist
in-laws and coworkers, chronic illness, government bureaucracy,
personal loss, and transformative heartbreak. Immigration is an
experience that varies wildly from person to person. My journey
up to this point, which began years before I even had a passport,
has been defined just as much by running toward something better
as it has been by running away from something worse.

When I decide to move, I don't feel as if I'm making a grand
political statement because I assume that the place I'm leaving
never wanted me there to begin with. It's the pervasive indignity
of feeling unwanted that lies at the heart of my relationship with
homelife and the environments within which it exists. And yet, I
know objectively that immigrants prop up entire economies. We
subscribe to the rhetoric of hard work while getting crushed by
the broken promises of politicians who use us as talking points
to get reelected before thanking us by turning their backs on us
altogether. When countries like the United States, Germany, and
Japan discuss immigration reform to address the labor shortage
caused by plummeting birth rates, immigrants flock from the
Global South to meet that demand. But the West treats immigration as a framework for all the things gone wrong, like drugs
and crime, never for the things that go right. When underlying
issues inherent to the hypercapitalism that led to those declining

birth rates and labor shortages continue to go unaddressed, and politicians need someone to blame so they can get reelected, it's people who look like me who have that welcome mat unceremoniously pulled out from beneath their feet. The result has been a frustrating but not-unpredictable rise in nationalism that hinges on a fragile social psychology where officials rely on an ignorant electorate to continue denying their collective role in oppressing whole ethnic groups, whole races and religious affiliations, which is to say—other human beings who are conveniently robbed of their humanity first at home and then abroad.

Having a U.S. passport has shielded me from much bureaucratic bigotry abroad, but it has not inoculated me from the toxic rhetoric of right-wing political campaigns in Australia or the anger I feel in watching my skin color weaponized for votes in Germany. It has not stopped me from obsessively following elections so that I can decide where to be—and how carefully to exist. Immigration is always a political decision because it is an indictment of the duty of care a country provides. No, I will not live in a country without socialized health care. No, I will not live in a country without gun control. Yes, I will question my future in a place where I'm more prone to state-sanctioned violence because of the color of my skin, my gender, or the person I choose to love. Always. So while these decisions are inherently political, they are first and foremost about survival.

I would never compare my circumstances to my grandparents' generation, though I do feel that their decisions to move in, around, and out of the South were similarly motivated. There were 6.5 million African Americans who completely transformed the demographic makeup of the United States between 1916 and 1970 during the Great Migration.[1] And still, for many Americans, it is difficult to accept that one of the world's greatest migratory phenomena was a direct result of the political disenfranchisement, economic exploitation, and sheer terror that came with being Black in the Jim Crow South. Detroit and Chicago became two of the Blackest cities in the country,* and both became hubs of political influence that gave rise to the Black Power movement of the 1960s and transformed labor unions in the industrial North, thus reconstructing the entire country's sociopolitical landscape.[2] Migration is responsible not only for reshaping the United States, but for creating the country as we know it, past, present, and future.

In 2016, after the United Kingdom voted to leave the European Union in a countrywide referendum, Dr. Ulysses Burley III coined the term Blaxit. This was initially a satirical response to the resentment that British voters felt toward immigrants, infuriating them to the point of leaving the European Union behind altogether.[†] But unlike Brexit, Burley's word was a response to the ubiquitous systemic, institutional, social, and economic racism that continues to mar the Black American experience. What began as a tongue-in-cheek hypothetical question that asked, "What if Black people decided to blaxodus their Black asses elsewhere?" is part of an actual global movement replete with online forums, relocation agencies, and communities that enthusiastically reject the idea that the cultures we're born into are the ones we have to live with for the rest of our lives.

While the term was only coined in 2016, Blaxit has a long, rich history spanning centuries. Frederick Douglass, then designated a fugitive slave, first traveled to the British Isles in 1845 to drum up support for abolition where he met Irish-independence activist Daniel O'Connell.[3] Their discussions reshaped Douglass's

---

* In 2022, Jackson, Mississippi, became the Blackest city in the United States.
† A poll conducted by the Savanta data-research group in December 2022 shows that 65 percent of Britons now favor a referendum to rejoin the European Union.

perspective on liberation. It wasn't enough to abolish slavery in the United States because oppression was an interconnected global system that had to be fought everywhere, in all its forms and functions. In 1848, he attended the first women's rights convention at Seneca Falls to support suffrage, even printing in his paper *The North Star* that "there can be no reason in the world for denying to woman the exercise of the elective franchise, or a hand in making and administering the laws of the land. Our doctrine is, that 'Right is of no sex.'"[4]

Black queer feminist, writer, and poet Audre Lorde spent eight years on and off in Berlin, working with Black German writers and activists like Katharina Oguntoye and May Ayim, who, in their collaboration, helped to articulate the Afro-Deutsch movement, which later formed Die Initiative Schwarze Menschen in Deutschland, an organization that incessantly pushed the German government to formally acknowledge, apologize, and offer reparations for the Herero and Namaqua Genocide in Namibia from 1904 to 1907—finally succeeding in 2021.[5*] The Great Migration chapter of Blaxit gave us writer and playwright James Baldwin, whose mother fled an abusive partner in Maryland and resettled in Harlem in 1924, at the height of its Renaissance. Baldwin navigated the insidious racial abuse of the "progressive North" before embarking on his own Blaxit quest to France in 1948. He left with only forty dollars in his pocket, convinced that no life anywhere else could be worse than what he had endured in the United States.

Even the Underground Railroad was a form of migration, one rooted in the simple idea that no human being can or should own

---

* In 2020, the German government offered €10 million in compensation but then increased it to €1.1 billion in 2021. The amount was agreed to be paid out over thirty years, but the declaration omits the words *declaration* or *compensation*.

another—the same tenants underscored in a constitution that many argue never applied to all its constituents. This horrific reality was validated in 1857, when the U.S. Supreme Court decreed that African Americans could not and never would be citizens of the United States in the *Dred Scott v. Sanford* case, a ruling that was upheld until the Thirteenth and Fourteenth Amendments were ratified in 1865 and 1868, respectively.[6]

Now, I look back on these histories of migration and immigration and I see how crucially they were rooted in survivalism. But while the United States is known for its racist history, as well as its ongoing struggles to recognize and atone for that history, I've seen how centering that history in global discourse has been used to overshadow Black histories in other parts of the world—including the countries I've called home. Racism has been designated as an American problem, and the rest of the world issues a collective sigh of relief whenever they're given an opportunity to deny the fact that Black people have existed, been oppressed, and resisted in countries far east, west, north, and south of the United States for centuries. Black people have also shaped the culture and political discourse in Japan, are the Traditional Owners of Australia, and have asserted their rights to self-determination as a radical feminist movement in Germany. I've tried my best to track down stories of individuals and movements with nuance, detail, and specificity, incorporating my own story whenever relevant. What I have discovered is that while racism has been mining from the same well of oppression and erasure for centuries, Blackness is vibrant, dynamic, and defiant in every corner of the world. And for the collective diaspora, our "lost home" has become an important symbol not only used to create communities everywhere we are, but a shared memory that challenges and rejects any discourse on national history that tries to sanitize the horrors of colonialism.[7]

There is no one way to be Black. That realization, however

simple, has changed me. It has changed how I see the world. It has changed how I see myself. It took until my early thirties for me to realize that, while no place is completely safe for a queer Black woman, the place I called "home" growing up wasn't even up to the task of trying. My decisions to move, and where, have always been about survivalism. But I haven't always been honest with myself about that. That would have meant admitting to a vulnerability—and a trove of anxieties that I wish did not exist. Identifying my political motivations only came when I allowed myself to acknowledge that I haven't always felt safe where I was—and developing that level of self-awareness and maturity took time. In some regard, immigration has forced me to confront the unconscious. Despite having had a girlfriend in high school and in college when I lived in Florida, I didn't accept that I was queer until I was thirty-three, kissing a beautiful Icelandic artist with bright-red lipstick in Kreuzberg's Roses Bar, beneath the sparkling disco lights surrounded by drunken couples of various genders who only looked up at me to smile, as they embraced their lovers to do the same. I could only accept that in myself once it felt safe to do so.

The pursuit of safety—safe environments, safe people, safe policies, and safe housing—has also exacted its toll, particularly on my mental health. The benefits to having a loose attachment style to a place or an environment are often romanticized in travel literature, but what is the actual cost? Exactly how stable is someone who has an overwhelming anxiety of hanging pictures up on the wall or unpacking pans from cardboard boxes? How secure can someone be when they're constantly worried that things will get so bad that they have to leave again? What is left of someone who quarters their heart into tiny pieces on different continents that are left bleeding in different languages? To put it in very Western terms: What is the price? Any immigrant of ordinary means, especially immigrants of color, can confirm that the mental and emotional cost amounts to more than all the currency in the world.

I have paid that toll in several significant ways: I have left my loved ones in a country that I am now watching slowly crumble from the outside. I have loved people who used the guise of "cultural differences" to cloak the bigotry that prevented them from loving me back. I have battled tooth and nail with anxiety, guilt, and depression that have, at times, left me paralyzed with despair and hopelessness. But it's when I return to the United States that I realize the biggest cost of all: the severe cognitive dissonance that comes with realizing I no longer recognize the beloved homeland in which my most formative memories were created; I see a burgeoning autocracy, an ultramilitarized hypercapitalist nightmare, and an ethnocentric empire on the verge of collapse. And that simple realization has left me with no option *besides* leaving. That is why I do, time and again, because everything I have sacrificed and endured has allowed me to have a significantly better life than the one I would have lived had I stayed.

No one place has proven to be my personal utopia, but that hasn't stopped me from trying to make one wherever I go. While this book will only focus on the places where I have lived, my life as an immigrant has involved traveling to more than forty different countries where race and gender have never failed to be a factor in how I was contextualized, and how I in turn investigated my surroundings. On the cobblestone streets of La Plaza de la Virgen in the southeastern Spanish town of Valencia, I encountered a young boy at a produce stand who stared at me as if I were a mythical creature. When I waved at him and said, "Hola!" his mother spat on me and pulled him away while others sneered at me. In Beijing, complete strangers approached me in a grocery store to rub my arm with their fingers to see if the skin color came off. In Marrakech, shopkeepers at the local souks tried to lure me to their stalls of colorful fabrics and polished silver by calling me Beyoncé. And on a daily basis in Berlin, when I catch the strident glare of a complete stranger on the subway or in the street, I have to ask myself the question: Does this person want to fuck or fight me?

This book is loosely inspired by my time as the Blaxit columnist at *The Root*, where I interviewed Black immigrants in Berlin, Stockholm, Jakarta, Melbourne, Seoul, Tokyo, and Auckland. Each person had a unique reason for relocating—money, love, and stable political environments—and while the terms of urgency may have varied, each person described the decision to uproot as a matter of necessity, not luxury.

In the conversations I had with interviewees for Blaxit, I have affirmed that not only do Black people have a multitude of stories to tell about their experiences as migrants, but that when we do, they're often coded in language that depicts us as invaders and unwelcome guests to otherwise sovereign land and a burden to their pure white inhabitants who are obviously more comfortable being the invaders themselves. In 2018, I watched in frustration as now-former Australian home affairs minister Peter Dutton used fearmongering and demagoguery to ascribe the violent choices of a few young men who had brawled and shoplifted to depict several different African communities as one monolithic criminal enterprise in need of state-sanctioned discipline. In 2016, I witnessed firsthand the rise of Germany's far-right political party after now-former chancellor Angela Merkel provided refuge to more than one million Syrian asylum seekers during a bloody civil war. Time and again, I've watched with complete bewilderment as Black and Brown immigrants and refugees become people who *leech off of government benefits* while white immigrants are given the tools to *work their way to the top.*

All the while, immigration has positioned people as a "problem" to be solved or a "question" to be answered, but never the

racist institutions and policies that create tidal waves of immigration every year. People living with disease or disability are problems for immigration authorities, not the immigration policies that
borrow from eugenics and ethnic cleansing practices more than
one hundred years old. Syrian immigrants were the problem, not
U.S. President Bush who invaded Iraq after September 11, creating
a power vacuum that gave rise to the Islamic State, which waged a
bloody civil war in Syria that led to the mass exodus of 1.5 million
people to Europe. But nobody has rallied to kick him out of the
country or strip him of his U.S. citizenship (much to my dismay).
People always pay the price for the barbarity of institutions.

Conversely, while writing about the racist bureaucracy of
predominantly non-Black countries for *The Root*, I was presented with another argument: if we, Black people, are to move
anywhere—it should only be back to Africa. That *did* surprise
me for several reasons: First, it relied on a flattening of the entire African continent into a single monolith that standardized
all fifty-four countries into one ethnic group with a homogenous
history and culture, a single language, and identical political systems. As if a cis-heterosexual Black man from Jamaica would have
the same experience moving to, say, Kampala as a trans-queer
Black woman from San Francisco. The other reason it surprised
me is that this attitude again organizes Black stories of immigration into those that are more valuable and those that are less. A
Black person deciding to move to South Korea isn't inherently less
important than a Black person moving to Ghana. Furthermore,
I've always felt that the argument "Black people only belong in
Africa" is a trauma response to governing bodies who perpetuate
white supremacy by constantly telling us where we *don't* belong.
By replicating those same oppressive ideas within our own communities, we do a disservice to the vast richness that is contained
within what it means to be Black, and why being Black in and of

itself is cause for celebration, regardless of where a Black person chooses to exist, because Black life enriches every corner of the world. More importantly, Black life *deserves* to exist in any part of the world, for no reason whatsoever. And when I'm told where I do or do not belong, I'm always struck at how that argument, regardless of who is sharing it, loses sight of that.

The biggest lesson I've learned, and the most important lesson I would like to impart, is that *all* Black people are entitled to these expeditions of self-discovery just as much as anyone else— regardless of where they are, regardless of who they are, and regardless of whom they love. That our relationships with home are also transient concepts, affected by politics, economics, love, and circumstance. And we are entitled to share them, to scream them at the top of our lungs, from the tallest rooftop on the highest mountain peak—whether it's Kilimanjaro or Fuji-san. They are diverse. They are emotional. They are courageous, powerful, maddening, heartbreaking, hilarious, and—because this is the time to say it as loudly as possible—they matter. My story is one of many that rests, sometimes uncomfortably, within all those parameters. And while it would not have been possible had it not been for the bravery of the people who navigated these spaces before me—it is still mine, and mine alone.

I hope it encourages you to write your own.

MY

PISCES

HEART

1.

Stick with the Devil You Know

I DO NOT MISS THE UNITED STATES. BUT I MISS "AMERICA" all the time. The first is a nation-state, and the second is an idea. I live between those two equally significant realities, knowing that the same austere jingoism that would have kept me tied to that place has kept me invested in its redemption—from a distance. I know that's a contradiction. Only after leaving did it become clear to me just how much the United States has failed so many people, especially Black families like mine who sacrificed intimate parts of themselves only to be compensated with a country's very conditional love. My family has served in wars that should never have been fought, went to schools where they were not welcome, and worked themselves into poor health under the requirements of late-stage capitalism only to retire with chronic diseases. Perhaps this is most starkly embodied by my own grandfather, a single soldier belonging to more than one million African American men and women who served in World War II. After leaving Europe, he returned to a war at home that is still being fought. The dementia that took him from me has been taking members of my family for at least 150 years, and I blame more than our bruised genetics.* I blame the memories that battered them. I blame the experiences that they tried to bury by forgetting, and I blame the way they always come back to haunt us. If my grandfather were alive and lucid today, I am certain that he wouldn't be the least bit confused about my conflicted feelings toward the country he helped defend, nor would he have any doubt about why I chose to leave. Leaving is better than trying to forget what the body always remembers.

People say I'm closer to my dad's side of the family because I act like him, but I think it's because I'm more like *his* dad—who disliked more things than he loved, especially being outside the comfort of his own home. He would visit us for only a few hours at a time, not staying over because it felt too much like being in debt, and he didn't want anything from anyone. He was fond of playing checkers with his friends outside of the community center in Haines City, a trucker cap pulled low over his brow, and a pencil 'stache on his top lip. He was quiet, something Mom described as prescriptive of men "from a certain generation." But he opened up about his life in letters to me, which were always lined with crisp five-, ten-, or even twenty-dollar (!) bills, and sometimes with photographs, like one of him shipping off to France during World War II in 1941, giving the camera every bit of the quiet attitude he was known for during his long life.

Georgia felt too small to my grandpa after he returned from France, so he joined the Great Migration. But he didn't join the exodus to the industrial North. Between 1910 and 1930, Southern urban areas' growth rate rose from 17 to 33 percent—expanding

---

* When I began to trace my family history, I connected with a distant relative in North Carolina who said that my great-great-great-grandfather suffered from either dementia or Alzheimer's disease and that there are accounts of him running around his farm in his underwear chasing chickens with a shotgun.

at an even faster rate than many Northern cities like Chicago and Detroit.[1] Choosing the comfort and familiarity of the agricultural South, my grandfather left Georgia for central Florida in 1946, where he picked fruit and drove a fertilizer truck for Haines City until he retired.

My singular visit to his birthplace of Woodland put my own family's migration into generous perspective. It's a single-stoplight town that stood at around 301 residents—mostly farmers—in 2022, and still shrinking year after year.* One day soon, it might not exist at all, except in the minds of people who remembered where it once was. In order for my family to get to where we are, someone needed to take a first step. So we picked up where he left off, and his life became the first chapter of a story that others and I are still writing. From the beginning, he was the iron rudder in my family's history, steering us in the direction of a better life.

When I was young, a lot of nineties movies made me romanticize kids getting into trouble in major cities like New York. They took the subway to school and went to MoMA for prom. I wanted to cut class and join them at the neighborhood pizza joint in Brooklyn, to run wild with them through the streets of Queens shouting curse words at one another with dropped Rs and gliding vowels. Being Southern felt, somehow, like being behind—chasing civilization through tall reeds of grass and sugarcane instead of skyscrapers made of glass and steel. Back then, Florida seemed like the last place on Earth where anything interesting ever happened. But my grandpa felt differently. His suspicion of anyone from New York became its own abiding personality trait—shared by every granny and every grandpa with a rusty screened-in porch across the Bible Belt.

---

* According to the 2021 U.S. Census. It's also one of many rural Southern towns with a decreasing population. In 2011, there were 401 residents.

It's a real stick-with-the-devil-you-know mentality, an attitude that spread across Old Black Dixie to caution against the perils of the Northeast and Midwest—for good reason. The South is a beast, but I saw how my relatives claimed it for themselves. Their resilience is forged from a kind of warped idea that, yes, our ancestors were once enslaved there, but why should *we* move somewhere else with the same problems and less sunshine? That only lets *white people* off the hook by making us invisible, so *they* can forget inflicting the trauma *we* carry with us. My grandparents would have just been trading in the Ku Klux Klan for the predatory housing policies of the New Deal's Home Owners' Loan Corporation, which began providing federal support to fund mortgage redlining as a means to segregate Black communities from white ones in 1933.[2] My uncles, aunts, and cousins continue to stick with the devils they know, each claiming a different corner of the South where, come what may, they have vowed to live and die. Even though I've chosen a different path altogether, I know there is something tremendous worth admiring in that kind of defiance.

My parents were the first in their families to attend desegregated schools and go to college. They were both born in what my mom once described to me as "the gutter beneath the poverty line" and chased money to eventually achieve financial freedom in North Carolina—the place where my father's family tree on the North American continent begins. Scottish plantation owner Alexander Torrey Purcell had a child with an enslaved woman that U.S. Census records recognize by the name of Sara, Sarai, or Darki, who gave birth to my great-great-grandfather Richard in 1840. Stick with the devil you know. If our family had an official coat of arms, that would be our motto, stitched across the sigil of a moving truck—but the unofficial slogan would definitely be "irony."

My brother and I were born in Charlotte. It's my birthplace, though I have no memories that would give me a sense of being *from* there. My recollection of Charlotte is distilled into a vague cluster of images: fireflies at night, white water rapids, blackberry bushes, dark carpet, and occasional views of Appalachia. Together, they weave the city's eclectic tapestry. And the more I learn, the more vibrant, complex, and dynamic that picture becomes: our biennial family reunions where distant cousins from five states remember the Scottish and Indigenous heritage of the farmers who owned our ancestors; visiting Chapel Hill's college campus during my senior year of high school; watching my best friend marry her husband in front of the charred palette of Greensboro's autumnal mountainscape; watching edited YouTube footage of Keith Lamont Scott's murder, shot by police; state representative Thom Tillis saying he didn't think of African Americans and Latinos as real North Carolinians in 2012, then winning a Senate seat in 2015 and reelection in 2020. That's where I was born: the Tar Heel State. Patron area of vinegar-based barbecue sauces and the racist slaughter that is the 1898 Wilmington massacre.*

God's country.

In 1986, Dad's job took us back to Florida. We landed in Clearwater, a city that is, in all ways good and bad, the fodder for a classic, vulgar Florida joke. If "Florida man" had a villain origin story, it would take place in Clearwater. He could have emerged from the sandy white shores, with a legion of stingrays at his back and a bucket of oysters in his hand. We lived in a middle-class neighborhood where citrus grew like weeds and a global Scientology headquarters has since sprouted. We lived across the street from a teacher who let me draw her pictures of mermaids and down the

---

* A coup led by white politicians, business owners, and uniformed police officers that resulted in the forced eviction of more than twenty-one hundred Black residents and the murder of at least sixty prominent Black magistrates, officials, and business owners.

street from a drug dealer whose son I scrapped with repeatedly. My memories from that place are potent with nostalgia, too obscured by sentimentality for an honest impression of the racist tensions. My memories of being sexually abused by an older white boy in after-school care are intercepted by the first time I saw *The Little Mermaid* in theaters—as well as the six times I dragged my mom back for an encore, and the time we drove around afterward singing "Under the Sea" with the windows rolled down and the salty air from the Gulf of Mexico all around us.

Clearwater was only two hours away from Polk County, so we saw my grandparents more often. Of all the things that blur together, I can still remember my grandma's house, lying on the living room floor while I colored with crayons. I still remember being picked up by my grandpa outside of the community center, hearing the chuckle through his throat when I wrapped my arms around his neck. Grandbabies are tiny people who give hardened old folks permission to become soft.

I will never forget what it felt like to come home to Clearwater after visiting them. When I push open the door in my mind, I can still enter our house in the city that taught me the meaning of the seasons and the sea, which I learned all over again through three more moves in Florida.

For my grandpa, Florida was the great land beyond, and I tried to keep that perspective by looking at every city as its own treasure trove of secrets, scars, and adventures. No one place ever felt or looked the same, not even in Florida. Tallahassee had hills like cliffs, Klansmen, and woods thick with ticks. It's a city that taught me about mud, snakes, and the cult of college football. Orlando was a stucco playground of theme parks and new megachurches that turned ripe with gospel each summer. It's a city that taught me about Jesus Christ, particularly when I began ballet lessons with an instructor who placed an empty chair across the studio and said that it represented God. She told us to "dance to Jesus," which sounded a lot like "dance for Jesus," and by the time my turn had come, had turned into "dance *on* Jesus"—and my young self gave his invisible lap the time of its life.

These homes never had a chance to solidify. My life from that period is drawn in wet sand. I tried to hold on to them when we left, as well as the people who lived there. Classmates and friends filled my packing boxes with goodbye gifts, notes, and cards—cursive promises of a lifelong friendship that magically expired after just a few months of protracted correspondence. When I left them behind, we exchanged a few letters. And when we stopped exchanging written letters, we made a silent agreement to move on and find new friends to break new promises to.

Eventually, I began throwing out the gifts as soon as I got them. There wasn't enough room in the truck.

I quietly shut away the part of myself that could attach to anything. I made it into a game where I always won, writing down estimates and calculations to see how long it took for me to forget someone. Six months became three, became one, became instantaneous—the moment our old house was out of sight, the memory of it blurred through a kaleidoscope of sharp, fragmented goodbyes. Now that I am invested in the idea of recalling and remembering, sometimes they come back to me in waves—and the feelings I repressed back then are no less devastating in middle age.

When I wrote to my grandpa, I complained about making new friends, about bullies, about being called racist insults at school. It must have sounded hilarious to a man born in 1919, but he never discounted what I said and was quick to offer empathy in his jagged shorthand—saying that I still had my family, and that was all that mattered. It was, quite possibly, the only thing we ever disagreed on. But I let it slide because he was my family too—and I *did* have him.

Our family's position improved each time we moved: a bigger house, a better school, a wealthier neighborhood with more successful neighbors. And yet within our home, there was always anxiety about cost. My parents would buy top choices of meat, then ration them out like we were going to war. They obsessed over cleaning our plates, washing everything in the sink to save water, even though we had a dishwasher. They bought fancy pantry items that then expired on our shelves because nobody was allowed to touch them. My parents had achieved that rare and incredible feat of overcoming the cycle of poverty in a single generation but struggled to relax into the affluence they had earned and deserved. They carted us from place to place while haunted by the threat that if we didn't stay mobile, we could be cast back to the badlands of scarcity. Still poor. Still Black. Still sticking with the devil we knew. They achieved their American dream, but the cost of social mobility also has a generational price—and it has exacted its toll.

As I finished my undergraduate studies, I weighed going to law school against going to art school, and somehow came up with "teach English in Japan," deferring my acceptance to the Chicago art school of my dreams. I didn't want to be a teacher in the long run, but I also knew that I wasn't ready to enter the U.S. labor market to work ninety hours a week with fourteen days of annual leave. If you had asked me then, I would have said that I didn't leave the United States for political reasons. I just wanted to see the world. But the fallout from the terrorist attacks on September 11, which happened during my freshman year, revealed the horrors of American reactionism I had always sensed lurking beneath friendships, in classrooms, across news reports, and deep within immigration policies that deported people, including one of my closest friends.

My brother had also enlisted in the army, and when the invasion of Iraq began, he volunteered for deployment. The military is a strong tradition in my family—seen as a favorable path for wayward youths of disinterested parents—and our parents encouraged him to enlist. I cried when he left. I tried begging, bartering, and then just refusing to believe it would happen—all the stages of grief. But he went anyway, and I ended my tenure at FSU fearing for his life. Halfway through his deployment in Iraq, he returned with all fingers, toes, and limbs still attached—contrary to the colorful ways in which my nightmares had dismembered him. He had left with a dream to be a musician and returned with pictures of bodies bleeding out in the desert. On his face, I recognized no discernible feeling besides contempt for the dark stains they left on the sand. No, my decision to leave wasn't political. But the world I was *leaving* was mired in political motivations to go. Shortly before he was shipped back overseas, we got into a massive fight. This was the kind of fight that wasn't about just one thing, but decades of things exacerbated by instability and transience. This moment in our shared history became a fifth family member that had been secretly lurking in the corner all along. And it was the final catalyst I needed to leave. So I did.

On my connecting flight to Los Angeles, I considered what my grandpa would have thought about me living in Japan, after he fought a war on the other side. Maybe nothing. After all, he left home as soon as he could and made it sound like the easiest thing in the world. I found that, for me, it was the same thing because I had been training for it my entire life. It was a part of me, practically in my blood. I didn't just inherit his wanderlust. I inherited his limits for bullshit. I inherited his wide-eyed curiosity toward life, his disdain for authority, and I inherited his Pisces heart because we were both born in the first week of February, in Aquarius season, sixty-four years apart. We're both deeply sensitive people with hard exteriors that disguise how we live our lives swimming through a churning sea of emotion toward the promise of something better. Maybe other members of our family stuck with the devils they know. But I see in my grandfather and myself how those devils have stuck with the families *they* know too. And they followed me to Japan, where I went in search of adventure, knowledge, and the distance I needed to gain new perspective—only to be confronted with the past of my own people everywhere I went.

In this book, I'm using astrology as a framework, but also as a thought experiment to help me identify the patterns between my grandfather's life and mine, while exploring how patterns of immigration, oppression, and resistance have been replicated the world over. To study history is to dismiss the idea of coincidences and confront the intentional design that connects past and present. But more than that, it's given me the opportunity to remember a man who made this life I have possible, with his courage and his conviction—which hopefully live on in me. Whoever reads this book helps to keep the truth of that connection alive by witnessing. And for that, I have to say to you in advance: thank you.

PART 1

*

Kudamatsu, Yamaguchi, Japan

August 7, 2006–August 6, 2007

My Aquarius Ego (Sun) in the Ninth House: A standout characteristic of those born under the sun sign of Aquarius is their unwillingness to follow the beaten track. They are intellectual, fiercely independent, eager learners, and value the pursuit of truth above all other things. They are curious about many things and can develop a philosophical outlook toward life. They also keep people at a distance—with an intellect that operates much like the rings of Saturn itself, needing a buffer between them and the world. The sun is in detriment in this position. Its domicile position being Leo, which is very comfortable leading, declaring their emotions to the world, and being the center of attention. Because Aquarius is the opposite position on the zodiac chart, they embody the opposite characteristics: being rebellious, resentful of authority, and extremely secretive about their emotions. When they feel emotionally vulnerable, they withdraw from the world. They're best understood by people who respect their need for space and solitude. For anyone who tries to force a closeness during this time, it should not come as a surprise that an Aquarius will defend their independence by any means necessary. By leaving the city, the state, or the country. They may, in fact, run to the opposite side of the world . . .

2.

The United Colors of Gaijin

THERE ARE CERTAIN KINDS OF PEOPLE WHO TEACH English in Japan, and I met nearly all of them on my flight from Los Angeles to Tokyo: scholars of Japanese culture and language who knew one thousand kanji characters already; cinephiles obsessed with Studio Ghibli who spoke in a series of obscure Miyazaki references; awkward romantics in long-distance relationships with locals they had met in online anime forums. Some were racists strung out on fetishistic stereotypes of Asian people and drunk on delusions of their own sexual prowess, which had, for some curious reason that they just couldn't seem to understand, endured years of homegrown rejection. Together, we were a veritable United Colors of Gaijin.*

Despite our vastly different backgrounds and knowledge, we all had one thing in common: rejecting the well-established path in which most college graduates go from an environment of learning

---

* *Gaijin* is the Japanese word for "outsider" and is commonly used to refer to foreigners of every persuasion—both as a descriptive tool and an insult, depending on the context and tone.

into a decidedly incurious workforce, then onward to marriage and families (and perhaps divorce inspired by unaddressed frustrations accrued along said path). Our journey was "derailed," veered off road, into the wilderness of teaching small children. A lot of us just wanted to evade that nine-to-five life for just a little bit longer. But, beneath that, there was an element of failing to launch, where some used niche Japanese counterculture to distance themselves from whatever responsibilities we had failed to meet back home.

When we landed in Tokyo, a group of teachers immediately wanted to commemorate the occasion with a bowl of udon.* We went to Shibuya, the city's financial district illuminated with JumboTrons and neon signs written in katakana. Most of Japan turned dark when the sun went down, but Shibuya was a dazzling, electric maze of commercial advertisements, noise, and hyper-dense crowds that ingested us into a static blanket of white light. We made our way across the district's major crosswalk, weaving in and out of what seemed like hundreds of people who were finally heading home at nearly nine o'clock in the evening. We rendezvoused with a teacher named Patrick, a tall, spindly Kiwi who spoke Japanese with the kind of authority that made it clear he would be far more popular in Nagano-ken as an English teacher than he ever had been in Christchurch.

Because I didn't speak *any* Japanese, I compensated by agreeing a little too enthusiastically with everything he said. Nodding vigorously as he waxed lyrical about the linguistic complexity of honorifics or the necessary merit of local neighborhood hostess

---

* Thick, white wheat noodles with a handful of conflicting origins stories—though my favorite is its invention in Shikoku during the Heian period, by a Buddhist monk named Kūkai, just because I went to Shikoku to taste them from the source, and I haven't been the same since. Food of the gods. World peace in a hot broth with dashi, soy sauce, and shaved radish.

bars. He moved through the city like he had traced his footsteps in his dreams. He knew exactly where he wanted to go, exactly what he wanted to eat, and he was as confident slipping through the crowd as I was unwieldy. We arrived at one of Shibuya's darkened alleyways—so narrow we had to twist to the side to walk through, knocking low-hanging red paper lanterns with my shoulders. I caught the smell of deep-fried batter, seafood, and miso as we headed farther away from the main foot traffic—and I thought to myself, *Please let that be the restaurant he's guiding us to.*

It was.

But the restaurant was more than a small kitchen lined with a tiny row of stools around an exposed countertop. Every seat was filled. In the shop's window, a tasteful display of bowls filled with plastic noodles were arranged neatly on a wooden table. And inside, the fresh ingredients smelled like they had been carefully picked for their ability to draw a symphony of hungry sounds from a stranger's stomach. If perfection is an illusion, then I had just walked into a dream come true.

We ducked beneath the noren curtains and sat together, nestled between uniformed students, sex workers, and businessmen in crisp dark suits with their ties slung casually over their shoulders. The sound of slurping noodles replaced conversation; the strict social behaviors that informed an even stricter social hierarchy upon which Japanese society is predicated overruled by loud noises of satisfaction. That was the precise moment when I knew the noodle shop would become my favorite hangout spot in Japan.

Patrick barely glanced at the menu before deciding what to order.

"I'm having the tempura udon," he said, adding another word I didn't understand. Carrie, another Floridian import, closed her menu and said the same. I stared at the foreign characters on the laminated paper for a long time before telling Patrick to make it three. He reminisced about his first time at that stall as I looked around, not understanding the signs overhead or the calligraphy on the curtains. I tried to eavesdrop on the conversation of the kitchen staff, actually thinking that *maybe something would just click*, and came up questioning the entire concept of language. I had succeeded in avoiding the workforce, but I had also regressed to a toddler's comprehension of her surroundings. I didn't even know how to get back to the hotel by myself. I began to sweat, realizing that after years of hyperindependence, I now relied on these people for my very life. A light meal had turned into a very heavy evening before our food had even arrived.

A few minutes later, we were staring at bowls of udon, filled with tender white noodles in a hot, fragrant broth, crispy fried shrimp, shaved radish, and a shiny, golden egg yolk in each one. I stared at the yolk. It stared back at me. I pushed it to the side with my chopsticks. Carrie slid it into her bowl, mixing it in with the noodles. Our mouths became synchronized hatches to devour noodles. There is nothing sweeter than the first meal after a long flight when battling a creeping case of jet lag, but *that* dinner in particular was medicinal: a warm, balanced, hearty bowl offering the reassurance that everything would be okay by the time I licked the bottom clean. This is the feeling that remains my litmus test for a good meal—its ability to sooth an anxious mind.

I laid down five hundred yen when it was time to pay, or approximately five dollars at the time, a quarter of which was for tip. As we left, the hostess charged after me in the alley, extending her cupped hands with the change that I had meant to leave behind, bowing her head deeply. People turned around from their bowls and stared. I leaned away from the change. Patrick swiped the coins and put them in my hand.

"Don't tip. She would have chased you all the way to the train station if she had to."

✳

I spent three days in Tokyo, where entire meals could be purchased from vending machines and my hotel came with a toilet
programmed with a rotating playlist of synthesized pop ballads.
So I didn't immediately know what to make of Yamaguchi-ken
when I arrived at the airport in the southern part of Honshu.* The
first thing I *wasn't* anticipating was the heat. The dark suit I had
worn to set a good first impression turned into a wet dishcloth that
stuck to, and chaffed against, everything. There was no escaping
the sweat, the exhaustion, or the smell of my own body rebelling
against it. The sounds of Tokyo traffic had been replaced with cicadas and air conditioners, and a harmony of locals with paper fans
cooling themselves at rapid speed while shouting "Atsui, atsui!"†
Even on the other side of the world from Florida, I had somehow
ended up taking residence in its distant Asian cousin.

The second thing I noted was the mountains—the way they
rose up and all around us like a crown encircles a royal head.
The prefecture's name—yama, for "mountain," and guchi, for
"mouth"—was appropriate. Hano-sensei and Hata-sensei picked
me up. They had a handful of silver fillings and gold teeth between
them, smiling at me as much as I smiled at them—perhaps from
the same nervousness I felt.

When we arrived at the high school where I would be teaching,
a woman strode up to the car before I opened the door, introducing
herself as my supervisor. Akari-san was tall, athletic, as serious as
she was organized—already impatiently pulling me from the car,

---

* A *ken* is the suffix used to reference a Japanese prefecture—a large geographic division within the country of Japan, similar to a U.S. state. Honshu is the main island of Japan.
† "Hot, hot!"

easy to do because my joints were loose from the heat. Once inside the school, I changed into a pair of house slippers, with half of my noticeably larger feet hanging off the backs as Akari-san guided me through an endless checklist of bureaucratic formalities and documents that required signing with my brand-new inkan.* The school was a multilevel concrete building, full of long, thin glass windows where kids lined themselves up to stare and whisper to one another behind cupped hands in each classroom we passed.

I see you, I said to them with a self-conscious bow while their shy giggles greeted me back. *Please, go easy on me.*

My predecessor had instructed me to bring meaningful gifts, or omiyage, for the principal and vice principal, along with something slightly more modest for the other teachers. The logic being that it was important to acknowledge each institution in Japan as its own ecosystem with its own hierarchy. Of all the things to focus on during my preparation, gift giving had stressed me out the most. What said "Florida" without saying "skin cancer on the beach"? How do I condense trash politics, Disney World, and very combustible meth labs off the turnpike into something enjoyable? I could have been practical, but I went in the opposite direction—large chocolate baskets for the senior school officials, and NASA key chains for everyone else. Predictably, the gift baskets had partially disintegrated in my suitcase on the drive to Kudamatsu, the once-solid chocolate pieces smeared across the wrinkled cellophane like you-know-what. I handed them demurely to the principal and vice principal, who accepted them graciously.

----

* An *inkan* is a stamp with the surname carved (in katakana, for non-Japanese people) on the head, registered at city hall—as official and serious as any photographic form of government identification. An inkan is required to sign up for anything: a gym membership, a cell phone, an internet contract. Getting mine marked my official residency in Kudamatsu.

Akari-san popped the trunk of her sporty yellow hatchback, kicking around the netball gear to make room for my suitcases before hoisting them into the back without letting me help. American rock music played from her stereo while I tried to bridge the cool distance between us with nervous conversation. Her replies were short, punctuated by laughter that she cut in half, as if having a foreign stranger in the car was typical Tuesday business. She slowed down to approach a group of students in uniform, rolling down the window to chastise them in aggressive Japanese, flattening their faces into pancakes as they receded in the side-view mirror. After an awkward beat, I asked what that had been all about.

"She changed her hair color. She knows the rules, and she broke them anyway. I cannot *believe* she would do that."

I straightened in my seat, but also exhaled with a bit of relief, realizing I could probably win the students over easily.

MY APARTMENT WAS in the suburb of Suō-Hanaoka, an even smaller division of the already very small town of Kudamatsu. I shared my neighborhood with a cluster of other apartments constructed after World War II and an endless view of rice fields, tended by farmers in knee-high rubber boots with thick layers of ropy muscle baked into a golden hue by the sun. They all stopped wading through the watery canals to stare as we drove past.

"You're in the real inaka* now," Akari-san said, waving to the farmers. "*Very* different from Tokyo."

I had a look on my face that can only be described as something of the no-shit variety but hard gulped anyway because she said this

---

* *Inaka* refers to the Japanese countryside—not a specific region, but any part of the country where industry relies on farming and agriculture for economic production. Yamaguchi-ken is very much so the inaka.

like it was a challenge or a warning or the grand introduction into my first major postgraduation regret.

Akari-san promptly castigated me in Japanese for stepping into my new apartment with my outdoor shoes, and I apologized profusely while clumsily kicking them off, letting my toes settle on the cool floor of my new apartment. We opened up the windows to let the humid, thirty-eight-degree (hundred-degree-Fahrenheit) air out before she half-heartedly showed me around my flat. I had two tatami rooms—one with a television set and a DVD player, a spacious kitchen with a microwave oven and a brand-new rice cooker—and a bathroom with a cube-shaped tub. We heard a knock at my front door, and a very tall man with slick black hair and yellow teeth peeked his head into my flat. He introduced himself in a thick Southern drawl as Scott from Texas and said that we would be working together at the high school.

"Great! Scott, now that you're here—maybe you can take Jennifer to get some food from the store? I have a hair appointment." Akari-san was halfway out the door before she finished giving her orders, slipping her shoes back on and leaving. It was such an efficient getaway that I had trouble even being upset—just impressed.

After her car disappeared, Scott and I stared at each other.

"I really wanted your dining room table," he said. "But when I arrived Akari took me to the store to get groceries, so I guess I can't complain too much." That's what he said with his words, but the look on his face said, *You're right—she doesn't like you. But she likes me, so it's not my problem.*

WE ATTRACTED DOUBLE the stares from double the people, even some decelerating their cars for a more comprehensive inspection, pupils dilating with disbelief at the gaijin spectacle. The smell of ripe mikan oranges mixed with the heat as we passed the millennia-old Hanaoka Hachimangu Shrine, the shinkansen's

concrete railway-support slabs towering above us, the 7-Eleven kon-
bini and its hidden stash of small glutinous rice cakes filled with red
bean paste and ice cream.* It was a visual landscape that positioned
the ancient and the modern side by side, indicative of Japan's firm
attachment to traditional customs and its gentle embrace of foreign
conveniences—a paradox that I felt allowed room within its extremely sophisticated culture for someone slightly less so, like me.

MY NONEXISTENT LANGUAGE skills were the star attraction
at SunLive, the local grocery store.† Aside from a few paltry greetings, I didn't know anything. The previous teacher in my position
had told me over email that this wouldn't be a problem because
my supervisor would get me settled. The same supervisor who was
possibly getting a trim and blowout when I stumbled into a grocery store with a man I had known for half an hour. And I didn't
even know the Japanese words for *ham, cheese, soap,* and most crit-
ically *body lotion.*

    Scott helped me collect most of these items, but he had the tem-
perament of a line cook: sarcastic, grating, condescending, with a
flourish of arrogance that brought it all together like a runny egg
yolk on an otherwise appetizing dish. When it came to finding body
lotion, I picked up and put down about a dozen bottles with illustrations of smiling strawberries and dancing flowers printed across
the labels, unable to read the characters around them. I eventually
grabbed the dancing fruit so Scott would stop looking so annoyed.

AFTER I GOT back to my apartment, I turned on the air condi-
tioner and unrolled blankets that had been stored in the closets,

---

* Mochi, as it turned out, would become an addiction of mine.
† SunLive is pronounced "SunLibu" due to *v* being a nonexistent conso-
  nant in the Japanese language.

emptying them of corpses from several large mukade.* I stripped to bathe in the smallest tub I had ever seen and washed off the day's humiliation with soap I had pinched from my hotel in Tokyo. In the second tatami room, I switched on the television to a colorful game show with an extroverted host, introverted contestants, and loud, flashy sounds and props, including a collage of every swatch on the color wheel. I opened the tube of dancing strawberries and rubbed the cream all over myself before melting into the sofa and dozing off.

I couldn't stand when I woke up. I was stuck from the shoulders down. After slowly peeling myself off of the cracked brown leather, taking care not to tear my skin, I saw iridescent strawberry-scented swirls patterned my skin under a brand-new blanket of sweat. I looked up the word for *lotion* in my Japanese dictionary. That wasn't it. I looked up the word for *soap* and sighed, then took my second shower of the evening. I was exhausted and frustrated, confused by the sounds and shapes of everything—especially the cube-shaped tub in which I spun around repeatedly to avoid splashing water on the floor. As the hot water hit my body, the tub filled with the most spectacular lather I had ever seen.

*

Scott and I took the train into Yamaguchi-shi† the next day, picking up about a dozen more English teachers along the way. Anyone who didn't look Japanese, and a few who did, was a teacher headed in the same direction. That's how I met Penny, an Aussie

---

* Venomous centipedes with very large, very thick, very scaly bodies. If bitten, most people of a middle age range will experience swelling and fever—but they have occasionally killed elderly people with weakened immune systems.
† *Shi* is the suffix added to a city. Yamaguchi-shi is Yamaguchi city, not to be confused with Yamaguchi-ken, which is the prefecture.

with a ferocious appetite for life and beer, and Lisa, an elegant woman with a posh English lilt that made her curse words sound like smooth jazz. I was grateful when Carrie joined us at one stop, if only for the shot of familiarity that brought me back from the murky haze of jet lag.

We arrived at a local school, and two teachers led us through a manual of emergency phone numbers, as well as hacks on how to get driver's licenses, how to register our travels with the embassy, where to go for health checkups, and what to do if you wind up in jail ("You're laughing, but this actually happened, guys!"). The bureaucracy was important, but it was mostly an excuse to have a very large, very loud, and very lubricated party. The organizers had rented a room at a traditional izakaya* where round after round of sake was brought out in small ceramic tokkuri containers, along with plates of grilled yakitori skewers, pickled vegetables, edamame, and fried chicken that were served between endless frosty pints of cold Japanese beer.

The more people drank, the more they moved around the table to talk to one another, sizing one another up as potential friends or sexual conquests. And the more alcohol consumed, the more people seemed willing to fit either category before the night was over—a drunken bacchanal of possibilities that reflected our chaotic and exciting relationship to this new place. The older teachers had grown frustrated by performing the impeccable behavior that was expected of them over the years; they were the first ones to get hammered, setting the tone for everyone else who patiently waited for cues of when to let loose.

New friendship formed over loud laughter, mixed English accents, and the smell of hops and yeast. Digital cameras were

---

* Japanese pub

deployed for rosy-cheeked selfies. Keitai* appeared, and phone numbers were exchanged. We had attracted quite a bit of attention from the other people in the restaurant, who watched us with a blend of annoyance and fascination. We were a bratty bunch, having the time of our lives, dancing like no one was watching, singing like no one was listening, loving like we were all we had.

*

When I returned home, a woman knocked at my door. She was stunning. It was 90 percent humidity outside, but there wasn't a drop of sweat on her—whereas moisture leaked from my body like a loose faucet. She introduced herself and handed over a basket of skin-care products wrapped in ornate paper as omiyage. I couldn't read the labels, but each gel and cream smelled more expensive than the last. I accepted the basket with a deep bow and a smile, thanking her for taking the time to gift me with moisturizer—a sign of deep respect where I come from. At night, I used one small tub from the gift basket to moisturize my hands, trying to stretch it out for as long as possible because the smell was divine.

A few weeks later, I noticed that the skin on my hands and wrists was lighter than the rest of my body.

---

* Cell phones

3.

The Myth of Homogeneity and
the Ballad of Yasuke

Iro no shiroi wa shichinan kakusu.
(White skin covers the seven flaws.)

—JAPANESE PROVERB

HEN I WAS AN UNDERGRADUATE STUDENT AT
Florida State, I frequented different student organizations for lectures, parties, talks by famous activists—
anywhere where there was free food. To that effect, the Caribbean
Student Association always delivered. One such event was a
group-wide discussion on colorism, which featured a PowerPoint
presentation on skin-bleaching creams that had been circulated
across North and South America during the 1950s and '60s—
mostly by a Jamaican brand called Nadinola. These were predominantly black-and-white advertisements that exclusively targeted
Black women, who smiled into telephones and next to men who
looked on adoringly—their expressions very approving of these
women with their confident light skin. The captions read, "The nic-
est things happen to girls with light, bright complexions!" And my

personal favorite came from an ad that appeared in *Jet* magazine in October 1963 that stated, "He used to duck me, now he dates me!"

Even though we all had plates piled high with rice and peas and plantains cooked in brown sugar and butter, one by one, we stopped eating as the images changed—some began to jeer or hiss. I didn't realize how much my own face had scrunched up until someone pointed it out, drawing laughter from several others. I had been cringing through the whole thing. When the slideshow ended, we discussed our personal experiences with colorism, along with what we called the burden of lightness, which had all begun at a very young age. I was surprised by the similarities. When I shared how my parents were horrified at how easily I darkened while swimming in the sun, someone mentioned that her own mom wouldn't let her out of the house once the temperature reached a certain point, even if she wore sunscreen. I also thought about how I had begged my parents to get my hair chemically straightened at the salon when I was nine years old, so that it would "lay down" like all the pretty white girls I went to school with. These weren't experiences that my older brother seemed to have, and similarly, most of the stories the men shared that night concerned how they had been conditioned by their own mothers to see lighter-skinned women as more attractive. Though we were young when first exposed to these products and attitudes, it seemed we had all developed an awareness that they were underpinned by anti-Blackness and how the business of self-hatred functions with or without our consent.

*

The gift basket of skin-bleaching cosmetics was the first time I had been confronted with anti-Black racism in Japan. *That was bloody short-lived*, I thought. To this day, I'm not sure if that woman gave me skin-lightening products because she thought I needed them or simply because she thought they would make a lovely gift. People often visited with gifts because Scott and I were the two new English teachers of Kudamatsu, and everyone knew who we were. Even for a small town, I was amazed at how efficiently word had spread of our arrival. I only saw that woman once more, and when I did, she smiled and bowed politely, and I did the same because that's just what you do. But Japan's history of anti-Black imagery, which includes the widespread commercialization of skin-bleaching products, makes it necessary to examine both the historic origins of the country's obsession with lighter skin and the myth of homogeneity that has been central in perpetuating racist depictions of non-Japanese people for centuries.

Japan is not as homogenous as I had often been told; in fact, Black people had been present in Japan centuries before I arrived. Encounters with Black people in Japan date back to at least 1546.[1] Throughout the sixteenth century, it was common for enslaved people and indentured servants from Africa to accompany Portuguese and Dutch traders and missionaries on their trips to Japan, where they became subjects of local curiosity. In fact, Black people were commonly used to make money. In 1570, an Italian priest named Gnecchi-Soldo Organtino arrived in Japan and wrote in a letter to his colleague that some Japanese people "would pay money to see slaves from Ethiopia," adding that "anybody could make money . . . by simply showing a Negro."[2]

In 1579, an Italian Jesuit priest named Alessandro Valignano arrived to Japan with an enslaved man from Mozambique, and in 1581, they visited the capital, then Kyoto, where the enslaved man caused so much commotion with his robust physical appearance and dark skin color that locals reportedly broke down the door of his residence to see him for themselves.[3] When the warlord and the first great unifier of feudal Japan, Oda Nobunaga, heard of the commotion, he invited the enslaved man to his quarters, where he was ordered to strip naked to prove to Oda that his skin color was not painted on.[4]

A chronicler of Oda's life, Ōta Gyūichi, transcribed the account in his 1610 biography of the warlord, writing, "His age seemed somewhere around twenty-six or twenty-seven. He is as black as a cow, and looks healthy and talented. He is stronger than ten powerful men."[5]

Oda was so impressed by the Black man's appearance that he offered him a place in his army and a new name: Yasuke, who is now popularly known as the first Black samurai. Because Oda was a powerful figure, nobody questioned the decision to include a foreigner in his personal army, and beyond that, Yasuke's presence in Japan wasn't viewed as unusual. During the sixteenth century, several hundred African people lived in Japan as interpreters, entertainers, and soldiers.[6]

Yasuke fought with Oda during his unification campaigns, implying they had a close and trustworthy relationship—until Oda was betrayed and ambushed in Kyoto by one of his most trusted generals, Akechi Mitsuhide. Yasuke, Oda, and his attendant and lover Mori Ranmaru retreated to a temple, where Oda committed seppuku, or ritualistic suicide, by slicing open his abdomen, before Mori beheaded him. Mori then performed the same ritual on himself, before Yasuke decapitated him as well.[7] Yasuke survived—making a bold escape from the temple carrying Oda's head, denying Akechi the chance to seize his enemy's remains to make a public declaration of victory.[8] It's a fantastical image that has fueled imaginations for centuries, as it is rooted in feudal ideas of honor, loyalty, and valor.* This story, as well as many others about Yasuke

---

* It feels important to note that the shōgun were de facto military dictators. For example, Oda Nobunaga's exploits included fratricide, taking people as slaves, and burning monks alive.

and Oda, puts Black and Japanese culture face-to-face and demonstrates a kind of solidarity between people of color before the term *people of color* even existed. I believe this solidarity is part of the reason Yasuke's legend has continued to fascinate Black people who are interested in Japanese culture.

My first encounter with Yasuke was sometime in the mid-nineties after I saw *Ninja Scroll*—now considered a classic anime feature. This film is largely credited with popularizing Japanese animation outside of Japan. I was blown away by the movie: the quality of the animation, the sophistication of the story, the narrative themes that tackle vengeance, redemption, and queerness, all while demonstrating an appreciation for Japanese history.

After watching it, I disappeared down the *Encyclopaedia Britannica* rabbit hole at school. The Tokugawa period, the setting for *Ninja Scroll*, led me to the Sengoku period and Oda Nobunaga. It was the first time I read about queer daimyō, or warlords, including Oda, who took many lovers from their own armies. And then, in a small blurb affixed to an illustration, I read about Yasuke. It was only a tiny paragraph about a man from Africa taken as a slave across the world, given a wakizashi and karuta armor, who then became a warrior and legend. How there wasn't an entire library dedicated to his story did not make any sense.

Despite being totally caught up in the romance of Yasuke's legend at a young age, there are one or two fairly dismal facts that have been harder to reconcile: Chief among them was that Yasuke had as much agency over his life as my great-great-grandfather Richard in North Carolina. After all, his choice was to remain a slave *or* go to war for a country that considered him more of an anthropological curiosity than a human being—which could be said of nearly every Black male enlisted to fight in the American Civil War. And despite the proliferation of his legend over the years, which has included longer encyclopedia entries, counterhistorical

novels, children's books, and full-length animated features, nobody knows Yasuke's *real name*—because he was a slave.

The rest of Yasuke's life is shrouded in mystery, and scholars
debate everything from his origins (some claim he was Ethiopian,
not Mozambican) to the manner and location of his death. According to Thomas Lockley, coauthor of *African Samurai: The True
Story of Yasuke, a Legendary Black Warrior in Feudal Japan*, Yasuke
may have been a slave as a young boy, but he was likely a free man
by the time he met Valignano. Lockley also says that Yasuke may
have been wounded and captured after Oda's death, adding that
he was definitely not executed.[9] Japanese historian and editor for
the Japan Black Studies Association Furukawa Tetsushi claims
that, after Oda's death, Japan's new leaders "looked down" on Yasuke, called him an "animal," and then returned him to European
missionaries—no longer a samurai, but once again a slave.[10] After
that, he vanishes from historical records.

Yasuke as a person has been subject to tremendous reinvention. Sometimes, he is depicted in less flattering terms, as in Kurusu Yoshio's 1968 award-winning children's book, *Kuro-suke*
(Black One). There, Yasuke is drawn with minstrel-like qualities,
replete with large empty eyes, thick lips, and apelike ears, which I
personally find much more offensive than any firsthand historical
account of his appearance. The 1973* book *Kuronbō* (Nigger) by
Endō Shūsaku is a "satirical" account of Yasuke's story, featuring
an enslaved African man named Tsumpa, who was brought to Japan by a Jesuit missionary during the sixteenth century. In this
account, Tsumpa is depicted as a witless entertainer, crude and
"semi-human," like an "oni" or demon.[11] This story also takes place
in Kyoto, where rumor of Tsumpa's large frame circulates around

* Several online sources indicate this book was published in 1971. The
source cited here states 1973.

the city much like the real-life story of Yasuke's did. Tsumpa is brought before Lord Oda, who orders him to perform, and the Black man responds by clapping his hands, dancing, smiling, and playing a drum—a performance that is brought to an abrupt end when he farts in front of the famous warlord.[12]

While Ōta Gyūichi's description of Yasuke as being "as black as a cow" would absolutely provoke an inflammatory response from Black Twitter today, it's impossible to divorce this statement from its context. This was the sixteenth century, when the blackest comparison most people in Japan had to dark skin color might have actually been a cow. Maybe the night sky. Maybe an eel. None of which inspire especially romantic analogies. Whereas Japanese society was *widely* aware of Black people by the 1960s, when *Kuro-suke* was published, which makes the 1970s narrative of *K*ronbō* just obscene.

Exposure to enslaved Black people on Japanese shores sets a stage for racist beliefs, even if those enslaved people were brought from somewhere else. But racialization of that skin color, where it was weaponized to institute forms of systemic discrimination and violence, came later—when the West introduced it.

*

Japan has a problematic history in regard to skin color—as far back as the Heian period (794–1185), which predates Western trade. Back then, a skin's whiteness corresponded to one's status, with whiter skin belonging to people who could afford a more leisurely lifestyle attributed to a higher class.[13] The adoration of whiteness can be seen in literature, poetry, and painting. In *The Tale of Genji*, an early-eleventh-century folkloric text by Murasaki Shikibu (better known as Lady Murasaki) that is widely considered to be a literary masterpiece, the author describes her beautiful character as follows: "Her color of skin was very white, and she was plump with an attractive face."[14]

In Murasaki's personal diary, she wrote about the people in her life with detailed descriptions of their appearances, and skin color was a notable means of describing noblewomen from court: "Lady Naiji has beauty and purity, a fragrant white skin with which no one can else compete."[15] And even though women in particular aspired to this standard, men also began to apply powders to their faces from the eleventh century onward to achieve a similar aesthetic.[16]

Whiteness remained the beauty standard throughout the Tokugawa period, when women were known to apply white powder to their faces and carry around parasols or cover their heads in hoods to prevent their skin from being darkened by the sun. To improve the whiteness and texture of their skin, they "polished" their faces with grains like millet or barley, rice bran, or excrement from the Japanese nightingale.[17]

Granted, these accounts discuss whiteness as a singular concept; dark skin doesn't feature at all. But Japan did have its own caste of outcasts called *burakumin*—a pejorative word that translates to "hamlet people," "pollution abundant," or "untouchables," a class who were segregated from the rest of the population during the Tokugawa period.[18] Their association with "lowly" jobs like undertaker, butcher, and leather smith marred them as defiled people.[19] And the ostracization of the b*rakumin combined with the use of whiteness as a beauty standard set a stage upon which dark skin would later be precariously contextualized. So when Western traders arrived with enslaved Africans, that's when the villainization of darker skin truly began.

Paintings from the Tokugawa period frequently included depictions of Spanish and Portuguese merchants, who were referred to as nanban-jin—translating to "southern barbarian."[20] The period in which Yasuke arrived in Japan is also referred to as the Nanban trade. After long voyages at sea, traders from these countries likely arrived with tanned skin and so were depicted in paintings as having darker flesh tones, lending itself to the correlation between darker skin and menial jobs or a working-class lifestyle that involved being in the sun for extended periods of time.[21] But the portraits of the Black servants or enslaved Africans belonging to those traders were given a skin tone of "leaden or blackish-grey" in paintings.[22] Wagatsuma Hiroshi writes in his paper "The Social Perception of Skin Color in Japan" that the physical appearance of Black people in Japanese paintings is "characterized and in some instances closely resembles the devils and demons of Buddhist mythology."[23] When the Tokugawa shōgunate closed off Japan from Western trade in 1639, Japan's interactions with the West stopped—with the exception of the Dutch, who monopolized the attentions of their Japanese counterparts by continuing to import their racist thinking for their Japanese business partners, students, and peers.[24]

This adoption of racist thinking is not abstract in the least, but rather a matter of historical record. For example, in 1787, a Japanese scholar who focused on Dutch studies transcribed what he had learned about Black Africans from his Dutch mentors:

> As their countries are close to the sun, they are sun-scorched and become black. By nature, they are stupid ... The black ones are found with flat noses. They love a flat nose and they tie their children's noses with leather bands to prevent their growth and to keep them flat ... Africa is directly under the equator and the heat there is extreme. Therefore the natives are black colored. They are uncivilized and vicious in nature.[25]

Not only did these Dutch mentors demonstrate how little they thought of African people, they also made it clear how little they thought of their Japanese students by negatively influencing their thoughts about an oppressed group of people. This sinister description is reminiscent of colonialist eugenics, where racial differences are weaponized to promote a false image of ethnic superiority. And admiration for Western innovation and military might inspired comparable ideas of the West's attitude toward African people. John Russell, author of the 1991 paper "Race and Reflexivity: The Black Other in Contemporary Japanese Mass Culture," described the adoption of Dutch learning and Western science and values like anti-Black racism as Japan's attempt to catch up with the West, writing that "Japanese views of blacks have taken as their model distorted images derived from Western ethnocentrism and cultural hegemony."[26] These prejudices were passed from one country in a position of influence to another and took root—not only "echoing" racist Western paradigms, but "borrowing" directly from them.[27]

Like so many things, U.S. intervention only made Japan's burgeoning anti-Black outlook much worse. In 1853, U.S. commodore Matthew C. Perry forced his way into Japan as an envoy to broker a trade deal.[28] Worried about a potentially lengthy negotiation period, he used "tall jet Black negros armed to the teeth" to accompany white sailors as they delivered Perry's credentials to Japanese trade ministers, in order to enhance the already intimidating American presence.[29] When the Treaty of Kanagawa was signed in 1854, Commodore Perry and his delegates celebrated by treating the Japanese officials to a minstrel show featuring white sailors in blackface and singing songs like "Mistah Tambo" and "Mistah Bones."[30] Knowing this information makes it difficult for me to dismiss Yoshio Kurusu's illustrated book of Yasuke; I could never excuse Endō Shūsaku's book in any lifetime.

Afterward, when Japanese envoys were sent to the United States in 1860 to establish diplomatic relationships, they accepted the conditions of African slavery as a mere "fact of life."[31] In the diaries kept by some of the delegates, there are entries that suggest how slavery was justified with the help of their white American counterparts: "The faces of these natives are black, as if painted with ink, and resemble those of monkeys. According to the Americans, they are the incarnations of apes."[32]

To help legitimize the enslavement of Africans in the United States, these envoys described Africans as subhuman, equating them with Japan's own class of outcasts—the b*rakumin, who, by that time, had been inflicted with "certain badges of status" that included assigned clothing, hairstyles, curfews, and "prostration before their betters."[33]

The West may have introduced dehumanization toward people of African descent, but Japan used these attitudes to implement near-identical racist systems of oppression against their own citizens, as well as other Asian countries and people. For this reason, it's important to understand that contemporary attitudes on anti-Blackness in Japan are directly connected to the country's racist imperial campaigns across Asia—which tackles the myth of homogeneity, a defining characteristic of the Meiji period.

The Meiji Restoration was a period of modernization that abolished the shōgunate (samurai rule) and reestablished Japan as an empire in 1868. During this time, government officials opened up the country to Western trade—this time voluntarily—deciding that it was imperative to renegotiate treaties that had been forced upon the country.[34] But engaging with the West again gave the country a sense of its otherness for the first time, and this compelled officials to study the race theories of Europe and the United States—including Charles Darwin's book *The Descent of Man, and Selection in Relation to Sex*, which was translated into Japanese only ten years after the English edition was published in 1871.[35] This text highlights Darwin's racism and praises the teachings of his cousin, Sir Francis Galton—the founding father of eugenics theory. In *The Descent of Man*, not only does Darwin argue the intellectual inferiority of women, but he legitimizes Galton's belief of imminent race wars, writing "the civilised races of man will almost certainly exterminate and replace throughout the world the [*sic*] savage races."[36] Tsujiuchi Makoto, author of the 1998 paper "Historical Context of Black Studies in Japan," argues that it was texts like these that "indoctrinated the notion of racial hierarchy that prevailed in the West as if the theory of superior and inferior races was a biologically proven fact."

What followed was a series of annexations to expand the Japanese Empire: including Hokkaido in 1869, Ryukyu in 1879, Taiwan in 1895, and Korea in 1910—absorbing native Ainu and Okinawans alongside Taiwanese and Koreans into the "Japanese polity."[37] Essentially, state officials concluded that modernization could not be achieved without adopting nationalism and colonialism. Inspired by the West's colonial conquests on the African continent, these policies were created to "associate [Japan] with the European/Western race and to, ultimately, establish the "Japanese race" as equivalent to the "white race of Europe."[38]

We see echoes of this in some of the teachings at major national universities, which served crucial roles in the dissemination of nationalist rhetoric. Tomizu Hirondo, an ardent nationalist and law professor at Tokyo Imperial University, was particularly concerned with the division of the African continent by Western powers. He articulated these collective fears in his 1899 book, *Afurika no zento* (The Future of Africa), thus:

A few years ago, Africa was called the dark Africa, but it would be the source of wealth in the next decade and it would be the white race that would gain profits from it, not the Yellow race. Yellow race do not think big like white race and unless they do so, they could become slaves of the white race themselves.[39]

Initially, Japan incorporated Western ideas of racial superiority

and classification by categorizing different Asian nations and eth-
nicities into an inferior hierarchy over which Japan presided.[40] This
was applied to citizenship, military conscription, and familial reg-
istration with the grand scheme to expand the country's "sphere of
influence" across Asia to support the concept of Japanese people's
racial superiority.[41] Obviously, race played a part in Japan's application of "race science," and this included concepts of representation
and identity.

Whereas eugenics was deployed by Western colonizers to
highlight racial *differences*, Japan's conquests depended on the concept of a "shared national" and ethnic identity alongside a "common blood" to force unification under the Japanese emperor.[42]
The imperial policies birthed during the early days of the Meiji era
are widely viewed as the point of origin for the myth of "Japanese
homogeneity."[43] Ethnic nationalism was used to forcibly integrate
not only colonized countries like Korea and China, but Indigenous Okinawans and Ainu people *within* current Japan, into one
Japanese agenda with the singular goal of creating a "pure Japanese
race."[44] To do so required degrading the people from these groups
to justify the erasure of their customs, religious beliefs, and values, so that Japan could "rescue" them from their own "backward-
ness."[45] Not only to "liberate" them, but to claim these territories
before the West did.[46]

Between 1937 and 1945, Japan began a "large-scale ethnic
conversion" of people in Korea, Taiwan, and China who were to
be "reprogram[med]" into "ideal Japanese" people.[47] This featured
the banning of local languages and cultures, as well as the quash-
ing of civil dissent.[48] One of the most horrific events from this period is the 1937 Nanjing Massacre, which involved the mutilation,
rape, and slaughter of between 150,000 and 300,000 Chinese
people during the Second Sino-Japanese War.[49] While "comfort
stations" were first established during the First Sino-Japanese War

(1894–1895), they continued during World War II.[50] Most came from colonies in China and Korea, but many others came from the Philippines, East Timor, Taiwan, Vietnam, the Dutch East Indies (Indonesia), and some even from Europe;[51] the majority of victims were young girls between the ages of eleven and twenty years old.[52] An estimated 200,000 women and girls were forced into sexual slavery during World War II alone.[53]

These campaigns and others share chilling similarities with Western colonial conquests in the ethnically diverse African, Middle Eastern, Caribbean, and American countries. Japanese officials even viewed their country's colonial campaigns in Korea and China as "analogous" to the British occupation of Egypt or the U.S. occupation of Panama: countries "reduced" to the "lowest abyss" by means of their own "uncivilized" nature and, therefore, incapable of governing themselves.[54] This was used as justification to unite Asia under Japanese leadership to form something not very dissimilar from the British Empire, and the resulting colonies were formally recognized by some Western powers like Italy, Spain, and Germany.[55]

This mass slaughter created generations of trauma across Asia, which can only really be seen when visiting those Asian countries, as it's gone largely unacknowledged within wider Japanese discourse.* It also created a paradoxical crisis of Japanese identity that the country is still trying to reconcile: While Japanese imperialism was branded as liberation of other Asian nations from *Western* imperialism, the country's concept of racial homogeneity is clearly contradicted by the widespread campaign of sexual violence inflicted across the continent.

And this myth has persisted in the country's national discourse,

---

* The Memorial Hall of the Victims in Nanjing Massacre by Japanese Invaders is a deeply sobering visit.

where it's still being used to silence claims of racist discrimination. In 2006, the same year that I moved to Kudamatsu, the United Nations Commission on Human Rights released a report stating that racism and xenophobia *were* problems in Japan that affected three groups in particular: national minorities such as the Buraku, Ainu, and Okinawans; descendants of former Japanese colonies from China and Korea; and foreigners and immigrants from other Asian and non-Asian countries.[56] The report described how people from these communities live in marginalization and that their access to opportunities like education and housing were limited. Described as of a "political nature," this kind of structural inequity only serves to make national minorities "invisible in State institutions."[57] But the Japanese government denied the presence of racism, claiming that the definition of *race*, as outlined in the UN's International Convention on the Elimination of All Forms of Racial Discrimination, did not apply to the Japanese people, citing the country's "homogeneity" as proof, which erases both Indigenous and migrant ethnic minority groups.[58] After all, racism cannot exist if there are no minority groups to be racist against.

The popularity of this argument only grew after Imperial Japan's defeat in World War II, during the development of Nihonjinron, a selection of writings and teachings that contemplate the discourse on Japanese identity and nationality.[59] The myth of homogeneity is often cited as a relic of the toxic nationalism that became emblematic of Imperial Japan's former campaigns across Asia; it's a folklore that erases the existence of minority groups through forced assimilation to create a single Japanese hegemony.[60] If an identity is created by manner of exclusion, then maintaining that identity requires disavowing the marginalized experiences endured by other ethnic groups. By making them invisible, it becomes easier to accept that myth as reality.

The 2006 report recommended that Japan formally recognize

the existence of racism, adopt a national law against discrimination, establish a national commission for equality and human
rights, and a rewriting and reeducation of the country's colonial
history. None of these suggestions were implemented. And in
2014, a follow-up commission by Amnesty International presented to the same UN council found that racism in Japan "is still
deep and profound," adding that "the government does not recognize the depth of the problem."[61]

Of course, it's difficult for *any* government to recognize the
depth of a problem when it actively exacerbates it. In 2015, Sono
Ayako, then an adviser to the now-late prime minister Abe Shinzo,
penned a column in the major Japanese newspaper *Sankei Shim-
bun* stating that importing skilled workers to address the country's
labor shortage would only work if Black workers were segregated
from white and Asian workers, citing South African apartheid
law as a model for Japanese immigration policy.[62] Sono wrote, "It
is next to impossible to attain an understanding of foreigners by
living alongside them."[63] She went on to add, "Black people fundamentally have a philosophy of large families. For whites and
Asians, it was common sense for a couple and two children to live
in one complex. But blacks ended up having twenty to thirty family members living in a single unit."[64]

Sono's comments sparked outrage and were heavily criticized
by Japanese human rights activists, as well as the South African
government. She was rightfully dragged across media outlets the
world over who described her as an "embarrassment."[65] The response was justified (and enjoyable). But the Western backlash was
notably absent of any significant commentary on the relationship
between Sono's anti-Black comments and the racism that underscores Japan's history of classifying people into inferior categories to prop up the idea of Japanese superiority. And maybe that's

because that would mean looking at how the West had helped create it . . .

While racism everywhere is about power, it tends to be discussed through a reductive lens of color: Black and white being the most obvious examples. And while whiteness does play a role in Japan's racist history, the subject of racism in Japan is unequivocally rooted in a system where one group *has* power—and another, as a result, is *powerless*. Because all systems of oppression are interlinked and reinforce one another. None can be viewed in isolation because transient racist and anti-racist systems are made up of transient people: traders, diplomats, politicians, even teachers. What I experienced in Japan was not experienced in a vacuum. Colorism and whiteness are relics of a history that is perennial and continuously felt. While racism may smell, taste, and look different from place to place, the outcome is usually the same. Whether it's death by a single blow or death by a thousand tiny cuts, it erodes the moral positioning of an entire country.

Since Sono's statements, efforts to address discrimination in Japan at a state level have been clumsy at best. After years of pressure from the United Nations, Japan's National Diet (the legislative branch of the Japanese government) passed an anti–hate speech law to comply with the International Convention on the Elimination of All Forms of Racial Discrimination in 2016.[66] This seems like a massive step in the right direction, but the law doesn't contain any penalties for breaking it, nor does it officially ban hate speech. In fact, it only seems to apply to threats toward the body or human life but not insults or other forms of discrimination. That same year, *The Japan Times* published an article that cited fierce condemnation from critics, who called the legislation "philosophical at best" and "toothless window dressing at worst."[67] Naturally, many people—myself included—question why it was passed to begin with. So when an additional 2020 report by the Japanese NGO Network for the Elimination of Racial Discrimination found that "no progress has been achieved" when it came to the establishment of a national human rights institution, hardly anyone was surprised.[68]

But there *is* something to celebrate in terms of representation. In 2021, an African American animator based in Tokyo named LeSean Thomas created a Netflix series based on the life of Japan's first Black samurai, simply named *Yasuke*. You can watch it now. It's a six-part limited series in English that takes a much more refreshing route with Yasuke's legend. In it, we meet Japan's first Black samurai in an existential crisis as he mourns the loss of his beloved Oda. Yasuke is reimagined as a robust, muscle-clad warrior battling with alcoholism and purpose before taking up his sword once again to defend the weak. In this rendition, there is considerable creative license taken with both history and plot: Mori didn't die by suicide and managed to escape the ambush at Honnō-ji temple. Akechi's army is depicted as a supernatural, fire-breathing legion of robots. But the best part is that Yasuke is given a name: Eusebio Ibrahimo Baloi. This name is made-up, but the surname may be a reference to the famous Mozambican jazz musician Gito Baloi. For me, the name provides the most significant avenue through which the audience can reimagine the legendary figure, not as some nameless entity—but a real person, who had ambiguity, subjectivity, and complexity. Those are the first things robbed from Black people when they become the subject of racist tropes. Giving them *back* to Yasuke is like acknowledging his humanity for the first time.

Yasuke's character reminds me a little bit of Jubei, the lead in *Ninja Scroll*. Yasuke is clever, sarcastic, and tortured—all the telltale signs of a multidimensional protagonist. The series works beautifully with the baritone vocalizations of LaKeith Stanfield, who both voices the titular character and is an executive producer. Most importantly, it moves *away* from stereotypes and toward representations of Black people that put Black voices at the center of Black imagery—even ones that border on the mythological. I keep waiting for this approach to become the standard for more discussions on Blackness in Japan, but I think that would need to involve more Black voices and a stronger Black presence in the rooms where decisions on representation are made.

But I'd like to see a few more changes. I'd like to see Black and Afro-Japanese people centered more in conversations on Black representation in Japan. I'd like to see makeup shades for people with dark skin in Japanese beauty shops (which seems to have become the case since I've left). I'd like to see an open conversation on the country's colonial past, and I'd like to see a more comprehensive federal antidiscrimination law with consequences and clear language that outlines what discrimination is. Maybe I have no right to ask, but I'd like to see it anyway. I don't expect Japanese officials to listen to *me*, but maybe they could listen to their own constituents.

I THREW OUT the skin-bleaching products. When I tell Black friends about that incident today, many are put off from visiting the country, but I need to be unequivocal: Japan is the safest place I have ever lived in. *Ever.* I'm conscious of the fact that I only lived there for a year, at a time rapidly approaching twenty years past. I still have friends in Tokyo and Hiroshima who have made Japan their homes for ten years or more, and they are consistently racially profiled by the police *now*. So I have to ask myself if I would have continued feeling that way had I stayed. Would my impressions still be the same if I had more time to become more fluent in the language? And will I feel that way if I go back to visit?

I plan on finding out one day.

4.

The White Myth of Exposure and the Ballad of Beyoncé-Sensei

WHEN I WAS IN THIRD GRADE, AT MY THIRD ELE-
mentary school, our teacher instructed us to draw one
another's silhouettes. Each student stood in front of the
projector against a piece of paper while another classmate traced
their shadow with a black marker. The teacher hung the profiles
on the wall, and we then guessed who was who. We paraded around
the classroom of elegant profiles, sleek foreheads, pointy noses, and
thin lips. It was easier than I thought: identifying the white faces
of people I looked at every day. *That's Jeremy. That's Travis. That's
Kristin.* And then, there was one I didn't recognize: a gigantic head,
bulging lips, and a distorted nose. I was actually shocked.

"That one's Jennifer." Someone giggled behind me.

Is that what I really look like? I thought.

Okay, I'm ugly, and it hurts. But there it is.

I hid the drawing in my desk, only to destroy it later. I never
mentioned it to anyone, but it stayed in my mind while lap
dancing for Jesus during ballet lessons. Every time I posed for a
photograph—something I grew to hate—the image would reveal

another grotesque feature that I hadn't known about. And those features became synonymous with my dark skin because that was the only visible difference between me and the other beautiful silhouettes. I compensated by getting weird in photographs: making silly faces, striking overly confident poses, and making obscene gestures when I got older. All were effective deterrents from the homeliness I was confident other people saw in me. I have a small collection of photographs of me in Japan posing with my hands behind my head, lips puckered up, one hip jutting out with attitude. Not a drop of self-consciousness in sight.

Imagine my surprise when I saw the photographs that showed me that I was, in fact, not a human aberration. I chalked it up to the skill of the photographer, or the angle, or the lighting. Anything but the idea that I was physically attractive—even, dare I even say it, p-p-pretty?

Years and numerous disordered eating habits later, when I was already living overseas, I reconnected with some of the people I had gone to elementary school with on Facebook. It just happened in that way things do: Someone thinks about someone they haven't thought about in years. They get curious. They do a search. They send a friend request. We connect, and the hook of nostalgia instantly takes over. Handy thing, that whole social media network.

"Holy cow, it's been years! How have you been?! You live where now?"

After all the polite small talk and pleasantries, things get deeper—usually when someone wants to unburden their conscience for some reason. In my case, the old classmate had become a mother and recently sober. She looked healthy in their photos: lightly tanned, hair dyed black instead of blonde, and who was this adorable brown-skinned baby in her arms? A daughter! A plot twist I didn't expect, but hey, *times they are a-changin'* plays somewhere in the recesses of my brain.

Then it comes out.

"You know that silhouette assignment? That was a stupid joke."

"What joke?"

But it had already clicked. In fact, by the time she finished explaining that the drawing was never actually my silhouette, just a racist caricature they had drawn out of jealousy—jealousy for a beauty that I rarely felt I possessed—it snap, crackle, popped into place. It twisted around my abdomen into some gnarly back pain that I've been holding in that specific spot since I was eight years old. They explain how all those recent unarmed police shootings have made them "reflect" on their behavior. And I can't think of anything to say besides: *How fucking brave of you.*

"But it's a good thing you already knew that, right? Ha ha!" They fill the screen with laugh emojis.

HAHAHAHAHAHAHAHAHAHAHAHAHAHAHA.

Hilarious.

She says that it's a good thing that I figured that out in third grade (and not, say, my early thirties, when I really did). It was just kids being young and ignorant. And besides, "look at you now—a knockout," she adds, as if they can't believe my self-esteem survived that silhouette from more than twenty years ago. As if they are, in fact, *knocked out* by how their efforts have failed.

But did they?

I wonder, as I block them across all known social media platforms, why some people are so compelled to make another person hate a body that they don't have to live in.

✳

I hold two versions of Japan in my memory. There was the one I experienced with my students, sharing my care packages of greasy

American snacks while they introduced me to a wide range of foreign Kit Kat flavors.* These memories are stacked on top of my introduction to Anpanman—the slightly creepy animated superhero made of bread who eats his own face—and next to Hard Gay, the wrestler turned comedian who dressed in skimpy leathers and harassed random strangers with his pelvic thrusts on TV. It's the Japan where a kind stranger guided me on her bike to the community center when I became lost, and where a glamorous bartender in flawless makeup kept my friends and me company when we found ourselves stranded in a hostess bar during a typhoon, each of us taking turns practicing English and Japanese. It's the Japan that showed me that everything deserves a chance to live, including bugs and snakes—something my students taught me while carefully evacuating a tiny spider through a cracked window after I had tried to stomp it with my shoe.† This is the Japan I love most because it gave me an opportunity to learn just as much as I was teaching my students, and occasionally, this would lead to hilarious impromptu lessons for everyone.

Hikari-san dreamed of going to the United States and becoming a professional dancer. She often asked me to watch her perform at her dance club after school, and I would cheer as the girls made up elaborate dance routines. Once, she showed me her journal, more like a mood board made entirely of magazine cutouts: Beyoncé, Rihanna, Janet Jackson, Alicia Keys. She pointed to the picture of Beyoncé and said, "That's you, sensei!"

I scrunched my face.

---

* Strawberry, crème brûlée, caramel, coffee, toffee, and green tea for the uninitiated.
† I cannot overstate this enough: Don't ever do this. Whether you're in Japan or not. Let the little guys live. They're not hurting anyone.

"Hikari-chan,* are you sure about that?"

She nodded with her whole head, and I kind of shrugged and smiled.

When Hikari-san brought up the Beyoncé comparison again, she invited the other club members to weigh in. It was a fun diversion from our typical exercises of practicing greetings and farewells and times of day.† I seized the opportunity to exercise their familiarity with other ethnic groups, knowing that, for many of them, it might have been the first time seeing a Black person who was, lamentably, not rich and famous. "Okay—let's sort this out once and for all. Does Jennifer-sensei look like Beyoncé?"

This was the era of *Dreamgirls* Beyoncé, the slightly blonde Beyoncé. The pre-marriage-to-Jay-Z Beyoncé—ten years before she released "Formation" and dragged "Jigga Who" across a bed of hot coals in the name of Black female empowerment. I asked Hikari-san for the photo, and I held it up, gesturing first to the glossy magazine and then to myself. The students became excited, whispering to one another in debate.

"What do we have in common? Do we look alike? Or do we look different?"

The mood turned serious as they scrutinized us. They began to second-guess their earlier assessment.

---

* The suffix "-san" is added to someone's name to demonstrate respect, whereas the suffix "-chan" is added to a name when addressing children. However, it can also be used playfully between close friends. I still refer to the friends I met in Japan with the suffix "chan" to demonstrate affection. The suffix "-sama" is used for more formal acquaintances: managers, bureaucrats, or a principal in a high school, for example. And while it's more common in Japan to address someone by their surname, my fellow teachers, students, and I usually referred to one another by our given names with the attached suffix "-san" or "-chan." Probably because I was a foreigner.

† "How are you?" "I'm good. How are you?" "I'm fine. How are you?"

"Beyoncé has lighter hair."

Mm-hmm. I nodded my head. "What else?"

Someone pointed out that our chins were shaped differently. Someone else said that our eyes were shaped differently. After enough deliberation, I put it to a vote. Two people voted yes, that sensei did indeed look like Beyoncé. Two people also voted no. It all came down to Kenji-san, a very thoughtful student who took his assignment very seriously. He rubbed his nonexistent chin stubble and made a show of holding the picture of Beyoncé next to my face while I tried very hard not to laugh. After sucking on his teeth and feigning complete agony, he sighed and held up his hands to imply that he had come to his final verdict.

"No, sensei. Sorry. You are pretty, but you're not pretty like *Beyoncé*."

"A-plus," I said, beaming from ear to ear, as I shook his hand, then pulled him slightly closer to ask, "But did you have to say it like *that*?"*

BUT THERE IS another Japan, and I think of it when I remember Ichika-chan and Himari-san. Both girls, along with a few other friends, often stopped by my desk in the teacher's office for help with their English pronunciation. One afternoon, I asked Himari-san to stay behind while the others left for netball practice. I wanted her to introduce her favorite Japanese pop stars to me, by way of YouTube videos, thinking it would be easier, and hopefully more fun, for her to describe her fanfare for B'z in English than, say, the colors of different pieces of fruit.

"Oh, you and Ichika-chan are exactly the same!" I said.

Himari-san kind of rolled her eyes in reply.

---

* I know, I know. I absolutely brought it on myself. Still, a worthwhile if slightly humbling exercise.

"No, sensei," she began, waving her hand to dismiss the comparison.

"Yep." I smiled. "Exactly the same. Two peas in a pod."

She stomped her foot in frustration. I thought it was a response to the expression *two peas in a pod*, which I had only just realized probably didn't make any sense. So I said that they were like sisters, really, because they had the exact same taste and the exact same interests. They even styled their hair similarly.

"No, sensei." She crossed her hands in front of her chest to silence me. "I'm *Japanese*. She's *hāfu*."*

I had never heard that phrase before, and after my student left, I had to ask one of the other teachers what she had meant.

"Hāfu, Jennifer. You know, half. Half Japanese," someone said, crossing her flat hand against the edge of the other.

"But half Japanese is still . . . Japanese . . . right?" I asked.

She nodded.

"Yes. Half Japanese."

I knew Ichika-chan had a white mother and Japanese father, but I didn't know what to make of this brief exchange, so I let it go. But clarity came to mind years later, in 2015, when Japanese model Miyamoto Ariana was crowned as the first mixed-race winner of a national beauty competition, chosen to represent Japan in the Miss Universe pageant. Born and raised in Sasebo with a Japanese mother and an African American father, Miyamoto experienced horrific racist abuse as a child growing up in Japan. Other kids at school threw garbage at her and called her racist names. It was the suicide of one of her close friends, who was also bullied for being multiracial, that drove her to enter the competition in the first place. While some people celebrated her win as a

---

* Hāfu: a designation used specifically for people of mixed or biracial Japanese descent.

positive step toward more inclusivity in Japan, there was also a lot of controversy, centered on one argument: She was not Japanese, she was hāfu. The term was used in a way that seemed to create a completely different racial designation, one that didn't *include* Miyamoto's African American heritage so much as it *excluded* her Japanese identity, moving her and other mixed-race Japanese people, specifically those with darker skin, into a separate category altogether. Despite winning the title by a selection of judges, it appeared critics didn't want to acknowledge that she *is*, in fact, Japanese because of an underlying fear that this would somehow *change* Japanese society itself.

I have no idea how Ichika-chan felt about this designation, though I did recognize a feeling of secondhand offense on her behalf. I have come across more stories from other hāfu people over the years, in person and on the news, reminding me that there is also an underreported diversity of experiences to match the underreported heterogeneity of the country's ethnic makeup. Governments can choose to erase certain histories or identities, but individuals can also choose to make them visible.

To some extent, my limited understanding of the language shielded me from seeing too much of this kind of discrimination, but it was easy to identify in other ways. The skin-lightening advertisements in magazines and brightly lit panels in SunLive featured models with radiant pale skin as they gingerly touched their faces in amazement as if to say, "Wow, I cannot believe it's *this* white." Or the savagely racist comments that one of my fellow teachers made about Koreans upon my return from a trip to Seoul. "They will eat anything with four legs except a table," one said.

Reconciling these two different versions of Japan has been as important to me as it has been uncomfortable. Perhaps that's just a feature of the foreigner's experience: seeing the country that locals want to present to you—the one you *want* to believe in—while being unable to look away from the contradictions that locals want to pretend don't even exist, the ones you wished weren't there.

I tried to discuss these subtle and not-so-subtle instances of racism with fellow English teachers, but many dismissed my complaints, citing a nebulous "exposure myth" that had no discernible point of origin, wasn't cited by any notable scholar, and did not seem to be present in any Japanese discourse in which I participated. All it did was preemptively invalidate how uncomfortable I sometimes felt as a darker-skinned person—which felt like a decidedly Western thing to do. My peers all came from English-language countries like the United States, the United Kingdom, Australia, New Zealand, and Canada, so I knew that they knew what racism was. Especially when one of the white male teachers from the United Kingdom became David Beckham–sensei to his students, or when a white female instructor from Australia was instantly compared to Kylie Minogue.* But they were also decidedly quiet when I mentioned my discomfort with the skin-lightening ads, which could be because *they* also used these products—and I got used to hearing, "Oh, Jenn, it's just a lack of exposure. Lighten up."†

I was the first Black person that many of my students had ever seen. Ever. In their whole adorable lives. And their wonderful curiosity made it easy to disabuse them of any preconceived notions and stereotypes—especially when I showed them my rapping skills.‡ But it was much harder to do with fellow Westerners, even people teaching in Japan, who didn't seem to grasp how this argument also implied that countries where exposure to Black and Brown people as a daily occurrence would naturally generate *fewer*

---

* I am sorry to say that no teacher in our prefecture looked like either of these people.

† Pun not intended, but I'm just going to leave it there.

‡ They begged me to stop.

racist systems, fewer racist politicians, and fewer traumatic racist experiences. That would mean that a country like:

The United Kingdom.

I mean, the United States.

Or Canada, France, Spain, or Australia.

Or South Africa.

... is a goddamn utopia. I don't have to dig at all to know how untrue that is. I don't even have to scratch the surface. Their discomfort in discussing racism in Japan may not have been about the discomfort of acknowledging the role that racism plays in Japanese history and society, but about a resistance to examining racism in the countries *they* came from with the same critical lens. The migration of anti-Black attitudes between countries of influence should indicate the need to have a conversation about how systems of oppression are designed specifically to determine who has wealth and global influence and who doesn't—an objective that underscores nearly every imperial strategy, whether it's the colonial division of the African continent, Western proxy wars in Iran and Iraq, or Japan's own imperial campaigns in China and Korea.

For my own sake, I chalked their resistance up to a *lack of exposure* to critical thinking, which I had to contend with whether I wanted to or not. Not long after my Beyoncé lesson, Scott came back into the office after a weekend in the city with friends. He was in a shit mood, irritated by me before I even had the chance to be annoying. Out of nowhere, he began to interrogate me on whether or not I believed that Black people could be racist because another Black woman had said that to him at a party.

I hesitated to reply before deciding on deflection. "What do *you* think?" I asked. I knew there was no way to win. Here was a man who sat across from me every single day, *exposed* to someone who understood racism better than he did, lecturing me on why this other mystery Black woman was wrong.

I don't think my taking the time to educate Scott would have made a difference when it was clear he had decided that reverse racism, an *actual* myth, was the cross he was prepared to die on— and forcing him to sit down and watch *Lemonade* on repeat, if it had existed at that time, would not have changed his mind, let alone peer-reviewed data and historical evidence that show how antiwhite racism anywhere in the Global North isn't the thing he thinks it is.

But maybe it would. Maybe that's just *my* ignorance about the power of "Formation." If any song could cause him to see the error in his thinking, it's that one. As the darker-skinned, non-blonde, pretty-but-not-pretty-like-Beyoncé-sensei one, I get to make that call.

When I tried to respond to Scott's question in more depth, he cut me off with my favorite classic Western proverb: "This isn't the United States, Jennifer."

And he was technically right because, in the United States, everyone knows that I look like Gabrielle Union—not Beyoncé.

5.

Tower of Babel

I MADE THE MISTAKE OF TELLING THE MUSIC TEACHER at my school that I used to play the flute in middle school. We hadn't interacted much outside of the polite nod she gave me while pedaling her electric bicycle uphill, and I was making a concerted effort so that other people felt comfortable around me until I could find a Japanese tutor to help bridge the language gap. With clear excitement, the music teacher introduced me to one of her students—a young flautist named Hina, who lent me her spare flute.

"To play together," she said, as if she had been waiting for an opportunity to trigger someone's preadolescent memories.

"Oh, like, for fun? As a hobby?" I asked, thinking she just wanted to hang out (with her twenty-three-year-old English teacher, of course).

She didn't say no. Neither did the teacher. But they both giggled. That should have been my first clue . . .

Hina-san began to fetch me from the teacher's office for band practice after school. I could read the music, and that felt good because it was a language I understood. Then, one day after practice, the music teacher pulled me aside to tell me what time I should arrive at the auditorium for the school-wide performance.

Performance?

Yes, performance. *For the school-wide festival.*

I blinked. Hard. I drew the line at public spectacle.

"I'm sorry, but no," I said in Japanese. *Gomen nasai. Iie.* I thought and made up an excuse about spending the weekend in Hagi, a seaside city located in the central part of the prefecture, for . . . a nondescript *thing* that didn't require further explanation because providing circuitous apologies was the right way to decline an invitation—wasn't it?

"Sō sō, Hagi," she said, expressionless, staring not in my eyes but left of them. A tiny spot that burned. Then she smiled, and we both bowed goodbye—me thinking that I had successfully evaded reliving seventh grade. When I sat back at my desk in the teacher's room, my supervisor, Akari-san, approached and tapped me on the shoulder.

"Jenn-chan," she began. "You're performing in the band show."

My stomach sank. Not only had I done something else culturally unacceptable (and been caught), but I could sense that I had disappointed her once again, enlarging the gulf between us that was first established when she had abandoned me at my apartment.

Then she leaned in closer, lowering her voice, and sighed. "You can't say no," she said. "That's very rude here."

∗

The school festival was a citywide event. Everyone came. Not just the students and their parents, but their grandparents, aunts, uncles, and neighbors. Retirees and shopkeepers, restaurants owners and city councilmen. In hindsight, I don't know what made me think I had the audacity to skip it. It was a communal event—an opportunity for everyone to show their support and belief in their local high school, a source of pride that distinguished it from every other high school in the prefecture. Tea club performed the meticulous matcha ceremony at scheduled intervals, long enough to allow enough room for each elaborate step of the four-hour-long process. The cooking club prepared takoyaki and sold them in batches with fish flakes, Kewpie mayonnaise, and okonomiyaki sauce for hyaku-en each (or roughly one U.S. dollar at the time). The baseball-team students had an exhibition game, and there were other sporting events. In a zealous attempt to participate in an obstacle course, I failed to clear a hurdle and face-planted in the red dirt of the track course, to the loud commentary of one of my students shouting into the loudspeaker, "And Beyoncé-sensei goes dooooooooown!"

I shared sheet music with Hina-san during the band performance and hit all the notes well enough. When the piece ended, the teacher said something in Japanese to the crowd, who all awed in response. And I knew, by nothing other than her tone of speech and their gasp of disbelief, that they were talking about me. She pointed in my direction, indicating for me to stand up—with Hina-san nudging me in the ribs. I did so, slowly, and was greeted by roaring applause from beyond the fixture of bright yellow lights shining directly into my face. I bowed as deeply as I could before sitting down in my own puddle of sweat.

✳

Switching between Japanese and English required the use of opposing thought processes—but it was a good exercise in mental agility that got me over the initial awkwardness of working with my fellow teachers. I began Japanese language lessons with an enthusiastic retiree who taught from her dark wooden house in neighboring Tokuyama. A demented miniature terrier that hated everyone but her ruled the domain.

I was given homework each week and practiced my phrasing in the hours between classes at school. Akari-san took an interest in my diligent efforts and began correcting me when I practiced telling the time, counting numbers, giving directions, or describing the colors of different fruits. When I felt comfortable, I asked her if she knew of any shodō or calligraphy classes that I could take to further my knowledge of Japanese characters and penmanship. Not only did she manage to locate a class at the local community center, she drove me to my first lesson and introduced me to my new teacher, who had prepared my materials in advance and charged me the equivalent of two U.S. dollars per lesson, what we called the "the gaijin discount."

Sato-sensei had short curly hair, a patient face, and a very kind smile. She had heard of the new teachers at the school and was very happy to meet me. Surrounding her was a gaggle of young kids, five- and six-year-olds who had already finished their shodō lessons and were mostly goofing around until their parents arrived. Sato-sensei explained to them that I also wanted to learn how to write, and they responded with enthusiasm. "Hello, goodbye!" and "Nice to meet you," they said, extending their hands for big shakes before hiding behind Sato-sensei. I sat at a table where my ink, brushes, and paper were neatly arranged. Sato-sensei pointed to her eyes and to the paper to say, "Pay attention," as she wet the ink stick to create a black puddle in the suzuri, or ink stone. I watched her carefully create the first kanji characters I was meant to learn: 山口県.

Yamaguchi-ken.

She placed the brush on the table and gestured for me to pick it up, which I did—with my left hand. She gasped. So did the children, who shook their heads with pained looks stitched across their young brows. I paused.

Sato-sensei made a sound like reverse whistling as she took the brush out of my left hand and placed it in my right. The children around us nodded in approval.

"Hmm, uh, how do I say this?" I began. I tapped my left palm with my right index finger, saying in English, "No, no, no." I buckled into myself.

She shook her head. The kids did the same, tsking loudly—an echoing sound of disapproval. Holding my right hand with the brush, she dipped the hairs in ink then pressed them onto the blank piece of parchment as she redid the brush strokes for Yamaguchi-ken. When she was finished, she pointed to the tiny inflections in the thickness of the brushstrokes, saying "Tome, harai, hane," which seemed to indicate that using my left hand to make the same brushstrokes would be impossible. It wouldn't be kanji—it would be some inverted and corrupted version of it.

I was astonished. I couldn't write with my right hand. It was, and remains, useless to me unless I'm eating, drinking, or playing an instrument (like the flute). I would have been better off finger painting than writing anything legible. But there it was, flopping around like a fish on a piece of parchment: tome, harai, hane, while a group of tiny jurors gave encouraging nods and grunts to help me along.

Sato-sensei balled her fists and smiled. "Don't give up!" she added emphatically. I concentrated as hard as I could, using my entire torso to try and control the right side of my body. And after a few minutes had passed, my right hand—to my complete surprise—remained utterly useless.

After my lesson, the kids wanted to make faces and compare body parts. They loved putting my hand against theirs, and I loved watching their eyes widen when they saw my fingers bend over theirs like earthworms. They stood next to me so that they could see how large my feet are, and when they begged me to pick them up, I twirled them around, letting them climb on top of me while running around the room for consecutive piggyback rides while they squealed in my ears. Everything about me was curious to them, and it was worth the late nights of ice packs taped to my lower back just to forget the strict social conventions of which I was overly self-conscious at work.

Akari-san seemed impressed when I showed her my first productions from Sato-sensei, and I occasionally found her looking over my shoulder while practicing between English classes—thawing, ever so slowly, the more I demonstrated an interest in learning the language and culture. I wasn't yet sure if it was enough to become the basis for a friendship, but the more she encouraged me, the more motivated I felt to continue learning. She started joking around with me, and the first time I made her laugh, I knew that we had made progress. At some point, when I shared anecdotes about my life in the United States, she stopped responding with a polite vocalization and started replying with stories of her own. She told me that she had studied in Kyoto, that it was the only big city that she really liked—she enjoyed the countryside most. She showed me pictures of her dog, and I showed her pictures of mine, the one my parents were watching in Florida. Once, I asked her why she had chosen to learn English over all the other languages. She actually kind of chuckled when she responded.

"When I speak in English, I feel that I can express myself in a more open way than in Japanese. It's not so easy in Japanese, but in English it's okay to express your feelings and thoughts. It's more accepted. And I like that."

So did I.

When the leaves began to change color, she suggested we take a drive through the countryside to take photos and go on long walks through the woods. Looking back, my love for hiking began with her. Exploring a place by train is very different than exploring by car, and I enjoyed the twisty turns up and down mountains with all the epic vantage points over cascading auburn forests. We took pleasure in wandering aimlessly together, finding hidden waterfalls and fresh springs where we could fill our cups with pristine drinking water. We sat in silence, listening to birds and watching sunsets—something she described as wabi-sabi: the simple, imperfect, and completely changeable beauty of nature.

As we headed back, we stopped at a tea store, where she showed me her favorite brands of loose-leaf tea and matcha powders. I bought way too many packages that smelled like cinnamon, hibiscus, and orange peel, and she seemed happy with my enthusiasm. On the way back to Kudamatsu, we stopped at an onsen.* They usually rest in the mountains, but there are also many man-made onsen throughout Japan. We showered sitting on short buckets and then plunged into the steaming-hot water, talking to each other as if we were meeting for the first time—and realizing that we did, in fact, enjoy each other's company. The onsen was nestled in some mountains, and we watched them get dark while we soaked. The heat from the spring had an intoxicating effect, and when the skin on my body began to shrivel and loosen, she suggested we end the night by visiting her favorite okonomiyaki† restaurant for dinner.

"Kansai style is most famous, but Hiroshima style is much better," she said. I took her word for it. The restaurant was filled with sweet-smelling steam and uniformed chefs busy slicing and dicing meats over a hot oiled skillet behind the counter. The hiss of the noodles and cabbage searing on the griddle was the sound that I

---

* Natural hot spring

† Okonomiyaki is a type of Japanese pancake made from diced cabbage and a unique flour mixture. While both styles include meat or seafood, Kansai style uses Kewpie mayonnaise and ramen noodles, whereas Hiroshima style includes cheese and udon noodles—making it clearly superior.

imagine angels make when you enter heaven. We were served massive okonomiyaki dishes with fish flakes, mayonnaise, sauce, green onions, and a generous flourish of dashi seasoning on top. We devoured our plates until there was nothing left and then looked at each other with approving wide-eyed expressions that conveyed a mutual admiration for the other's appetite.

The satisfaction of a gorged belly gave me the confidence I needed to finally ask her about the first day I had arrived in Kudamatsu. I couldn't understand why we hadn't gotten on this bandwagon of friendship earlier—we could have been hiking, onsen-ing, and eating from the beginning.

"What happened that day? You know, when you took off for your hair appointment? Scott said that you had done all these things with him."

She fidgeted at first, but then her face shifted in a manner that pretty much said, "Fuck it," and she told me about a former assistant language teacher (ALT) whom she hadn't gotten along with.

I could tell that she was choosing her words carefully, and maybe I should have left it there, but I couldn't. I tried to keep my tone even, but I sounded like a robot.

"So you thought . . . it would be the same with me?"

She nodded demurely. I asked if it had been the same with Lindsay, my predecessor, whose correspondence had helped me prepare for my arrival.

"No, Lindsay was great. She really put me at ease, and I felt much more comfortable around her. She really repaired things."

I pushed to see what else came out, but a part of me braced for the answer that I already expected. I asked Akari-san what this other teacher looked like.

"Well, she had braids. And . . ." She looked at me.

"Well, you know." She stopped speaking.

Yes, I did. All too well.

6.

Flowers Return to Their Roots

W E ALL HAD DIFFERENT WAYS OF HANDLING THE colder months when winter finally arrived in Kudamatsu. Many of the English teachers passed the season with drinking parties and karaoke—at which I had become a natural with my colorful rendition of "Beat It" by Michael Jackson. But I'm an introvert, and was then a very strict nondrinker, so my social activities were naturally limited by my unwillingness to cross certain thresholds of debauchery. On the other hand, I developed some pretty bizarre behaviors of my own: chopping off my hair and going natural for the first time since I was nine years old, prompting all kinds of commentary about my sexual orientation; daring a friend to meet me in Osaka, where I spent six hours in a chair getting a tattoo from my shoulder to my hip bone; and becoming Myspace pen pals with an Australian named Matteo, a man twelve years my senior, in whom I confided all the things I didn't feel comfortable discussing with Akari-san or other English teachers. It was a series of strange decisions that elicit the same kind of cringe I feel when I read old diary entries, recognizing an inability to articulate my struggles with mental health. And all these things—my haircut, my tattoo, my new friend—were in some way an attempt to reassert control.

Since arriving in Kudamatsu, I had been battling with panic attacks that came out of nowhere. They left me feeling powerless, and I often had to pull out of plans last minute to recover, only telling people that I suffered from a stomach thing. Nobody questioned it; some just advised laying off the imo-kenpi.* I didn't know that I was having panic attacks at the time. In my isolation, without much access to mental health services—or even the awareness that I *needed* them—I just learned to adapt. I leaned into an idea of self-empowerment by quietly, and violently, battling these feelings alone.

On the evening of the annual winter party, I had a major panic attack. It was the worst one up until that point. After showering in my square tub, I rubbed myself down with cocoa butter sent by a friend in the United States who had read about the strawberry-lather debacle on my blog. I had bought a red dress especially for the party, which I put on with a festive string of jade pearls I had picked up in China several years prior. My hair and makeup were the final touches, and by the end, I looked immaculate. I took some pictures of myself and smiled back at the image of me in the digital display window.

I called my parents just to check in, and they, once again, urged me to reconcile with my brother. I sighed deeply to compose myself and explained to them, as calmly as I could, that I would not. I asked them to respect that decision. We went back and forth like that for a while before I ended the conversation, knowing

---

* Deep-fried sweet potato chips, covered in a thick sugar syrup. One of the heavier snacks you'll find at the grocery store but absolutely delicious and worth every single tummy ache.

that Scott would be arriving shortly so we could cycle to the train station together. I made myself a cup of tea, choosing one of the many flavors I had bought with Akari-san on our autumn date. I poured the matcha powder into the cup and waited for the water to warm, looking out of my window at the waxing moon rising above the thicket of trees behind my apartment. My heartbeat began to speed up so fast that I remember feeling it in my head, hammering between my ears, knocking me completely off-balance.

The next thing I knew, I was blinking myself awake on the kitchen floor—bathed in moonlight that was so bright I had to shield my eyes. I tried to turn, but pain shot through the left side of my body. I pulled myself up slowly, wincing as I noticed the new aches and pains in my knees, my elbow, and my wrist. I had hit a chair and a table on my way to the floor, where I finally fell on my now-bruised arm. Hobbling into the bathroom, I turned on the light and checked my face. I looked fine, but my eyes were wild and bloodshot—half-lidded and exhausted, as if I had been drinking for hours.

I heard a knock at the door. I quickly threw on my bathrobe and limped to find Scott waiting outside.

"So, you're *not* coming." He frowned. I must have looked like quite a sight. A bathrobe, jade pearls, red lipstick, crazed eyes.

"Sorry, it's my stomach again. I better stay home."

He didn't seem convinced, but he didn't question it either. He looked me up and down one more time and stepped away.

"Okay . . . I'll tell the others you said hi."

I forced a smile and an apology and watched him cycle down the street.

That was just the way winter was for me.

✳

My first hanami* was pure witchcraft. The cherry blossoms opened, and every street in the country was transformed by hues of light-pink flowers in every direction. On some streets, cherry blossoms were all you could see, blocking out buildings, noodle shops, and cafés. Kintaikyō, or Kintai Bridge, in Iwakuni turned into the prefecture's busiest hanami picnic grounds, where locals laid out blankets to eat mochi, drink tea, and sit in silent meditation beneath thickets of flowers so abundant they blocked out the sun. The air was filled with a sweet-smelling perfume that followed us into every store, restaurant, shrine, and temple. And it wasn't just Yamaguchi. Akari-san and I traveled to Kyoto where I filled an entire roll of film with photos of us posing in front of the trees and between budding branches, giving sultry side-eye in halos of fully bloomed flowers.

She was excited to take me to her old university, where we visited a professor of hers, who served us tea and mochi. I felt closer to her than anyone else in the ken and became enamored with the smallest things she showed me from her younger years, including her favorite kimono shop, where I bought a yukata† and shoes, with several people wrapping garments around me and showing me how to stand—penguin toed and knock-kneed, "for grace," they insisted. I saw a pair of geisha walk down the cobblestone streets in the Gion district, keeping their heads down as foreigners stopped to snap photos before disappearing behind the sliding wooden door of an izakaya that Akari-san said was invitation only.

"Some of them are gaijin dressed up as a tourist thing," she said. "But those were real because foreigners aren't allowed there."

She took me to Nishiki Market, where craftsmen and vendors

---

* Cherry blossom festival: when people take time to sit, picnic, and stroll outside to enjoy the cherry blossoms, which only last about two weeks, typically in early April, though I wonder if climate change has affected this.

† Like a kimono but made out of cotton instead of silk. Better for hot weather.

sold a buffet of cherry blossom products: tea, perfume, mochi, ice cream, and candy. I tried to be cool, but it was difficult when everything was handmade, artisanal, and delicious. The moment someone caught me looking at their goods, they smiled at me, then I smiled back, and Akari-san poked her head between us to say in Japanese, "Yes, she wants to try some of this." Many of the vendors were retirees who would tell the stories of how they came to be tea producers, or ice cream makers, and confectioners, as well as why the cherry blossom was a unique flavor that could only be enjoyed in Japan. They spoke about how their respective sweets recipes had been in their families for a century. Some said they had started selling sweets during the war to make money, but since retiring, they only did during hanami. Some said that they enjoyed selling sweets more than they had ever enjoyed their desk jobs because of the joy they found in feeding people. I listened to their stories, putting the pieces together through my broken comprehension— but, as always, I found that I could convey an entire paragraph of conversation through facial expressions, sighs of empathy, and the look of complete satisfaction as something sweet hit my tongue.

"Su-ggoi oishii desu,"* I said. It was an easy way to win favor from vendors, who responded by giving me more samples and adding extra items in my bags—insisting that I take them because it would have been criminal not to give them to someone who genuinely enjoyed them.

We sampled so much food that we skipped lunch and went to more temples and shrines, filling my goshuincho† with each sacred site's unique shodō signature. I lined up to watch the monks and

* Meaning "very delicious!" The bigger the pause before and emphasis on the *ggoi* in *suggoi*, the more emphatic one sounds.
† A book used especially for collecting signatures from Japanese temples and shrines. Each one has its own unique signature, and it's a popular activity with tourists.

attendants sign my book with flourishes of thick black ink, consisting of all the correct harai, tome, and hane strokes—with the right hand only. My favorite was from the Kiyomizu-dera, the oldest Buddhist temple in Japan. The brushstrokes looked like the temple itself surrounded by trees and old kanji characters, the kind I had seen carved onto pagodas and statues at cemeteries, in red ink.

Kyoto is one of the larger international cities in Japan, but everywhere we went, we found pockets of peace and quiet isolated from the noise that came from the trams, buses, and heavy foot traffic nearby. This was especially true at Ryōan-ji, a temple where Akari-san and I took a slow stroll around what is called Japan's most beautiful Zen garden—a yard made of tiny pebbles raked around large rocks. Monks in long robes moved slowly through the garden in silent meditation while Akari-san and I watched from behind the glass. Nobody else was allowed in the Zen garden itself, though we could continue through the other parts as we liked. She hooked her arm through mine, like so many other pairs, who nodded and smiled as we passed one another. We briefly separated to enjoy the blossoms, but she called me back over. Her hand beckoned me by fluttering in a direction that had initially felt like being shooed away. She knelt beside a bamboo pipe from which water dripped slowly onto a stone basin, next to a long wooden ladle.

"This is it," Akari-san said, whispered as if she was afraid to disturb the drip's rhythm. "That's wabi-sabi."

I looked at the fountain, and I looked around us: cherry blossoms, birds chirping, a slight chill in the air, dew pooled on the jagged edges of green leaves, and the bluest sky of the season. I wanted to connect deeply with the environment like Akari-san had—some kind of catharsis to match the splendor of my surroundings—but wabi-sabi still seemed abstract. I was looking through her view of the world but only understanding fragments of it.

"I know that winter was hard on you, Jenn-chan. But it gets better."

This caught me off guard. I thought my act of stability had been convincing. She tilted her head.

"We wait all year for the cherry blossoms, but they only last two weeks. Then we let them go and get back to our everyday lives. Appreciating all the simple things in nature. Like a bamboo water fountain." She pointed to the basin. "Or a walk around the Zen garden. You just have to learn to let things go and appreciate the beauty where you find it."

She squatted down next to the water and poured some in her hands, letting it fall through her fingertips back to the ground. Then she gestured for me to do the same, and I mirrored her movements.

"Nothing lasts forever. Not even difficult emotions. You just have to let them happen. Then let them go."

We continued walking through the garden, meandering next door to the Kinkaku-ji. The air was thick with the promise of rain, and the temple's golden surface was slightly dimmed. Birds overhead flew toward shelter while ducks paddled in the water between tiny islands of bonsai trees. Our appetites had returned by then, and Akari-san suggested udon noodles and miso soup. I told her that I didn't need convincing. A delicious meal with my good friend, whom I loved very much.

As we headed toward the park's exit, a breeze from the approaching storm swept through the manicured leaves of the bonsai trees, smelling like earth, rain, and death at the same time—the lifeblood of spring. The birds went quiet. All I could hear was the branches shifting around us, their leaves curling in anticipation.

I stopped in the wet dirt; Akari-san did the same.

"Aha," I said out loud.

She looped her arm into mine again, smiling, and nodded.

7.

Problematizing the "Meaning" of Japan

Amicus meus, inimicus inimici mei.
(The enemy of my enemy is my friend.)

—ANCIENT PROVERB OF THE OPPRESSED

AS MY TIME IN JAPAN DREW TO AN END, I BECAME curious about expressions of solidarity that may have existed between Black and Japanese communities, either while I lived there or at some point in history. After all, if negative stereotypes of Black people could be adopted, then more educated perspectives could also reasonably be expected to exist in history as well. I started with Yasuke again, and then moved to more contemporary examples. That's when I came across one of the most important figures in African American history. I already knew that W. E. B. Du Bois was an author, scholar, historian, sociologist, and famed Civil Rights activist. I had *been* a member of the W.E.B. Du Bois Honor Society at Florida State. The club's focus had been on volunteering and mentoring to support the tenet of moving forward while giving back, which had been very important to Du Bois. He was, after all, a key figure in the early development of critical race theory, Civil Rights, and Black pride. The society specifically emphasized the last point for its members: we should feel *proud* about being Black, especially as minorities at a predominantly white academic institution. But, like most of our heroes, there is another side to Du Bois that is pretty problematic.

While coined by white Northern liberals, the Talented Tenth theory was made famous in Du Bois's essay of the same name, which first appeared in *The Negro Problem*, a collection edited by Booker T. Washington, published in 1903. At the time, most of the jobs available to African Americans required manual labor, and Du Bois was concerned that the exclusion of Black people from intellectual spaces would set the community back. Du Bois's essay argued that a select tenth of African Americans should be granted access to higher education so that they could in turn lead the remaining 90 percent of the race post-Reconstruction.[1] Du Bois argued that these cultural missionaries were sacrificial roles, and these selected "leaders" were expected to forfeit their own interests for the "noble cause" of racial advancement, which was meant to benefit all African Americans.[2] Du Bois also wanted Black people to consider not just how we see ourselves, but how we're seen by others, especially white people.[3] He believed that doing so made it easier to appeal to their goodwill, but this belief always felt like it was tying the personal dignity of Black people to white approval, positing that this approach made it easier to respect *ourselves*.[4]

The Talented Tenth concept was criticized early on by other Black leaders, including Booker T. Washington, who accused Du Bois of having an elitist agenda that would set him and a select few apart from everyone else; Washington thought that the Talented Tenth philosophy would create an internal power struggle within an already beleaguered people—a critique that haunted Du Bois.[5]

I would argue that it still haunts us today in the form of respectability politics—the idea that if Black people behave with a certain degree of decorum, as defined and recognized by white people, that we can then earn their respect.

And I personally feel that respectability politics is an extension, or perhaps even a perversion, of the Talented Tenth. Du Bois was a very educated man. He completed a graduate program at Friedrich Wilhelm University (now Humboldt University) in Berlin and was the first African American person to earn a PhD from Harvard University; he was also one of the seven African American founders of the National Association for the Advancement of Colored People, or NAACP. He is a giant in African American history, but Du Bois's essay and its meaning continues to be debated by Black scholars—with a fair split between people who mostly describe him as an elitist or a visionary. In reality, he was both. But these debates primarily focus on his activism *in* the United States. I feel that his elitism—and perhaps the communal trauma it was responding to—is made much more apparent by examining his interest in Asia, especially Japan. There, he fostered relationships to grow global awareness of anti-Black racism in the United States by propping up the Japanese Empire as a shining example of how white racism could be defeated.

Du Bois saw Japan's positioning against the West as "analogous" to the struggles of Black Americans.[6] This is not without basis. At the time, U.S. immigration was waging a bureaucratic war against Japanese immigrants. Like many other Asian laborers, Japanese immigrants came to the United States to work on railroads, in oil refineries, and on farms in California during the 1800s.[7] But by the turn of the century, the U.S. public had grown resentful of the country's changing demographics. The U.S. government responded by enacting a series of xenophobic policies: the Gentlemen's Agreement of 1907 largely restricted Japanese immigration to the U.S.,* followed by the California Alien Land Law of 1913, which forbade Japanese immigrants from owning land.[8]/† The Immigration Act of 1924, which included the Asian Exclusion Act, banned Asian immigration altogether‡—a racist-controlled process that created the country's very first, and equally as racist, Border Patrol. These horrific campaigns were waged against Japanese immigrants to the United States, but it seems that Du Bois couldn't separate the *people* it affected from the institution that was Imperial Japan, and he conflated the struggles of one group with the colonial ambitions (and atrocities) committed by the other.

For more than thirty years, Du Bois looked to Japan as a shining example.[9] To him, Japan was an instrument of "righteous punishment" against the West, a therapeutic projection of what he viewed as a "colored race's" successful revolt against white colonial interventionism.[10] He likened Pan-Africanism to Pan-Asianism and, in echoes of his Talented Tenth philosophy, believed that Japan was the right nation to lead the latter.[11] He expressed admiration for the emperor and called Japan's occupation of Korea after the First Sino-Japanese War in 1894 a "necessity" to defend itself from the threat of Chinese intervention; to Du Bois, China was a naive vassal state of white Western power.[12] His writings from this time are rife with condescension. In 1931, he wrote a letter describing the people of China as "utterly deceived as to white opinion of the yellow race," adding that the Chinese people were just as "despised as Negroes."[13]

---

* This was an informal agreement where Japan limited the number of passports it issued to citizens migrating to the United States so that the United States would not restrict Japanese immigration on its side. The result was the same.

† This affected all Asian immigrants.

‡ It also set quotas for white immigrants from southern and eastern European countries.

He further justified the Japanese occupation of China with comments that regarded the two countries as relatives, flattening the immense ethnic diversity of Asian people into a single monolith while feeding directly into the idea of a shared commonality that was being simultaneously used to justify Japan's colonial conquests. In either a column or a letter, Du Bois wrote that "they are so near akin that Westerners cannot tell them apart."[14] Du Bois also used Japan's victory in the Russo-Japanese War in 1905 to praise the country as a "a colored people [who] successfully defied Europe."[15] To him, Russia's defeat changed everything; it set a new standard for how non-white countries should stand up to Western military powers, and this sentiment was echoed in many corners of Black America. After 1904, Japanese fashion became popular in Black communities, a Black theater program in Indianapolis staged a rendition of the opera *The Mikado*, and there was even a Black baseball team that had proudly named itself the Japs.[16]

Du Bois fulfilled a long-term dream when he visited Asia in 1936, specifically China, Manchuria, and Japan, to witness the conditions of Japanese imperialism firsthand.[17] His first stop was to Manchukuo, the new name given to Manchuria after being invaded by the Imperial Japanese army and turned into a puppet state.[18] He didn't view the people of Manchuria as victims of a colonial campaign, instead praising Japan's work there as "nothing less than marvelous," describing a fully employed people who seemed peaceful and happy.[19] In newspaper columns he published during and after his trip, he wrote at length about "little Japanese touches," the cleanliness of his hotel and blue kimono, and the "courteous" service he received.[20] Rather than denounce colonial projects altogether, which would seem to better align with his values, he instead wrote that "no nation should rule a colony whose people they cannot conceive as equals," and this—he asserted—was Japan ruling over Manchuria, a country where he said "a lynching would be unthinkable."[21]

But there is something less "unthinkable" that was also happening during Du Bois's trip to Manchukuo. Between 1936 and 1945, a covert Japanese warfare research facility located there called Unit 731 committed war crimes on an estimated three thousand civilians who were vivisected without anesthesia in grotesque human experiments that included deliberately freezing human limbs, contaminating shrapnel with pathogens before inserting it into the human body, and pressure-chamber experiments comparable to the ones performed by Sigmund Rascher at Dachau concentration camp in Germany.[22] Du Bois didn't see Emperor Hirohito authorize Unit 731 to use bubonic plague, cholera, typhus, and anthrax as biological weapons to kill an estimated 200,000 people.[23] Or when Unit 731 purposely injected fleas with bubonic plague and dropped them on Chinese cities.[24] And if Du Bois had known, he probably would not have believed that this all took place under the supervision and with the full cooperation of the medical, scientific, and academic communities.[25] These war crimes were safely guarded state secrets at the time; now, they are considered so atrocious that their scope has been compared to the horrors of the Holocaust.[26]

Letters from this visit read like a proxy critique of the European presence that controlled a significant portion of Chinese mining, commerce, and manufacturing. In a meeting with several important Chinese diplomats, educators, businessmen, and journalists, Du Bois railed against their continued relationship with white countries, demanding to know "why [they] hated Japan more than Europe when they had suffered more from England, France, and Germany than Japan."[27]

This was one year before the Nanjing Massacre.

Du Bois finally made his way to Japan at the invitation and
thanks to the efforts of Hikida Yasuichi, a Japanese diplomat.[28]
Hikida is a controversial character in his own right. He spent a lot
of his time in the United States visiting historically Black colleges
and universities and meeting with Black intellectual elites like
James Weldon Johnson, Rayford Logan, Mary Church Terrell,
and Walter White.[29] Hikida also translated a number of books by
African American authors into Japanese, including *The Souls of
Black Folk* by W. E. B. Du Bois and *The Fire in the Flint* by Walter
White, which he translated without White's permission.[30] These
texts were promoted by the Japanese state to expose the cruelty of
white America toward African Americans; by doing that, the state
used Black suffering to validate its colonial offensive in China.

In 1938, Hikida started working for the Japanese consulate in
New York and began attending Black community meetings in Harlem that were sometimes used as a platform to defend his country's
invasion of China. According to Roi Ottley, an African American
journalist, Hikida said that the Japanese occupation was part of
their effort to "rid China of whites" and modernize it in the spirit
of Pan-Asianism. Walter White, then the president of the NAACP,
opposed the Japanese occupation. But Du Bois, obviously, felt very
differently.[31] Hikida and Du Bois had fundamentally misaligned
agendas. Both were invested in exposing the hypocrisy of white
Western racism. But Hikida, on behalf of Japan, repackaged the
horrors of Black Civil Rights as cause for the Japanese *subjugation*
of other Asian countries, while Du Bois aligned himself with a for-
midable Eastern military power to bolster Black *liberation* at home.
And while there are half-truths and rationalizations found in both
perspectives, there's no acknowledgment of the exploitation and
imagined superiority in which they were both couched.

Du Bois arrived in Kobe, where he was received warmly by
a delegation, reporters, and escorts who personally handled his

visit. During his time there, he gave lectures at Kobe College and was taken sightseeing by the governor's secretary in the governor's private car.[32] Upon arriving in Osaka, Du Bois was received as a "world famed scholar," and when he moved on to Kyoto, he gave lectures at several universities.[33] By the time he made it to Tokyo, word of his travels had already preceded him, and he was greeted like a celebrity by journalists and photographers. The Japanese Office of Foreign Affairs* treated him to a party with geisha, whom he described as "modest" and "charming," and he bragged that in Japan, he was treated with the respect he deserved even in the presence of white people.[34]

Du Bois needed to leave the United States to be treated with even a modest level of respect, and the indignity of this is felt in the written accounts of his trip. But I *also* wonder if Du Bois was consciously sanitizing what colonialism *means* to further what he saw as Black liberation. In reading his columns and letters, I can see why he found the idea of defeating whiteness at its own game so intoxicating, but that also involved weaponizing the trauma of another brutalized people, which he tacitly participated in by praising their colonizer. And I *have* to believe that this tested his value system. Perhaps he believed that true liberation—which would demand an end to all settler colonialism—was too idealistic. After all, choosing a "lesser evil" is (still) a common feature of American ideology and politics. I'm a little uneasy critiquing his motivations while sitting comfortably in a time decades removed. But as one of our most important figures, and a self-appointed member of the Talented Tenth, Du Bois's role as a leader implies that there are also followers. And I find myself asking the question: Where would he have led us if history had been different?

---

* In Du Bois's letters, the Office of Foreign Affairs is used. But he was likely referring to the Ministry of Foreign Affairs.

After returning to the United States, Du Bois drafted a speech simply titled the Meaning of Japan in 1937. Equal parts travel writing and analysis, it's a discursive love letter that seems well-intentioned but also exoticizes the country. As he speaks of the nation's cultural curiosities, he engages in a reductive gaze that calls Japan a "country of little things with dwarfed trees and tiny gardens."[35] Many of the observations he wrote during his trip are on full display in this speech, which he uses to demonstrate how economic and industrial interests can unite a people under one cause. Du Bois attempts to explain the country as a whole—from the Heian period to then present day, including the Buddhist religion and Confucius. In one section, he circuitously positions Japan as the underdog left with no choice but to invade China to protect itself:

> The Japanese were compelled by the concert of European powers to take nothing from China but Korea and Formosa [Taiwan] which meant that China, now revealed as weak and tottering, was to be divided by Europeans with Japan left out ... From this time until today Japan has presented a problem for those who think of the future of modern civilization as a problem of white folk.

In another section, he justifies the puppet state of Manchuria (Manchukuo) as a project that defied the West because it was accomplished by a non-white race:

> Japan in 1931 seized Manchuria and made it into a puppet state and later dominated two districts of North China. The reaction toward Japan was bitter and the feeling throughout the European and American world would, under other cir-

cumstances and in other ages, have led immediately to war. But Europe, as Japan well knew, could not fight and for the first time since the Turks threatened Vienna, a colored people successfully defied Europe.[36]

Du Bois's words read like propaganda, which, in a way, they were. He was hoping to use Japan's strengthened global position to draw parallels between two "colored" ethnic groups standing up to white supremacy—but it doesn't take into account whether or not Japan sees *itself* as a "colored" nation. That's an important distinction to make given the country's troubled relationship to race. To me, Du Bois's essay is written through an internalized Western gaze that takes the position of defining the identity of another people for his personal use. Perhaps this speaks to the way his own racial trauma had shaped his thinking. I say that as a person with her own fair share, belonging to the same people *he* did, and we have more than enough to go around.

This goes without saying, but the Meaning of Japan isn't really the "meaning" of Japan. It's what Japan meant to *him* and, possibly, what it could have meant to others who shared his agenda and vision for a different future for African Americans. And the "meaning" of Black studies in Japan also served its own purpose.

The United States' anti-Asian immigration bills fueled outrage and deep concern among scholars, professors, and journalists in Japan, who rightly identified the underlying cause of anti-Asian racism as anti-Black racism.[37] During the Paris Peace Conference in 1919, Japan proposed including a principle of racial equality into the charter of the budding League of Nations, which six of the seventeen representatives rejected.[38] U.S. president Woodrow Wilson, chair of the conference, declared that it was not unanimous and, therefore, would not pass.[39] Japan responded by condemning the West's "callous" attitude toward oppressed people around the world.[40]

This was a pivotal moment for several reasons. First, it put President Wilson in an extremely awkward position by showcasing his own hypocrisy and only reinforced Japan as a "leader" of non-white nations to Black people who were closely watching.[41] Du Bois, who was also in Paris at the time for the Pan-African Congress, used the ruling to further press African American solidarity with Japan.[42] The second unintended effect of the rejected initiative was that it led Japan to abandon the idea of equal treatment with the white Western world.[43] Japanese leaders turned away from Western white teachings like Darwinism and turned instead to African-American studies.[44] Kitazawa Shinjiro, then a professor at Waseda University, rebuked the United States for building "their country with a view to enhancing freedom and equality, but [who] deprived the colored people of their natural rights, by regarding the white race as superior and the colored as inferior."[45] Kitazawa also adds, "The cultural stage of the Negro today is as low as an infant in every respect ... It is striking how much progress they have made over the last fifty years. They are developing just like little kids." It's a much less flattering comparison that mirrors some of the infantilizing statements of Du Bois, but the fact remains that white hypocrisy brought the Black and Japanese communities closer together.

In 1925, Mitsukawa Kametarō, founder of the radical Japanese Pan-Asianist nationalist organization the Yūzonsha, authored the 1925 text *Kokujin Mondai*, or the Negro Question. In it, he effused over the intellectual contributions of people like Booker T. Washington, Harriet Tubman, Sojourner Truth, Marcus Garvey, Frederick Douglass, and W. E. B. Du Bois. Mitsukawa believed that "the next world war would be a war between the Blacks and the whites," and that "the [American] negros would side with Japan" should that come to pass.[46] Du Bois wasn't the only person who agreed with that statement. Black feminist leaders like Mary Church Terrell and Mary McLeod Bethune also rallied around the cause.[47] And even Du Bois's longtime rival, radical pan-Africanist Marcus Garvey, also believed that there would come a time of war between Black people and white people, which he said could be won by forming an alliance with Japan.[48] It was one of the most significant perspectives on which many members of the Black intellectual sphere agreed.[49]

In fact, radical Black organizations worked hand in hand with pro-Japanese nationalist groups to undermine the U.S. government. Groups like the Peace Movement of Ethiopia, the Colored American National Organization, and the Brotherhood of Liberty for the Black People of America worked closely with and were funded in part by Japanese diplomats to promote their causes.[50] Garvey's organization, the Universal Negro Improvement Association, or UNIA, also had links to the Pacific Movement of the Eastern World (PMEW)—a pro-Japanese African American organization that believed Japan would play an almost "messianic" role in liberating the non-white world.[51] The PMEW was founded in 1932 by self-proclaimed Japanese emissary Takahashi Satokata.* Takahashi's campaigns aimed to mostly subvert Black military conscription while forging economic bonds, and besides Hikida Yasuichi, he might have been the most significant Japanese figure influencing African American sentiment.[52] The PMEW was primarily tasked with rallying African Americans to support Japan and commit treason against the United States.[53] Founded in Chicago, the PMEW initially operated in Northern cities like Detroit

* Takahashi's status as an emissary has never been substantiated.

but expanded its operations to Southern states like Missouri and Mississippi, where lynching was rampant. There, the PMEW found an enthusiastic audience in people who were also repeatedly brutalized by white America. Takahashi recruited new African American members in deeply segregated cities like St. Louis and Kansas City while preaching about the sins and amorality of white men at such historic institutions as the Bethel AME Church.[54] He was also a member of the Black Dragon Society, an ultranationalist Japanese group that funneled money into radical Black Muslim groups like the Nation of Islam, which was run at the time by Malcolm X's mentor, Elijah Muhammad. Takahashi reads like a true believer. He was known for refusing to speak in meetings if white attendees were present, and his speeches were emotionally charged declarations that described Western civilization as a "sinking ship," which he urged African Americans to flee.[55]

In one lecture he gave, titled "The Sinking Ship and the Lifeboat," Takahashi said:

Leave the sinking ship. Civilization's march westward has reached its farthest western shore on the Pacific Coast of America. West of America is what? Hawaii, the Philippines and your friend Japan, the lifeboat of racial love made radiant by the star of the east, Japan.[56]

Around the same time that Takahashi was sowing pro-Japanese sentiment among Black communities in the United States, literature by Black luminaries was becoming more popular in Japan. A number of books were translated, published, and then studied as a means to subvert and defeat white Western racism and rule. More NAACP members were invited to speak in Japan, including James Weldon Johnson. Johnson is perhaps most famous for writing "Lift Every Voice and Sing," the official song of the NAACP, and he was the only Black American invited to speak at a conference held by the Institute of Pacific Relations (IPR), which took place in Kyoto in 1929.* Local reporters inundated him with questions about the NAACP and the future of African Americans.[57] He was presented as a "world figure" committed to the "emancipation of non-white races of the world." In his memoir, Johnson wrote of his surprise at learning how familiar the Japanese people were with Black issues. He was treated like a local celebrity and even invited to dine with Emperor Hirohito himself—an honor that, up to that point, had been bestowed upon fewer than two hundred foreigners.[58]

Praising Imperial Japan obviously placed Black American leaders in morally ambiguous terrain. When Du Bois described Japan as a country standing up to the white Western world, he wasn't wrong. Nor was Japan wrong to fear Western invasion of the continent. The Dutch held a colony in Indonesia from 1602 to 1949. Britain had colonies in Penang (Malaysia) from 1786 to 1957, Singapore from 1819 to 1963,† and Malacca (Malaysia) from 1824 to 1957 (previously ruled by the Dutch from 1641 to 1824 and the Portuguese from 1511 to 1641). An excoriating critique of Western greed and interventionism is richly deserved and a righteous reflection of the hypocrisy of a region that has fashioned itself into the global arbiter of freedom. There is probably some truth to the claim that the West would have continued its expansionism without militaristic resistance like the one presented by Japan, whose victory in the Russo-Japanese War was a significant milestone.

---

* Organizers of a previous IPR conference requested a "negro of distinction" to attend two years prior, in 1927, but because that conference took place in Honolulu, it did not happen. The American delegate believed this could invite discussion of white-Black relations, providing evidence of how white people viewed Asian relations, which they sought to avoid.
† Singapore became self-governing in 1959, but Britain still retained control of its defense and foreign policy. Only when Singapore became part of Malaysia in 1963 did British rule come to a complete end.

But I keep coming back to this previous statement that Du Bois wrote during his travels to Asia: "No nation should rule a colony whose people they cannot conceive as Equals."

There can be *no* equality where any nation rules another because that dominion is only claimed through subjugation. To think otherwise is a very, well, *elitist* position to take. If Du Bois saw himself as part of a Talented Tenth leading the Black American diaspora, then perhaps Japan was the Asian equivalent in his eyes. And he saw himself in Japan, which also means seeing the *inferiority* of others.

I feel compelled to compare Du Bois's elitism with contemporary attitudes of respectability and how it makes us carry the representation of others. When individuals are forced to be the best of a whole group of people, it creates distance between that person and everyone else—but most importantly, between the individual and their authentic self. And that can feel like spinning on an axis shaped like a high horse light-years away in outer space with your own intellectual ambitions revolving around you like the rings of Saturn—far away from the causes you represent. In *that* sense, I relate to Du Bois more than I can say.

In 1940, Japan joined the Tripartite Pact with Nazi Germany and Italy, creating the Axis Powers. This shocked many African Americans, who were repulsed by Hitler's savagely racist philosophy of Aryan superiority, which included open disdain toward Asian countries. In a 1937 column for the *Pittsburgh Courier* titled "A Chronicle of Race Relations," Du Bois wrote that Italy's colonial campaigns in Libya, Somalia, Ethiopia, and Eritrea had turned its hands "red with the blood of Africa."[59] And he went on to describe Japan's decision to join the alliance as an act of self-defense, blaming the racism of the United States, France, and Britain for "driving" Japan "into the arms of Hitler."[60]

Clearly Du Bois was demonstrating confirmation bias, but

many other people shared his sentiments. After Japan's attack on Pearl Harbor, the United States began to imprison Japanese Americans without due process. In 1942, President Roosevelt's Executive Order 9066 led to the forcible removal of an estimated 110,000 Japanese Americans from their homes, two-thirds of whom were U.S. citizens.[61] By the end of the war in 1945, 125,000 people— nearly half of whom were children—had been imprisoned in what Roosevelt later admitted were concentration camps.[62] Their living conditions included sleeping in livestock paddocks surrounded by barbwire, food shortages, and executions of disabled and elderly people by military police who shot and killed them under the claim that they were "attempting to escape."[63] It's one of the most horrific human rights violations of the twentieth century, and it, unsurprisingly, led many Black Americans to render the U.S. government's criticism of Japan's fascist alliance as hypocritical and irrelevant.[64] Some even saw it as an indication of what they would themselves have to face one day. African American author and satirist George Schuyler, a ferocious critic of Du Bois and Garvey, went so far to suggest "this may be a prelude to our own fate."[65]

In 1942, the Office of War Information conducted a private survey of African American households in New York to "gauge" their views on Japan. Eighteen percent believed that life would be better under Japanese rule if they won the war, and 31 percent said that things would be the same.[66] Whether that was an indictment of U.S. treatment or a resounding endorsement of Japanese support, it definitely didn't bode well for the Roosevelt administration.[67] That same year, the FBI led raids and arrested many members of the PWEM, including Elijah Muhammad.[68] Takahashi, who had been arrested and deported several times, was imprisoned in 1939 and released in 1942.[69]

Regardless of the government's concerns, Du Bois used his platform to assert Japan's victimhood, while offering little examination into how Japan's policies, history, and ambitions may have been a *cause* for joining the Axis Powers. When Hitler declared the Japanese people to be "honorary Aryans," it obviously wasn't because they were white.[70]/* Infantilizing Japan as a besieged nation forced into joining one of the most monstrous alliances in history only emphasized the differences between the main Axis Powers, without ever pointing out that all three nations were ruled by nationalist leaders, had colonies in other countries, and were governed by officials obsessed with racial purity. At the same time, it displays a kind of paternalism that I see in the Meaning of Japan, as if Du Bois alone was the conduit endowed with the ability to explain the essence of a country he had only visited. It's equally as absurd to think that anyone in Japan could translate the "meaning" of African Americana to the rest of Japan—though, that's kind of what people like Takahashi tried. All these efforts to marry the values of African Americans to Imperial Japan were clumsy—and, at times, dangerous. When a colonized people empathize with an imperial master, they abandon themselves. But I want to extend Du Bois the additional courtesy of recognizing how trauma can push people into making unholy alliances. In his reimagining of Japan as a freedom fighter, perhaps he was also reimagining the United States as the colonized, Europe as the enslaved, and the West as the region in need of moral guidance—putting Japan in a position to liberate white rulers from their own uncivilized nature, and to lift *them* from the abyss of their own depravity.

But that could just be my own interpretation.

After Japan's defeat in World War II, Du Bois did issue a very soft reversal of his position by criticizing Japan's caste system:

"So far as Japan was fighting against color caste, and striving

---

* The concept of Aryan is also an appropriated term, which originally references people of the Indo-Aryan race and doesn't mean "white" at all.

against the domination of Asia by Europeans, she was absolutely right," he wrote.

> But ... so far as she tried to substitute for Europeans an Asiatic caste system under a superior Japanese race, and for the domination and exploitation of the peasants of Asia by Japanese trusts and industrialists, she offered Asia no exchange for western exploitation.[71]

But though he "abandoned" the idea that Japanese superiority was a better option for Black people than European supremacy, he did not explain when or what had led him to the conclusion that Japan's purpose was no longer "liberation" but "self-interested imperialism."[72] In fact, he never offered any substantive criticism that matched the rigor of his earlier statements of support; rather, he continued to add that he believed that the "ideas" Japan had started— while temporarily derailed—would continue to grow.[73] I can only determine that these are the musings of a wounded ego, whose champion had been humiliated on the world stage by another U.S. atrocity. Not so much an "admission" of erroneous or misguided beliefs, but a concession of defeat. With all the support that Japan had received from the Black community, what happened in Hiroshima and Nagasaki wasn't just a blow to the country of Japan; it was a dramatic blow to everyone who had wanted Japan to succeed.[74] Once a shining beacon of non-white liberation, the nation was defeated and then occupied—yet another victim of U.S. aggression.

And when I visited the Hiroshima Peace Memorial Museum, I saw just how crushing that blow really was.

8.

Problematizing the "Meaning" of Solidarity

GROUP OF FELLOW TEACHERS AND I DEBOARDED the shinkansen alongside a cluster of chatty families and tourists. It was a bright, humid day—beautiful even beneath the towering shell of the so-called A-Bomb Dome, a rusted skeleton of the Hiroshima Prefectural Industrial Promotion Hall originally designed by Czech architect Jan Letzel. The fragments still harbor traces of that distinctly Bohemian aesthetic: the corroded metal outline of the dome and the curved brick walls. I let my mind fill in the rest of the structure, rebuilding the concrete and brick that had been gutted by the nuclear blast of Little Boy on August 6, 1945. It was like remembering the life of someone while visiting their grave.

The monuments were vibrant displays of grief, each more somber than the last. The Children's Peace Monument, a statue dedicated to Sadako Sasaki, hit me the hardest. She had folded one thousand paper cranes as a meditation for world peace while dying from leukemia that had developed as a result of the nuclear blast. Her story, which has come to represent the countless children who died from radiation poisoning, felt even more poignant as I watched young children playing around the monument.

The memorials lead to an unsuspecting, modern museum. Looking back, it reminds me of a little of the brutalist apartment complexes I've seen in Berlin. Walking past the manicured flower patches and engraved placards, I was inundated with a growing sense of dread—as if we were being lured inside under a false sense of security.

Inside the museum, we were greeted by the Dangers of Nuclear Weapons, a hall lined with a panel of celluloid black-and-white images that stretched across the theater. The images flickered, showing first what these schools, these buildings, and these hospitals had looked like before the bomb, then the skeletal aftermath—like a body that decomposes leaving only the bones. Whole neighborhoods wiped off the map, images of people born with birth defects for decades in the aftermath, children without limbs or faces, human shadows burned permanently into concrete slabs. Centuries of history vanished in an instant, replicating the sudden impact of the bomb on the prefecture. Text panels below the images asked us to try and pinpoint where specific places had once been, to find some shred of evidence that two images captured the same stretch of land.

The display created an image of near annihilation. And yet I found myself instinctively reaching for comparisons, not because there are any—and there definitely are *not*—but because the black-and-white images reminded me of others I had seen. Specifically, the photograph of Sarah Carrier's house in Rosewood, Florida, which was burned to the ground during a white massacre in 1923. Or the smoldering ruins of Black Wall Street after the Tulsa Race Massacre of 1921, with plumes of black smoke still curling up into the sky when the sun rose. Or what I imagined the scene resembled after the Wilmington massacre of 1898, or the Colfax Massacre of 1873. To be clear, they are completely different events from what took place in Hiroshima and Nagasaki, but all of these are acts of state-sanctioned violence by the United States against people who are not white and assaults on the very humanity of civilians—men, women, children, aunties, grandparents.

And those instruments of war have also been used on U.S. citizens. On July 16, 1945, the Manhattan Project scientists, led by J. Robert Oppenheimer, conducted the Trinity test, detonating an atomic bomb two hundred miles away from the town of Los Alamos in New Mexico. Nearly half a million Hispanos and Native Americans lived within a 150-mile radius of the blast zone, some as close as twelve miles away.[1] Nobody was evacuated beforehand, nor were any warnings of radiation poisoning issued. Some were impacted immediately, including young girls at a summer camp, who fell out of their bunk beds, then danced and played in the "debris like it was snow" letting it fall on their tongues and rubbing it on their faces.[2] In 1947, a health-care worker named Kathryn S. Behnke wrote to Stafford Warren, the scientist responsible for radiation safety during the Manhattan Project, to report that thirty-five infant deaths from the area were recorded a month after the test was conducted. Warren wrote back denying any breach of safety protocol and saying he had not heard of the spike in infant mortality. In the following decades, people who lived through the bomb testing developed various health problems like cancer and heart disease. People who were affected became known as "downwinders." In 2010, the Centers for Disease Control and Prevention concluded that radiation exposure from the Trinity test reached levels "10,000 times higher than currently allowed." A formal apology has never been issued.[3]

As I kept moving through the museum, I could feel the weight carried by the people who had cataloged and rendered that history in such meticulous detail to ensure that it would never be forgotten. In the next room, someone had sculpted clay effigies of young children in school uniforms and backpacks with skin melting off their arms, stumbling through rubble and choking on atomized air. My friends and I became quieter, separating into our own pods of

solitude to process and reflect. When I arrived at the permanent exhibit, I stopped short, trying to figure out what I was seeing, slowed
by the burden of confronting America's finest hour from the other
side. There were personal objects left behind by the victims, and I instinctively gravitated toward the personal items. Handbags, shoes,
tricycles that had once belonged to small children, all bleached to
the same charred rust color by the blast of radiation. A blast that
had aged young children into ghosts, into artifacts, into historical
records that only asked us to remember, and never repeat it again.

When we left the museum, the sky was cloudy. None of us had
kept track of the time, each lost in our own thoughts. Walking
into the night, I felt myself release a deep, shaky breath—feeling
the blood rush from my head as I bent over to catch myself. I felt
nauseous. Connecting the dots between the horrors that had been
inflicted on Hiroshima and Nagasaki and how it had ended the Second World War left me feeling completely twisted up inside. I had
learned more about the war in the Pacific from that single visit than
I had during all my years in school—and I understood why. It turns
the same people who have fashioned themselves as heroes into
people who are also very comfortable playing the role of the villain.

It wasn't the solidarity I had been looking for, but it was undeniable. I wanted to believe that there had been other acts of unity between both cultures. Ironically, W. E. B. Du Bois was the one who
led me to the organization working on exactly that. After the bomb-
ings of Hiroshima and Nagasaki and Emperor Hirohito's unconditional surrender, scholars once again revitalized the subject area of
Black studies. Living under U.S. occupation after the war, Japanese
academics found solidarity in the struggles of Black Americans.[4]
In 1954, the Society for Black Studies at Kobe City University of
Foreign Studies was formed—now called the Japan Black Studies
Association (JBSA).[5] Initially comprised of academics, the group
quickly expanded to include politicians, unionists, housewives,

and African American soldiers stationed in Japan.[6] They also began to publish a journal of Black studies, called *Kokujin Kenkyu*, which published Marxist articles on anti-colonial movements on the African and South American continents. However, after being asked to provide a list of its members, the Japan Black Studies Association turned its focus to more cultural articles.[7] The group studied translated works like *Native Son* by Richard Wright, *Invisible Man* by Ralph Ellison, *Go Tell It on the Mountain* by James Baldwin, and *Not Without Laughter* by Langston Hughes.[8] Throughout the 1950s, '60s, and '70s, the Kobe branch of the organization held public lectures on American and African history and did radio lectures. In 1963, the Tokyo branch held an event commemorating the hundredth anniversary of the Emancipation Proclamation, including a discussion by Nobel laureate Ōe Kenzaburō.[9] In 1966, the group published a collection of essays by Dr. Martin Luther King Jr., Malcolm X, James Baldwin, W. E. B. Du Bois, and others titled *Black Liberation Movement in America: Emerging Negro Leaders*, a milestone that marked the organization's ten-year anniversary. In the 1980s, the JBSA began to focus on more feminist texts by emerging African American writers like Alice Walker and Toni Morrison—who still features as a central figure in Black studies across Japan.[10] In the 1990s, the JBSA expanded its literary focus further to include Caribbean authors like Jamaica Kincaid and Edwidge Danticat. The group is still active. The journal still publishes regular articles on Black studies, but only in Japanese. They also hold bilingual events in Japanese and English, monthly meetings, and annual conventions and curate activities to educate larger parts of society on Black and African culture and history.[11]

I didn't learn about the JBSA until years after leaving Japan, when I began to write this book. Their work feels like a significant and evolving conversation that marks a turning point in discourse. If I had known about the organization sooner, I would have tried to seek out members to discuss some of my favorite books, which, in and of itself, would have completely changed my relationship to the country. Imagine discussing Toni Morrison with Nishida Kiriko, who wrote her doctoral thesis in large part on the themes in *Playing in the Dark: Whiteness and the Literary Imagination*. Or *The Souls of Black Folk* by W. E. B. Du Bois with Kato Tsunehiko, whose paper introduced me to the JBSA's work. Or discussing the life of Yasuke with Furukawa Tetsushi, trying to peel back the layers that separate the man from the myth. Would we do it over yakitori and beer or matcha and mochi? And would that feel too elitist . . . or just like home?

*

I had my own tender and unexpected moments of solidarity while living in Japan. Kiyoshi-san was one of the teachers I had taught with, but he was different from the others. When everyone typically spent their Friday nights drinking at the local izakaya, he was mostly absent. He was an expert at seamlessly removing himself from social gatherings, then reappearing at school the next workday and behaving as if he hadn't missed anything. One day, just out of abundant curiosity, I asked him when his birthday was—he whispered that it was that very day. And then it made sense: we were both Aquariuses, both happiest when left alone to think up weird and unusual ideas.

Once, he stepped out of his shell to ask me and Scott if we would come to one of his Toastmasters events. He explained that he had joined the club to become a more confident public speaker and said it would mean a lot to him if we came and provided feedback—because his speech was in English. Scott and I both agreed and sat in the middle of the auditorium, right where he could see us. We both smiled for encouragement, and I already knew that I was going to be very positive regardless of his actual delivery.

I recognized the first words instantly because they're seared into my brain, a part of my culture and identity, a cornerstone of American history: I Have a Dream by Dr. Martin Luther King Jr. Kiyoshi-san took his time, savoring the words as he scanned the room—looking at me, then the other members from his group, and finally the emptier corners of the auditorium. At first, I couldn't hide my surprise. Then, I found myself getting defensive, even critical, feeling that those words belonged to me and not to him. I wondered why he chose that speech, what Dr. King's message meant to him, and why he had chosen to deliver it in front of us. But as he relaxed into the speech, I saw him become more emotional, pausing and thinking about the gravity of the words before he said them. I could feel tears coming to my eyes. I was moved by how deeply those words inspired him because I realized that he *did* understand them. That he loved them. When he finished, Scott and I gave a standing ovation—breaking character temporarily to yell and cheer like the loud, obnoxious foreigners we normally were.

When Kiyoshi-san dropped us off later that night, Scott got out of the car first. As I followed, Kiyoshi-san leaned back and stopped me.

"I'm really glad you came, Jennifer-san," he said. "It really meant a lot to me."

I smiled and told him it was my pleasure. It was the truth.

I'VE THOUGHT ABOUT that evening many times since leaving Japan. Kiyoshi-san came top of mind again in 2020, when the murder of George Floyd triggered a tidal wave of Black Lives Matter demonstrations around the world. I was heartened to see several took place in Tokyo. Thirty-five hundred protesters marched from Yoyogi Park down Omotesando and through the same crossing in Shibuya that had made me feel like I was sinking into the asphalt on my first jet-lagged night in Japan. I could almost count the footsteps from the demonstrators' path to the udon shack. The African American founder of Black Lives Matter Tokyo, Sierra Todd, led the march, surrounded by Japanese allies, holding up signs in support of Black and trans Black lives, shouting phrases like, "Racism is the real pandemic!" and "Black pride!" and "Enough is enough!" It was a sight that covered me in goose bumps because I never thought I would see something like that: a public acknowledgment of the exact problems I had quietly kept to myself during my time in Kudamatsu.

"It is not enough to just send our prayers. We need to change society, not only for George Floyd, but also for those who died in the past," said a twenty-two-year-old student named Fukui Shu.[12]

"In Japan, there are far-right people who discriminate against other races. And Koreans and Chinese in Japan are exposed to a lot of hate speech. These things must not be allowed and we need to oppose this," said forty-four year old Ida Naho.[13]

As I read the articles reporting the protests, I came across a curious news bulletin from *The Japan Times* posted on Facebook: Hiroshima is one of the few cities outside of the United States that observes Martin Luther King Day with equal significance. It was an initiative spearheaded by the former mayor, Akiba Tadatoshi, who frequently mines Dr. King's speeches for inspiration in his diplomatic efforts for nuclear disarmament. In 1967, Dr. King even addressed a letter to "the people of Japan," writing, "Japan knows the horror of war and has suffered as no other nation under the cloud of nuclear disaster. Certainly Japan can stand strong for a world of peace."[14] He had also expressed hopes to visit the country one day. Today, when residents in the United States choose a place for a peaceful demonstration against nuclear proliferation, the Martin Luther King Jr. memorial in Washington, D.C., is a popular gathering spot. I recommend seeing it as I did for the first time in 2014—during spring, with his likeness carved in stone illuminated by a thick halo of Yoshino cherry blossoms.

Jennifer Neal and Catapult acknowledge that the city of Chicago has long been a center for Native peoples. The area is the traditional homelands of the Anishinabe or the Council of the Three Fires: the Ojibwa, Ottawa, and Potawatomi nations. Many other nations consider this area their traditional homeland, including the Myaamia, Ho-Chunk, Menominee, Sac and Fox, Peoria, Kaskaskia, Wea, Kickapoo, and Mascouten. We acknowledge all Native peoples who came before us.

PART 2

✳

The Chi, Illinois,
United States of America

August 20, 2007*–December 13, 2008

My Libra Moon (Inner World) in the Fifth House: Individuals with their moon in this sign have a deep need for harmony and balance in all of their relationships, but especially their personal relationships. They enjoy sharing, balancing, and harmonizing with other people. They have a reasonable and fair-minded approach to society and the world around them. Caring, charming, witty, and sympathetic, they're excellent planners and strategic thinkers. People naturally gravitate to lunar Librans for their ability to find middle ground in almost every situation.

Trouble normally arises when it comes to their romantic relationships, which they take very seriously and can be very intense. They have a strong need for partnership and can be impulsive in love. This is why many people with this position get involved in marriages or living arrangements at a very young age. They're very instinctive, take unnecessary risks, and can be irresponsible with their emotions. Lunar Librans tend to battle with two primary fears: being alone and making the wrong decision. Unfortunately, the only way for them to overcome those fears is to accept the fact that both will eventually happen, especially because they can be prone to compromising too much of themselves in an effort to please others.

9.

That Inescapable Delicious Feeling

The years, after all, have a kind of emptiness, when we spend too many of them on a foreign shore. We defer the reality of life, in such cases, until a future moment, when we shall again breathe our native air; but, by and by, there are no future moments; or, if we do return, we find that the native air has lost its invigorating quality, and that life has shifted its reality to the spot where we have deemed ourselves only temporary residents. Thus, between two countries, we have none at all, or only that little space of either in which we finally lay down our discontented bones.

—NATHANIEL HAWTHORNE

MY FLIGHT OUT OF TOKYO WAS A MAUDLIN ODYS-sey across an ocean of time. I counted the list of things I was losing as I traversed the international date line once more: the smell of incense beneath the pagoda at sunset, the individually wrapped cakes filled with red bean paste and vanilla custard, the students who wrote me notes on decorative paper with affection-ate words framed by drawings of sad kittens—they apologized for any grammatical mistakes made over the past year. Still, I was sure that it was time to leave. I was certain that Kudamatsu was only the first stop on a very long journey ahead, and yet I still agonized as I left it behind, knowing that time would one day dim my memories of its tree-lined mountainscape.

Kudamatsu might have been the closest place to home I had experienced up to that point—and I said so during my leaving ceremony, reciting a carefully rehearsed speech in hiragana, written with my left hand. I dressed in my brand-new sakura yukata, embraced by my tearful students—who wanted to arm wrestle one last time. Even though they knew I had let them win, they embraced me tightly. My colleagues laminated an okonomiyaki recipe as a gift especially for me. I didn't cry in front of them, but tears later fell against my chest as I fingered my gifted notes and trinkets while waiting for the train in an udon stall on the shinkansen platform taking me to Narita International Airport. As I'd come to expect, I felt better by the time I licked the seasoning at the bottom of the bowl. I battled mixed feelings all the way to the airport, and during boarding. As my plane landed in the United States, my doubt was still the width of the blue-and-white sky that welcomed me home.

There was no time to adjust to life in Chicago. Just do. I moved into a new studio apartment on the Gold Coast, with a single window that barely opened enough for me to drop eggs on drunken passersby who made way too much noise early in the morning. My neighbor was a man from Paris whose French woke me up every time he was humping someone to death in the middle of the night. The hallway had dark-red carpet, and the air frequently smelled like soup. My dad arrived to help me unpack and put together some pieces of furniture. He walked into my studio and plopped down at a small kitchen nook. I didn't even blink when I pointed and yelled at him to take off his shoes.

*

The first thing I noticed was the size of things: the meals I could no longer finish, the buildings that perforated the sky, the wide streets accommodating even wider vehicles that more closely resembled armored tanks. But if they were tanks, then where were their guns? As it turns out, everywhere. In their trunks, in the glove compartments, on hip bones, in kitchens and nursery closets. All over the five o'clock, six o'clock, seven o'clock, and early-morning news—along with pixelated photographs of the victims whose lives they had claimed. Some guns looked like complex machines. Others could rest in the palm of my hand, which then shook through the *pop pop pop* of target practice with my cousins before I politely asked if we could "just fucking leave."

Relatives and family friends looked me up and down, remarking on my weight and size. They wanted to know if I saw a geisha (yes). They wanted to know if I met a yakuza boss (maybe—who's asking?). They wanted to know if it's common to worship plants and animals, and when I began my preamble of "It's more complicated than that . . ." the instant response was "'Cuz you *know*, cousin . . . Jesus is *Kang*."

I became angry. *This* United States wasn't the place I remembered and had, at times, longed for during my time coveting Little Debbie snacks in Japan. Someone had scooped it all up in a black bag when I wasn't looking and replaced it with something louder, dirtier, newer—more *pop pop pop*–ier. This new place was a distortion of the one I remembered, and everyone in it was a paid actor. I wanted to crawl begging back to Japan. I missed the rice fields and noodle stalls. I thought about my neighborhood of rich landscapes filled with ancient cultural artifacts in Kudamatsu whenever I was confronted by Chicago's Confederate monuments and the tiered pagoda-shaped outline of P.F. Chang's neon sign. I asked questions that surprised even me:

Why do people throw their garbage *on the ground*?

Why are there so many people sleeping *on the streets instead of in homes*?

Why are men I don't know, don't even want to know, *grabbing me on the sidewalk and telling me to smile?*

Why did I need three referrals to get a gynecological examination that my insurance provider then would not cover?

Why did the sound of my accent from other people's mouths give me a headache when *I had missed hearing it for so long?*

The answer to these questions is a phrase known as reentry or reverse culture shock. Culture shock was first identified by Canadian anthropologist Kalervo Oberg, described as something "precipitated by the anxiety that results from losing the familiar signs and symbols of social discourse," whereas *reverse* (or reentry) culture shock is the kind of disorientation a person experiences when returning to their country of origin.[1] For a long time, both forms of shock were misunderstood. Oberg characterized culture shock as an "occupational disease," a "psychological malfunctioning," and an "affliction" because the dissonance that comes with questioning one's immediate surroundings can operate similarly to a mental illness.[2] But both culture shock and reverse culture shock, in fact, have some of the same symptoms: anger, irritability, mood swings, even suicidal or fatalistic thoughts. But there is general consensus that reverse culture shock is *much* harder because home stops being home and becomes uncharted terrain.[3]

Reverse culture shock can be such a disturbing experience that the U.S. Department of State has a section on its website addressing the challenges of readjusting back to American life: things like an abundance of materialism and waste and the high-speed pace of life. But the most hilarious bullet point is the list of "myths & misconceptions" that anyone returning to the United States may be struggling to reconcile—like the concept of American exceptionalism. If the U.S. Department of State doesn't even believe its own publicity, then why does anyone else?

Older thinking on culture shock and reverse culture shock

pinned the source of the "psychological malfunction" and the distressing effects of a "strange new culture" on the poor foreigner.[4] Now, we understand that this discomfort is part of a natural process when we are confronted with new information. And reconciliation between two different cultures can lead to learning and growth. After all, it *was* the same United States I remembered. With the same culture I remembered. With the same toxic politics I tried to forget. The only thing that had changed was me—and how I saw things anew. My old personal truths had been challenged, resulting in a revelation about my place in American society. Other people noticed my struggle to readjust as well. When relatives dragged me to church, I curled up in the pews, hissing at the pastor like a rattlesnake. I still threw up peace signs in all the photos the way I used to with my students, and people poked fun at me for changing.

But wasn't that the point?

Chicago wasn't just an experience in reverse culture shock. I was experiencing white-liberalism shock. White-*everything* shock. And deeply segregated–city shock, where white people were so sequestered from the rest of us that it felt as if the entire metropolis was conspiring to make almost everyone else invisible. Chicago is a concrete mecca in the sternum of America's heartland. Its unique brand of mobster movies, South Side hip-hop, and radical leftist movements have made their way onto television screens, onto radio stations, and into our social discourse. I could see how a duel between progress and the status quo had built a city as culturally rich as it is segregated, fostering a pernicious rift that was as visible in 2007 as the intersection of State and Madison, dividing the North Side from the South. And suddenly, it was my home. Chicago was still the United States, but for someone raised in Florida, it may as well have been a different planet.

I began to understand why my grandpa had turned his back on the so-called Progressive North, burrowing even deeper into the South—a rare example of how "you'll understand when you're older" actually proves to be true. For the first time, I truly *felt* Southern as a person, in the core of my genetic makeup. I realized how polite I was, how unusual it felt to stand in a line at the grocery store without talking to the person ahead of me, how strange it felt to not know someone's cousins from a nearby town. It was obvious, from my habits to the rustic aphorisms that spilled out of me like blackstrap molasses. In short, Chicago made me as nervous as a long-tailed cat in a room full of rocking chairs.

I had enrolled in the painting and drawing program at the School of the Art Institute of Chicago, which was very different from Florida State University. For one, it was a private school, meaning it had an endowment, which is a very aristocratic euphemism for being filthy rich. Buildings had names I only recognized from finance classes and corny conspiracy theories, and many of my peers were printmakers from Connecticut with English accents, photographers from old Southern oil money, and international students descended from long lineages of diplomats and statesmen. Everyone was studying to become a gallerist, curator, or artist—hyperrealists with an obsessive eye for detail, abstract sculptors, performance artists, and run-of-the-mill misogynists trying to disguise their craft as some state-of-the-art development in evolutionary philosophy. Is it a painting of a woman with distorted reproductive features being sodomized by a robot or is it a Stuckist critique of the role that artificial intelligence is playing in our own ontological destruction? Who can say? It's *art*!

I thought of myself as an artist, but at SAIC, I found myself described as "a Black artist," expected to create Black art, on Black issues, Black pain, and Black trauma. Black art had to be readily identifiable, featuring Black bodies and Black faces. Black artist statements were expected to incorporate references to Black hip-hop and Black history. None of these expectations seemed to have been established by the Black student body. It was the whim of some prominent white lecturers who taught my classes, led my critiques, and wrote assessments on my body of work. I didn't mind being called a Black artist because I am, but I resented the expectation to perform that for white gatekeepers who needed me to spoon-feed them clues to identify what was Black and what wasn't, only to then critique my work based on their perceived value of my race.

My frustration with these contradictions was exacerbated by how few Black people I actually saw in my classes, in my neighborhood, at my local grocery store. North of State and Madison, I rarely saw anyone who looked like me, unless they were homeless. But I did get a lot of looks whenever I walked down the street with a white classmate or peer—from Black people, and white ones, as if I were violating the city's unspoken terms and conditions and would be issued a residency-infraction notice from a faceless council who kept watch from Sears Tower.

People describe the South as the most racist place in the United States, but I had grown up with friends of almost every ethnicity and background. I knew the difference between maduros and tostones, challah and rugelach, jollof from Nigeria and jollof from Senegal. I knew how to make fry bread, and I knew how to pronounce pho before Anthony Bourdain and Barack Obama ever shared a bowl on the streets of Hanoi. The South's Confederate legacy needs no explanation, but it would be easier for me to accept its appointment as the scapegoat for American racism if I hadn't also lived in Chicago.

It wasn't unusual to meet people who had roots on the North Side going back at least two generations. People from the South Side had similar stories. Each side had its own layout, its own dining institutions, its own magnet schools, and its own baseball teams with their own baseball stadiums. During a visit to the Renaissance Society in the South Side, I grabbed something to eat at a packed bakery. People were shouting over one another in a long line that snaked out the door, but everyone was served quickly. That is, until it came to one person.

The cashier was a burly gentleman with arms like stone pillars who looked at the customer's Chicago Cubs cap, then looked back at him and said, "Not until you take off that hat. This is White Sox territory."

And he did.

Wherever I went in Chicago, I had an inescapable feeling that everyone around me had taken a side. It was like being the odd person left out of dodgeball-team selection. Everyone seemed to have their place, their spot, their crew. No one was taking new applicants. I was watching from the sidelines, not actually involved in what was going on, not understanding why it was happening, and, most importantly, uninvested in whether or not it happened at all. Even after several months had passed and I had developed a routine of classwork and studio time, that feeling did not go away.

That's when I had the idea to make my own community consisting of a small group of friends who didn't seem to mind my melee of weird readjusting behavior. I didn't think much of it at the time, but we were a diverse bunch: Black, Cuban, Chinese, Korean, Jewish. Our first meeting was at an Indian restaurant, eating garlic naan and rogan josh until we were kicked out for other dinner reservations. We complained about U.S. politics, talked about our travels, and complained about U.S. politics even more. We all shared a similar sense of humor and spoke openly about race and racism in a way we couldn't with others. It was such a wonderful night that we decided to make it a monthly restaurant meetup, choosing a different international cuisine each time. We even decided to give ourselves a name, which you'll have to excuse because it *was* 2007: Foodies International. We gave ourselves designated titles: president (sorry, it was me), vice president of restaurant selection, vice president of publicity, treasurer, and secretary. We wrote a list of rules for members: Everyone had to bring cash to make check division easier, everyone had to arrive on time so as not to hold up ordering, any new members had to be introduced by way of a core member who had attended our first meetup at the Indian restaurant. And no conservatives were allowed.

Over the coming months, we savored cheesy pierogi and stuffed cabbage rolls at Polish restaurants, devoured bulgogi and kimchi pancakes at Korean-barbecue shacks, relished dunking steaming-hot injera into vegetarian curries at Ethiopian hideaways and licking the oil from jibaritos off our fingers at Puerto Rican diners. I began to appreciate Chicago for its rich food culture. Each new plate had a regulating effect, and I found an equilibrium less affected by the transition from East to West. I followed Chicago's calendar of international food festivals on offer. It was my way of venturing offshore again, every month, in the company of like-minded friends. If I couldn't be traveling the world, then Chicago would bring the world to me in fragrant, delicious increments—as much as I could handle, as often as I wanted. It was how I found my place in the city and a way to be part of it. It was how I picked my side—the eaters, the pleasure-seekers, the people who launched into passionate speeches about socialism over smoked sausage.

Iconic historical photos keep a record of Black activists and leaders coming together over meals, napkins folded over their laps, fingers steepled in contemplation as they discussed important chapters in their respective movements: Martin Luther King Jr. at a table with his children for Sunday dinner; the Black Panthers feeding young children for their free breakfast program; Rosa Parks smiling at a dinner table with actress Marla Gibbs and Elaine Steele, cofounder of the Rosa and Raymond Parks Institute for Self Development, smiling with empty plates and tea glasses in front of them and a painting of Langston Hughes in the background; Maya Angelou in her signature sunglasses, grinning widely while gripping a plate piled high with food.

Few people know that, in addition to being a Pulitzer Prize–winning author, poet, activist, and musician, Angelou was also a passionate cook who wrote several cookbooks toward the end of her life. Characterized by *The New York Times* as someone who had a way with words and spices, she once compared inviting someone to sit at your dinner table to inviting someone into your life. She spoke lovingly about the many notable figures she had shared meals with and cooked meals for: James Baldwin, Louise Meriwether, Nina Simone, and Toni Morrison—to name a few. Angelou was known to frequent places like Paparazzi in New York's East Village and order takeout from El Faro in the West Village.[5] Photographs of her laughing and smiling over elaborate half-eaten dinners are some of the most joyful images you'll ever see because they show her, not as some unflappable feminist symbol, but as a human being who needs the same things we all do: connection, community, nourishment.

To me, Maya Angelou has always been a symbol of pleasure and rest, which she spoke about at length whenever someone tried to prop her up as some flawless figurehead. She encouraged young Black women in particular to find joy and community, and she led by example. I wanted to create something similar to Angelou's legendary gatherings, albeit on a much smaller scale. And while it would take years for me to build up the culinary skills needed to host someone in my home, I developed the social skills early on: be friendly, be polite, be open, and curate a group of people as excited to eat as I am. We weren't changing the world with our dinners, or even the city of Chicago. We were just changing the experience of that city for ourselves. Far from radical. But in my case, a potent example of how communion can be a healing act.

Our meetups had an unintended effect: it became clear that Chicago wasn't going to be my final destination. I enjoyed being immersed in the global world more than the local. I knew how to be at restaurants—but it was everywhere else that was a challenge. The classroom, the studio, the streets. I fantasized about travel and escape. I still struggled with the noise of traffic and restaurants. I stared at the evening news in confusion. The collage of talking heads that spoke, dressed, and deflected in exactly the same way, forming a spray-tanned legion of liars banging the drums of war against any form of universal health care because they "supported the troops" too much to adopt socialism, which was what the war in Iraq was all about anyway: Freedom. Guns. America. I briefly considered burning the "greatest country on earth" to the ground and rebuilding with whoever was left. When I confided this to a friend, she scowled and replied, "Okay, Doctor Manhattan."

I was having what I can now recognize as the early stages of an identity crisis—perhaps my quarter-life crisis, as it's often referred to. I couldn't see a future in Chicago, or anywhere else in the United States, and at the same time, I had trouble remembering the past, which felt like an illusion whenever I tried to analyze and compare it to what I saw in front of me. Sometimes, when other art students were going to open-studio nights and drinking in bars, I was just lying in bed—paralyzed by the vastness of a single city block. Other times I was loud and convivial, striking up conversations with complete strangers, such a force of energy that I could start or end a party by entering or exiting a room.

I could clearly see the United States for what it was, and perhaps for the first time ever, I no longer saw myself *in* it. That's when I began plotting where to move to when my program ended. I had no idea where I would go, but I was open to the signs—any sign, pointing in any direction, as long as it was far away.

Then, one evening, when I got back to my apartment, I had a message on my answering machine from Matteo.

"Just thinking about yoooOOOooooou," he said, his Aussie diphthongs exacerbated by alcohol.

"Oh," I said to myself.

I put away my groceries and pulled out a frying pan to make some eggs, stopping just before I could pour them onto the hot skillet.

"Oh no . . ."

10.

An American Werewolf in Australia

If he can't use your comb, don't bring him home.

—AFRICAN AMERICAN PROVERB

FELL IN LOVE WITH MATTEO EASILY BECAUSE IT HAP-
pened from a distance. It was safe, secret, and obfuscated by ten
thousand miles and an ocean so vast that I couldn't even picture the owner of the voice I had been speaking to over the past
year. It was just a voice. Just a melody of sounds that clustered
together, bouncing off a satellite in outer space and into my ear
late at night—early in the morning his time—saying things that I
believed were true. Things like, "I can't stop thinking about you,"
"I think I'm developing feelings," and "I needed those extra twelve
years just to be able to keep up with you."

His behavior seemed to justify our age gap. He was affable,
kind, funny, consistent, and gentle—all attributes that *seemed* in
short supply among people my own age. In return, I showed him
how smart, creative, witty, and affectionate I was—all signs of my
advanced maturity. Our connection lured me out of a period of

self-isolation and into a shared intimate space with a person who, I felt, knew me so well because he was a complete stranger.

We began at the start of 2007, on Myspace, right before my twenty-fourth birthday in Japan. Then we transitioned to MSN Messenger, onward to email and phone calls—learning each other platform by platform. Matteo suggested we switch to Skype, a fledgling technology at the time, but I resisted. I didn't want an *actual* image of the person I had developed feelings for, as it could shatter the *imaginary* image of the person I had fallen in love with.* I wanted him to permanently exist as the insanely beautiful person I saw in his scanned photographs: short, slender, a thick, dark mop of black hair, olive skin, black eyes, and a toothy smile. That was enough for me.

I flew to Sydney to visit him during my winter school break, and it wasn't until my airplane began descending that it hit me like a tidal wave of ice-cold water—and I began to laugh at myself.

The person sitting next to me seemed nervous and asked if I was alright. We restored our trays and pulled our chairs upright. I turned back to him with the intent of saying that I was, in fact, very much so not okay, but that thought was interrupted with another one.

"Mind if I ask you two questions?" He shrugged to indicate, *Why not?*

"One, what's the tipping culture like in Australia?" The first thing that came to mind: how *not* to inconvenience someone else.

"We don't tip," he said. "Maybe if you go to a fancy restaurant or something like that. But unlike *you* lot, we pay our servers a livable wage, so don't bother."†

---

* And it would have. But, more importantly, it *should* have.
† Tip your Australian server anyway. They deal with a lot of abuse. It's not Japan.

He stared at me, and I nodded while the new landscape appeared gradually as we descended through the parting clouds.

"And . . . the second question?"

"Oh, right." I turned back to him.

"What's the number for emergency services in case I get, like, kidnapped or something?"*

*

Matteo was in Melbourne, but I landed in Sydney first. I didn't fly ten thousand miles just to hang out with him. Well, *I had*, but I also figured I could see a few other things while I was there. Sydney was huge. Big green rolling hills, extensive beach in every direction, with humidity that punched me in the face when I walked out of the airport. My flight had landed at seven the morning, so it was too early to check in to my hostel. I wandered around Hyde Park, then hopped on a bus that took me through Sydney and its surroundings suburbs: Liverpool, Darlington, Croydon, Epping, Paddington, and Blackheath—Australian places with English names that had a decidedly British feel, but with better weather and tanner people. These names were juxtaposed with Indigenous Australian words like Woolloomooloo, Coogee, Bondi, and Bennelong. These are the things that I notice when a place feels interesting and new.

On Christmas Day, I ate English fish-and-chips on a beach with an Aboriginal name, while surfers in Santa hats angled their golden abs across rolling teal waves. It was a simple but exciting leap into unfamiliar territory, and I felt my senses on high alert—entertaining possibilities I didn't dare say out loud.

The night before Matteo flew up from Melbourne, a couple of people from my hostel invited me out for Korean barbecue, and

---

* It's 000, in case you needed to know.

a young woman from Texas let me call him from her prepaid cell phone to discuss the plan for how we were going to meet the next morning.

"I cannot wait until tomorrow morning. I won't be able to sleep tonight!" he said on the phone. The electricity that had sparked between us when I lived in Japan, and I finally acknowledged after moving to Chicago, felt more intense than ever.

"We hope we get to meet you too!" the others shouted, whistling in the background.

"I can't wait either," I said. "I can't believe this is happening," I replied.

I was shaking.

I didn't fall asleep until very early in the morning, and I woke with kimchi and bulgogi solidified in my belly. I pressed on it from the sides and groaned; when I saw my German roommate staring, I slapped the bulge and asked her if being "too constipated to make out" was a thing. She laughed and dragged me down to breakfast, talking me through my nerves, knowing he would arrive any minute. After picking around my bowl of cornflakes, I decided to give the bathroom another shot, but as I turned toward the elevator, Matteo walked through the door.

My feet sunk into the ground, and my knees went completely weak. I'd heard stories like this, but I never would have imagined looking at someone and seeing *only* them. When people spoke about falling in love, I used to think they were describing a mental illness. When it happened to me—it was like having a physical episode. I became sweaty and shaky, and my vision blurred. I don't remember moving toward him, but I do remember him walking toward me. When he picked me up, I suddenly remembered that my legs worked, and that I had arms I could wrap around his neck. I withered into him and remembered to breathe. When he put me back down, I looked into his face, and we both giggled like lunatics.

It was the final piece of the puzzle—his face. Matteo had a subtle beauty that matched his personality: calm, confident, unpretentious. He had eyes like giant puddles of ink and lush black hair pulled back into a tight ponytail. A chin like soft clay. Arms that felt like home.

We were surgically attached to each other for the thirty-six hours we spent in Sydney. Talking and wandering in and out of bakeries, gardens, museums, and the zoo—making a spectacle of ourselves by throwing our blossoming romance into everyone else's face.

Although I would join him in Melbourne in a few days, his departure to Melbourne was emotional and intense. I spent my time waiting at a nearby internet café, responding to emails from friends who demanded updates in the crassest terms possible.

When I arrived in Melbourne, Matteo put my luggage in his car and told me he had a surprise for me.

"Are you ready?" he asked, as we buckled our seat belts.

"For . . . ?" I had canceled the hostel I'd booked in Melbourne—just in case he turned out to be a serial killer—but the emergency services number was still committed to memory.

"You've been invited to Shabbat dinner!"

I laughed nervously, and then quickly agreed to attend. I didn't immediately realize what he meant.

"You can say no, but Mum is really looking forward to meeting you."

Oh . . . I thought . . . Oh no.

MATTEO LIVED WITH a woman named Hazel, a butch lesbian whose vocabulary was equal parts self-help jargon and RuPaul song lyrics that later became *Drag Race* references when the show premiered in 2009. I ran into her in the kitchen the next morning, and she sized me up and down while Matteo made eggs. I did the same, eyeing her striped boxer shorts, tight singlet, and the color-ful tattoos that stretched across her skin in every direction.

"You seem like a lot of work," she said, eyeing the curly coils on my mini-afro, then making a quick crucifix type of motion across my torso.

"Shantay you stay!"

I laughed. "Thanks."

"*Condragulations*," Matteo whispered. "She approves!"

SABBATH DINNER BEGAN at around seven o'clock in the eve-ning, but Matteo told me that a revolving door of relatives were expected to come and go throughout the rest of the evening, each with hot dishes covered in steaming aluminum foil. When I asked if I had anything to worry about, he asked me what I meant. I ges-ticulated to myself in a broadly sweeping motion that said, *You know, the whole Black thing.* He scrunched up his face and assured me that his family would welcome me with open arms.

"Mum teaches English to refugees, and she's remarkably edu-cated herself. You're going to get along great."

Matteo's mum, Maria, hosted the dinner, alongside her hus-band, Matteo's stepfather, Michele. I didn't see her, but I heard oven and cabinet doors slamming in the kitchen. She shouted that she would just be a minute, then five minutes, then ten. While we waited, everyone else arrived: Matteo's younger brothers, Luca and Dante, flew over from Perth and Brisbane, while Matteo's cousins and their small children perched around the table in high chairs banging their spoons for attention while we tried to get to know one another. The only person who didn't attend was Tomaso, Mat-teo, Dante, and Luca's father, whom I would meet at a later date. I met the cousins, uncles, and siblings who Matteo collectively de-scribed as "the syndicate." They laid out dishes of pasta, meatballs, burrata, salsiccia, prosciutto, and bruschetta on the table. It wasn't a typical Sabbath dinner. Matteo said it was really just an excuse to get together. The only traditional food I recognized was a rogue jar of gefilte fish. And somewhere in the background, the faceless Maria prepared the roast, lasagna, and salad.

It seemed that they had all been briefed on me. They asked questions about my studies, how I was enjoying Melbourne so far, and what it was like to be with Matteo after all the time we had spent as digital friends. Nobody was smiling. Nobody was laughing. They were polite, but after about an hour, it began to feel forced, as if they had already made up their minds about me and I was interrupting a meeting where they could deliberate on a shared consensus.

One of Matteo's cousins with perfect curly blonde hair asked if I had ever been to Sicily, and I said I had not—but had enjoyed my time in Venice, Rome, Florence, and Tuscany.

"So, not Sicily then?"

I looked to Matteo to say, *Is this how it usually is?* But he just smiled at me, oblivious to the atmosphere, and I questioned if my imagination was just running away with itself. I shook my head no. She nodded curtly, satisfied by a moment that felt as if she were trying to catch me in a lie. And that's when it clicked. They had been coached. It was the werewolf effect—a series of behaviors and mannerisms that some white people adopt when interacting with a Black person for the very first time, which, to them, is no less bizarre than interacting with the mythical creature. Despite seeing movies and TV shows and reading books about werewolves, it becomes a different matter altogether when there's one sitting at your dinner table—so they require guidelines.

It's an instinct I've come to depend on. I'd recognize it anywhere.

I suspected that direction came from Matteo, but perhaps it was Maria, who suddenly burst into the room carrying a stunning tray of lasagna. I stood to greet her, and she politely tapped me on the back before pulling her son into a full embrace, keeping her arms wrapped around him as she kissed him anywhere she could reach from her short stature. He pulled me closer to him with his free hand, saying, "Look, this is her, Mum. Isn't she beautiful?"

Maria gave a quick "yes, mm-hmm" before moving to the dinner table, where we all sat down again. She asked rapid-fire questions and answered them before I could.

"How many people live in Chicago?"

"I'm not sure, I think . . ."

"Oh, I heard it's three million people. So, similar to Melbourne. You know everybody says that Melbourne is a lot like Chicago."

"Yeah, people keep saying that to me. But I don't know how they're making that comp—"

"Well, they're both cultured cities with diverse populations and a heavy European influence, so I think it's an appropriate comparison."

Well, without all the Black people, I thought to myself.

"Have you ever been to Chicago?" I asked.

Maria laughed and tore a piece of bread, not looking at me while she replied. "No, I have no desire to go to America." She opened up her arms as if to embrace the entire table. "Everything I want is right here. I have my family, I have my husband, and I have my grandkids. Why would I want to ever go to America?"

I shrugged and smiled passively, while she continued to list all the reasons why the United States didn't appeal to her in the slightest and how incurious she was about the country's attitude toward guns, politics, and health care. My agreeing nods seemed to annoy her, but she continued on to the food and the noise, and I allowed her to say whatever she pleased. Meanwhile, Matteo only twirled the stem of a wineglass and smiled at me—and I thought, *We are not hearing the same things.*

As we were preparing to leave, I noticed a wooden Al Jolson–like statue, painted black with gaping red lips, white teeth, and a black tuxedo, holding a silver tray in which people had been placing their car keys and loose change. I didn't mention it to Matteo at the time, but I thought about it a lot—when he introduced me to more of his friends, when we went out to dinner, even on our trip down Great Ocean Road a few days later, swimming, surfing, and eating fish-and-chips by the beach.

I couldn't forget the wooden statue or the awkward dinner—which I began to question even more in the presence of Matteo's optimism. I wanted to enjoy the trip, but I also knew that a future with him would be impossible unless we cleared the air. I just didn't know when to bring these issues up, and I was afraid that my observations could have been off—that I could offend Matteo and hurt what we were building in the early stages of our relationship.

On New Year's Eve, we returned to Melbourne and counted down to midnight in the water. Tiny sea creatures swam around our legs, lighting up the ocean in patches of blue and indigo. When fireworks began to crack in the sky, Matteo wrapped his arms around me, and we made resolutions to each other to find a way to make a relationship work.

I became sick when I returned to Chicago. I couldn't keep anything in my stomach and developed a fever that made my below-zero apartment feel like a furnace. It was a mysterious illness that didn't respond to the usual over-the-counter treatments or prescription drugs. When I went to an emergency clinic, I was diagnosed with nonspecific gastroenteritis and told to stay home, stay hydrated, and rest. I picked up a bag of Pedialyte on the way home and curled up next to my heater in multiple blankets for two days. My dreams circled around my trip to Australia, including one in which Matteo and I were about to get married on a beach. As I approached him at the altar, his side of the aisle was full with the people I had met at Sunday dinner: Maria, Michele, his younger brothers, cousins, and babies on their laps.

My side of the aisle was empty.

When I woke up, I called Matteo and let it all out. Not the dream, but the feeling of discomfort I had had around his family. He seemed genuinely surprised. I mentioned Maria's coldness toward me, her possessiveness toward him. That awful statue. How I had felt awkward sitting at that table. Eating with people from different backgrounds wasn't anything new to me, but it seemed like it had been a very different experience for them. I asked him if his mum acted that way with any of his previous partners, and he said that his first serious relationship—with an Indonesian woman—had presented some "challenges" for some of his family members.

"But that's in the past now. I guarantee you they're just happy to see me happy."

I didn't hide my skepticism. If they had been unwelcoming to her, then that would have been resolved when their relationship had ended—which, admittedly, had *something* to do with time, but not in the way he clearly meant. He asked me if they had said or done anything to make me feel discriminated against, and I said no, but that it was just a feeling. He said that I had just been nervous, but that they probably were as well—and he implored me to give them a chance. Then the conversation shifted to my insecurities, and he asked if there was anything he could do to alleviate them. There was one thing: I told him I would not compete for his love or attention with his mum or anyone else in his family. If I was going to move across the world to be with him, I needed to know that we were on the same side and would grow together as a team.

"Jenn, you don't need to worry about that, ever," he said. I was willing to consider the possibility that my suspicions might have been wrong, but I also noted how he didn't seem to consider the possibility that I might have been right. "Really, she can't wait for you to be here, so she can take her time to form a more meaningful relationship with you. I promise—that won't be a problem. Okay?"

"Okay."

"Just remember how lucky we are to have found each other."

Lucky.

"That's true."

11.

An Australian Werewolf in America

I BEGAN THE PREEMPTIVE APOLOGY TOUR TO TELL MY family that I would be leaving the United States—again. This time with an indefinite return. Matteo and I had discussed a long-term strategy for how our relationship would work: I would finish my program at SAIC, and he would visit during the summer break to meet my family and friends, as well as check in with each other about the relationship. Barring any major problems, I would move to Melbourne after my last semester in December 2008—one year after I had met him for the first time in Australia. In the meantime, I downloaded Skype, and we dedicated Saturday nights my time and Sunday mornings his time to bridging the distance as much as possible.

This was the tail end of a period when online dating was still viewed as the sole domain of weirdos and pedophiles. I had to explain to relatives and friends that Matteo was, in fact, an employed professional with advanced degrees in business and law—and not, say, a deranged lunatic who lived in his mom's basement surrounded by the mummified corpses of the teens he had preserved in formaldehyde and pickle juice. My closer friends understood that falling in love with someone through long, intellectual phone calls and emails was probably the only way I could let my guard down. Everyone else was a hard sell. None more so than my family—understandably. A man. A *white* one. Who was *twelve years older*. In *Australia*. Whom I had met on *the internet*. People repeated the information back to me as if they were trying to proof a formula that would solve the riddle as to how their baby cousin and niece could be so fucking stupid that ended with exclamations like, "But you're supposed to be the smart one!"

I had a list of Australian facts and figures prepared, from the unique flora and fauna to socialized health care and heavily re-stricted access to firearms. If I had told them that I was moving down under for those reasons alone, they probably would have been more understanding. But as logical as these reasons were, they didn't overrule the fact that I was shacking up with a white guy, out of wedlock, in glorious, glorious sin. Some were more vo-cal than others. My cousin Aisha took the lead. Five years older, and a die-hard member of a founding Black sorority, she had al-ready preselected a Kappa to spend her life with. She was Black. He was Blacker. Together, they would have Blackass babies* and construct an empire built on white tears.

"If he can't use your comb, don't bring him home," she said emphatically. When I told her about the age gap, she screamed so loudly I had to pull the phone away from my ear.

Mom was understanding. She wasn't even surprised. After all, as she reminded me, I had "always been so mature for my age." And being the youngest person in a family where everyone else was one to three generations older, she reasoned, was bound to have some influence over the company I chose to keep. She asked me when she would get to meet him before passing the phone to Dad. He

---

* And I love them all to the moon and back.

had his own way of taking in the news. It was the same way he always dealt with disappointment, and the reason why leaving became much easier—threats reinforced by radio silence that lasted for months.

✳

Six months flew by, but it felt like only days had passed since I'd met Matteo in Sydney. My train to pick him up at the airport was late, and I arrived just as he was let out of immigration, wandering around with his chin craned to look over everyone else from his unimpressive height. I hid behind a column until he caught sight of me—smirking. I walked over to him, and he dropped his bags, wrapped me in his arms, and squeezed me tight.

Each morning, we woke up as if we were looking at each other for the very first time. "I can't believe you're here" became the soundtrack that played in the background as I dragged him to my favorite restaurants: Ann Sather, Chicago Pizza and Oven Grinder Co., Twin Anchors, Lou Mitchell's, and Gibsons Bar & Steakhouse. When he was cranky, I took him to Intelligentsia for coffee and showed him around my art studio and campus. We went to Buddy Guy's Legends club on the South Side, where his Aussie timbre sounded even more alien in the midst of chords that Bryan Lee played while serenading a whiskey-drunk audience on the pre-Katrina glory days of New Orleans in his signature raspy warble that now is missed the world over. Finally it was just the two of us—and Maria, who called on a daily basis. I asked if she wanted to speak to me, but she usually declined, and when the calls ended, Matteo stomped his foot like a toddler and yelled, "You're costing me a bloody fortune!"

Chicago was buzzing. Hillary Clinton had just suspended her campaign for president, and Barack Obama was the presumptive nominee for the Democratic Party. The city was filled with pride for being the adoptive home of the nation's first Black president. His photo and cardboard cutout adorned the doorsteps of hundreds of shops and restaurants, where it was common to see BARACK LOVES OUR CHICKEN WINGS! written on whiteboards that otherwise advertised daily specials. At SAIC, a student had created a portrait of Barack Obama out of scratchboard with the caption: H.N.I.C.*

There was a lot of love for Black couples and families. Less so for interracial ones. The ire came from every direction. We were walking and holding hands on Michigan Avenue after an extended visit to the art institute's museum when someone shouted at me, "Sister, what the *fuck* are you doing??" It was so surprising that it didn't hit me until about twenty seconds later, when I stopped and kind of turned. "Was he talking to me?" I asked Matteo. He kept walking, pulling me forward by the hand. "I think so, but just ignore him." I couldn't. I began noticing all the looks we attracted. From everyone, in every direction—like we were suddenly the center of the fucking universe.

White women looked from him to me and back to him, shaking their heads like they had just read someone's disappointing report card. Sometimes it was accompanied with a sinister narrowed brow. Some stares were so corrosive they could have scraped the paint off walls. At a club, white women literally threw messages at him to get his attention, as if I weren't sitting right next to him. Other times, I would ask for service at a restaurant only to have the white server look over me as if I were the squeaky

---

* "Head Nigga in Charge." Widely associated with the rousing 1989 education drama *Lean on Me*, starring Morgan Freeman, who plays a hard-nosed, tyrannical principal assigned to a failing inner-city school to turn things around and give us all the feels in the process.

suitcase Matteo had rolled into the establishment that everyone just had to tolerate.

"What the fuck?" I asked out loud.

Some Black men took it as a personal challenge to critique my relationship—saying vile things inches from my face. Never to Matteo's, whose presence almost seemed inconsequential. They approached *me*, spat at *my* shoes, and pushed *me* back as they aggressively walked through us, forcing us to let go of each other's hands. More than once, Matteo had to pick me up and carry me away from getting into a fight, citing a (problematic) fear of violence that I did not care about. As if the words they were saying weren't an act of violence on their own. As if actual wars haven't been started for less.

Matteo insisted that the reactions we got from people on the streets of Chicago would not happen in Melbourne. And when I thought about my first visit there, he seemed to be right. We had not attracted an ounce of maliciousness from anyone. People smiled at us then looked away, and we did the same. Even though I knew that racism was not a uniquely American phenomenon, I thought that, perhaps, the iterations I would find in Australia wouldn't make it so difficult to be together.

From an historical perspective, I was aware of some of the grievances held within the larger African American community toward interracial relationships. For example, I knew how the mythology of the "Black beast" ravaging the poor, innocent white woman had been used to reinforce the color line and anti-miscegenation laws during Jim Crow. I also knew that relationships between white women and Black men had been strictly prohibited, and how manufactured tales of harassment, assault, and rape had led to the horrific torture and murder of countless Black boys and men like Emmett Till in 1955, or the razing of entire towns like Rosewood, Florida, in 1923. I also was aware that, while these anti-miscegenation laws sought to establish white women as property that could only be accessed and owned by white men, that white men had freely raped Black women at the same time. The policing of white women's bodies was about preserving the so-called purity of the white race by preventing them from giving birth to Black babies—thereby eroding the power of white men.[1] Whereas the unbridled assault on Black women's bodies, which also produced Black children, was about increasing slave labor and reinforcing white male supremacy by establishing that Black women did not have the same humanity as white women. In fact, to them, we had none.

This has, naturally, influenced the attitudes that many African American women have toward interracial relationships today. Our demographic remains the most resistant toward dating anyone who is not Black. According to a 2017 Pew Research Center report, Black men are still twice as likely to date outside of their race as Black women.[2] Once again, this comes down to male privilege. Men aren't judged nearly as harshly for their choices in romantic partners as women because women have historically relied on their male partners to secure their social positioning. If a woman married a man with the "wrong" social background, from the "wrong" family, or from the "wrong" race, it would permanently harm *her* place in society.[3]

While that might have historically applied more to white women, who have historically had more to lose, I had observed this among some of my Black female friends and peers who were deeply conscious of the social stigma that they would have faced had they chosen to deviate from the expectations imposed on them by their families or community members. As a close friend said, "I just don't know how I would explain that to my daddy." She didn't have the opportunity to meet Matteo, but like my cousin, she expressed her concerns—including several crude stereotypes—before resigning herself to accepting my situation with a "Well, I wouldn't. But you can." Eventually, she came around and expressed her excitement for "little octoroon* nieces and nephews." I understand the pressure that a community can have on individual decisions. What I did *not* understand, and refused to accept, was why Black women are subjected more to those communal standards than everyone else. Why do we always have to follow rules that were written by someone else?

In other words, if the person *I'm* with isn't using *your* comb, then you'd do well to leave *me* the fuck alone.

In 2008, there weren't a lot of interracial relationships featuring Black women and white men in popular culture. Shonda Rhimes's prime-time Capitol Hill drama *Scandal*, which centered on a passionate love triangle between Kerry Washington's Olivia Pope and two emotionally stunted white men, didn't air until 2012. *Insecure*'s colorful array of dysfunctional multiracial romantic relationships didn't air until 2016. And *Love Is Blind*'s golden couple Lauren and Cameron Hamilton didn't capture hearts until the early stages of a global pandemic in 2020. Supreme Court justice Ketanji Brown-Jackson and her biracial family didn't make headlines until 2022. These are relationships where Black women are the main characters in their marriages, and where, at least in the fictional worlds, Black women aren't victims to anything except their own bad decisions. I believe that this representation is part of what has shifted public discourse to be more accepting of interracial relationships in recent years.

---

* A derogatory term for someone of one-eighth Black ancestry, originating from slavery. Misused in this sense, since my hypothetical children would have been one-half Black. But, as one of millions of African Americans with European ancestry originating from rape, it's used more commonly in partial jest between close Black friends and relatives. More on that later.

Many of the critiques that I heard while dating Matteo were underpinned with an assumption of material gain—that I was getting something financial out of being with him. Love seemed to be the last thing on anyone's mind except for mine. But love could be the only motivating factor because why else would I volunteer to *lose* so much?

At least my family had a reason to hate him, and to that effect, I was relieved when we finally got down to Florida. I missed the artificial airs of Southern hospitality where people preferred judging me in silence. Matteo was nervous when we arrived. Dad had finally begun to act normal around me again, but when Matteo attempted to dap with him, he gave up after an awkward moment of handheld freestyling. "I stopped knowing what you were doing two seconds in," he said. They had their manly discussion on duty of care and responsibility, and Matteo was generous enough with his answers that my dad relaxed, which meant that everyone else could too.

We drove to Haines City, where Matteo met my grandmother in her signature T-shirt and blue-jean shorts. Her husband Sonny greeted him with the requisite Crocodile Dundee references, which Matteo took in stride—having already been told to expect them. Grandma cooked us macaroni and cheese, fried chicken, collard greens, and green beans. It was all seasoned to perfection, and yet Matteo felt the need to add more salt. I got up to get seconds, and Grandma leaned close to me, saying with a Southern inflection that sounded like she wanted to fight, "He don't like my food."

"What do you mean, Grandma?" I asked, reiterating that he definitely did like her food.

"Then why he adding salt?" She shook her head.

"Oh, you know, white-people stuff . . ." She harrumphed, stacking a pile of five-flavor pound cakes in their plastic carrier cases for us to take home. I went back to the table and gave Matteo a rundown of the conversation in Japanese, casually pushing the saltshaker aside and eyeing him intensely.

"Mary-Edith, this is so delicious. Can I have more?"

She instantly brightened. "Of course you can!"

He spooned heap after heap of greens and cheesy macaroni back onto his plate, each forkful widening the smile on her face by inches.

After cleaning his plate, he asked for her opinion on "this strange, white Australian with the funny accent swooping in to steal her granddaughter away." Everyone went quiet, including Dad, who leaned in with his eyebrows raised, ready for one of her trademark retorts. Matteo didn't know it, but my grandma had been married five times. I admired her willingness to leave situations that didn't suit her, her ability to put herself first, and the delightful ways she would curse out anyone who tried to tell her how or who to be. Dad may have felt that he was about to have a vindicating moment, but I *knew* it was mine.

She put down her fork, eyeing Matteo like a spotlight.

"Since the world's been a world, people been mixing. What of it? As long as two people love each other, that's all that matters."

I exhaled. It was all the blessing we needed.

"Now pass me them green beans."*

Matteo reached for my hand, smiled, and winked.

---

* Rest in peace, Grandma. You are very missed and much beloved.

Jennifer Neal and Catapult acknowledge the Traditional Owners of the unceded land upon which the following section of this book takes place.

Aboriginal and Torres Strait Islander people are advised that the following section of this book contains the names of people who have died.

PART 3

*

Naarm (Melbourne), Victoria, Australia

December 15, 2008*—July 31, 2016

---

* I was meant to arrive in Melbourne on December 14, but a six-hour de-
lay of my first leg leaving Chicago resulted in missing my connection to
Sydney in L.A. I had to stay the night and leave the next day, eventually
arriving in Melbourne on December 15. This was a common occurrence.
Somewhere in the multiverse are the days and days of time I've lost fly-
ing United between the United States and Australia, stuck in Los Angeles or Las Vegas, stranded in Denver or Dallas. It must amount to at least
two weeks of just disappeared time that I'll never get back. As Meat Loaf
once kind of said, "I'd do anything for love," but if I can help it, I will
never fly United again.

My Sagittarius Jupiter in the Seventh House: Individuals with this placement want nothing more than to share an adventure with their partners. They want to build a life with people who share their values. They're passionate about their loved ones, supporting them in their endeavors as if they were their own—especially in romantic relationships. In the right atmosphere, individuals with this placement love with a generosity that is off the charts. They're attracted to partners who bring opportunities for expansion and growth. They enjoy breaking traditions and disregarding social expectations.

Their pursuit of pleasure in relationships isn't always realistic. They can jump into relationships too quickly with an overly idealistic attitude—and are most likely to wind up with someone from a different culture, country, or religion. Disappointments come when there isn't time for things to unfold naturally. It would be wise for these individuals to investigate why they feel the need to rush into situations that may not be in their best interests.

12.

The Blackface, the Minstrel, and the Golliwog

THE GLOBAL FINANCIAL CRISIS FAILED TO HIT AUS-
tralia as hard as the United States, but it certainly didn't
seem that way when I landed with my working-holiday visa
in 2008. I submitted applications to more than two hundred businesses, interviewed with exactly one, and was rejected decisively
by every single company. Very few people wanted to take a chance
on a recent art-school graduate with only a little teaching experience when there were thousands of midcareer workers with long
résumés and mortgages pouring into the job market. I applied for
what I thought was most suitable to my talents: administrative
work at art galleries, tour guide at art museums, studio assistant
for successful artists. The rejections ranged from radio silence to
borderline hostility, like this one:

"I didn't even read your application. We are not hiring. Please
do not contact us about this specific request again."

My search grew a little wider with each wave of repudiations:
account manager, personal assistant, babysitter, private tutor,
cleaning lady. I went from restaurant to restaurant asking if anyone
wanted or needed a new server, haunting the streets of Elwood and

St Kilda as I submitted résumés that would wash up on the beach hours later, picked apart by seagulls like clumps of stale bread.

I landed a handful of short-term assignments with ramshackle employers, including a position selling magazines on commission only. After shadowing a young woman from Finland with blonde hair and blue eyes who kept making sales based purely off the attention she attracted from men passing by, I called the next day and left a panicked voicemail declining the position. No one returned my call. I worked as the personal assistant—or as she described it, "the Jennifer Hudson to her Carrie Bradshaw"*—for a woman who sold mineral makeup in South Melbourne Market, which involved using my face for advertising, managing the local distributors she absolutely despised, and learning how to build websites so I could discuss them with her graphic designer, who absolutely despised her. I did a little freelance work for Matteo's best friend, who grilled me about my talents with art and writing before deciding that he was "going to make a lot of money" off me. Ultimately, I just ended up writing some copy for one of his dentist clients.

Matteo's dad, Tomaso, took pity on me and brought me to some of his construction jobs refurbishing small eateries and kitchens. He picked me up from the flat early in the morning, and we drove to a Woolworths where he bought bread rolls, sliced meats, cheese, and bottles of water for both of us. I rolled thick globs of white paint

---

* The 2008 film *Sex and the City* was the movie adaptation of the long-running HBO series, in which Jennifer Hudson played a woman named Louise, who became Carrie Bradshaw's personal assistant—sorting through her emails, mail, bills, and personal belongings to better organize the main character's life. Many believe she was cast to address long-standing criticism of the show's complete lack of diversity. But critics pushed back, describing Hudson as the sassy Black woman, a trope that places her as a secondary character to uplift her white female boss. The woman I worked for absolutely expected me to embody all the same attributes. And she was visibly disappointed when I didn't.

onto spackled and sanded walls of chicken shacks and chipperies while he talked about how much Australia had changed since he relocated there from Sicily in the 1950s, and how glad he was that I had moved there to grow his family even more—which I genuinely felt. Initially, we'd shake hands when he dropped me home at the end of the day. But it wasn't long before we began to hug instead.

When I wasn't working for Tomaso, Matteo's cousin Emilia frequently stopped by unannounced. She would honk her car horn in the driveway until I came out, and then we'd go to the park to watch her three young boys play while she outlined all the ways life had let her down, including her unrealized dream of becoming a photographer. Then we'd drive to craft stores to buy items that she was enthusiastic about assembling together in her home, only to later announce that she was too tired to make crafts, proceeding instead to detail the inadequacies of all the people who had disappointed her. She said that she had always wanted a sister, but I felt cast into the role of a therapist instead, one with poor personal boundaries who really wanted to be liked by her new patients, who were also her partner's family members. When Matteo picked me up after work, he said that he could only "endure her" for so long. When I said how difficult I found those afternoons with her, he would hmm and then silently drive us home.

The one thing Emilia and I seemed to have in common was an interest in art, though from different perspectives. She didn't know about any of the artists who excited me, and I didn't know much about crafting or Art Deco pieces. That changed when we began to discuss children's books. I told her that, perhaps, one day, I would like to write and illustrate my own. We were in her car, driving back to her house when she responded enthusiastically.

"There's something I want to show you."

We pulled up to her house. Her two eldest boys went back to their Legos and model trains. We went into her toddler's room,

filled with bookshelves of colorful picture books. She ran her fingers over several of them before selecting a few. She removed them
carefully and placed them in my outstretched arms. I looked down
at illustrations of golliwogs on the covers.

"Aren't these fabulous?"

She cooed over them while turning the covers proudly, flip-
ping through the pages and smiling at me—looking for a similar
response. I gaped at their covers as she piled one after the other
into my hands. Illustrations of garish black dolls with big red lips
and white teeth, dressed in colorful tuxedos and striped clown
pants, hitting the country road for adventures in enchanted forests and the big city. I stared at them in horror. I realized that I
was holding my breath, and when I reminded myself to exhale, the
words that came with it just blurted out.

"These are . . . very racist."

She snatched them out of my hands.

"They're not racist! They're children's books! They're *just*
dolls," she said angrily, her eyes narrowed into beady arrowheads.
"There's nothing racist about them, nothing at all! Don't be ridiculous. Anyone who looks at these"—she flipped through the pages
aggressively—"and sees racism, well then there's something wrong
with *them*!"

"I mean . . . I can explain if you give me an opportunity.
This"—I gestured toward the covers—"is based on racist minstrel
performances."

Emilia waved away my words and continued to sternly talk
me down, insisting that, because they were children's books, they
couldn't possibly be racist—implying that racism was the sole domain of adults. The irony is this statement was lost on her, but not
me. I stood there, stunned. It was an early introduction to something I would see many more times in Australia—that passionate
impulse to defend the indefensible with a neurotic, preemptive

assault. In a way that appears to be a national pastime, Australia has mythologized the golliwog's racist origins for guilt-free white consumption. Books, television, and merchandise have all been placed on the front lines of this revisionist history, so ubiquitous in their appearance and marketing that indicting the image of the golliwog feels to many like an indictment on Australia itself.

Like many facets of white Australian culture, the country's love of golliwogs can be traced back to its colonial British parentage and an early American influence. This begins with Florence Kate Upton, a children's book author born in the United States to English parents. Upton's first golliwog book was published in 1895. *The Adventures of Two Dutch Dolls and a "Golliwogg"* was published by British publisher Longman's, Green & Co. (now known as Pearson Longman). The titular black-faced character of the book is described as "a horrid sight," "the blackest gnome," whom Upton illustrated in bright-red trousers, a red bow tie with a collared shirt, and a topcoat with long tails—common attire for minstrel performers at the time (or for wooden statues darkening the doorways of people's homes in 2008). Upton said that she was inspired to create the book by the black rag doll she had played with during her childhood in New York. It won't surprise anyone that the doll shares many physical similarities with minstrel acts commonly performed in the southern part of the United States in the nineteenth century.

The first minstrel shows were performed in New York in the early 1800s. Thomas Dartmouth Rice, a white American stage performer from New York known as the Father of Minstrelsy, first developed the popular blackface character Jim Crow in 1830.[1] He applied black face paint, usually shoe polish or grease paint, and wore tattered clothing while mimicking enslaved Africans on Southern plantations. It was a grizzly spectacle that became raucously popular among white spectators around the country—drawing the praises of politicians, prominent authors, and celebrities alike. Minstrel shows are widely considered to be the first American theatrical form. It wasn't long before other performance troupes picked up on the act and began staging their own productions. A group called the Ethiopian Serenaders even performed for the tenth U.S. president John Tyler in the White House in 1844.[2]

In his autobiography, Mark Twain wrote how much he enjoyed watching minstrel shows as a young boy, describing how the audience was "shrieking with laughter" as the performers fashioned their mouths like "slices cut in a ripe watermelon" while singing songs like "Massa's in de Cold, Cold Ground" and "Sing for the White Folks, Sing!"[3] These songs were sanitized of the horrors of American slavery and conveyed messages of sad enslaved people, mourning over their masters' deaths, bragging about their mischievous behavior, or crooning about the amazing conditions of their captivity. These "comedic" productions performed two important services for their racist white attendees: helping them to process complex feelings on the subject by convincing them that slavery was good and laughing about it as a communal activity. Comedy has always served as a powerful tool to help people process (or disregard) human complexity. For this reason, when a white comedian *today* tries to disguise their racism as the trappings of comedy, minstrelsy is always the first thing that comes to my mind.

Blackface can also be recorded on British stages as early as the 1600s, including performances of Shakespeare's iconic tragedy *Othello*. But American-style minstrel performances also began to spring up around Great Britain in the 1830s. Many American performers took their shows across the Atlantic—including Thomas Rice, who brought his form of minstrelsy to Britain in 1836.[4] His performances were so popular that he returned several more times. The Ethiopian Serenaders toured England in 1845. Queen Victoria of England was a big fan, and multiple troupes staged private performances for her at Arundel Castle in 1846 and 1868.[5] British comedians like Charles Mathews became popular for plays called "at homes," where he performed onstage in blackface for audiences as if they were in his home, telling comedic anecdotes and stories. After returning from his U.S. tour in the early 1820s, he amended his performance, naming it *A Trip to America*, using an amalgam of ethnography, travel, commentary, and what some people may have classified as comedy to create some of the first depictions of African Americans on a London stage.[6] Transcripts of the show listed his characters using names like Othello and Agamemnon, and one describes the role of "an African-American coach driver with reins around his neck and steered the horses with his fiddle tunes."[7] Historian Tracy C. Davis described the racist depictions as the self-indulgent musings of someone who likened himself to Christopher Columbus, or someone "discovering America."[8]

Australia was a sparsely populated country in the 1850s. Minstrel shows still found their way to shores down under via three troupes arriving from overseas—one from England and two from the United States, including the Ethiopian Serenaders.[9] Up until the 1880s, Australia was part of a "regular and established minstrel circuit" that was referred to as "the nigger business."[10] Though minstrelsy declined in popularity toward the end of the nineteenth century, it remained common to see blackface imagery in Australia for decades to follow—which mocked not only people of African descent, but also Aboriginal Australians and Torres Strait Islanders.*

---

* Aboriginal and Torres Strait Islander people are ethnically distinct groups, both indigenous to Australia. There is tremendous diversity of Aboriginal peoples, communities, and cultures around Australia. Unless overwise stated, I'm using the terms *Aboriginal*, *Indigenous Australians*, and *First Nations* to include all people of Aboriginal and/or Torres Strait Islander descent.

Many people from the hundreds of Aboriginal nations in Australia
also refer to themselves as Black. Sometimes, that's spelled *Blak* to
differentiate from the experiences of Pan-African people, although
Blackfella and *Blackfulla* are also common terms used by Aboriginal
people.[11]/*

In 1925, during a small revival of minstrel performances in
the interwar years, American playwright Edward Sheldon's popular play *The Nigger* was performed in Melbourne. It's an anti-
miscegenist wet dream about a man "ruined" by the discovery that
he possesses "a trace of Negro ancestry."[12] And in 1927, when Al
Jolson's infamous blackface film *The Jazz Singer* came to Australia,
it enjoyed an unprecedented twenty-week sales season.[13]

To me, it's clear why these shows enjoyed such international
acclaim and success. They were passed between countries that
shared a similar language, culture, religion, and attitude toward
people who were not white. These performances reinforced
the network between colonized and colonizing nation-states,
strengthening diplomatic relations that could then facilitate trade
alliances and beneficial economic agreements. But, equally as
important, they created a place for all three countries to relegate
Black people to the fringes of society on three continents. Where
so many remain today. Blackface was also deployed in Australia
to target Aboriginal peoples who, like African Americans in the
United States, weren't allowed to perform in theater productions.

In fact, Aboriginal people didn't play Aboriginal characters until Charles Chauvel's controversial 1955 film *Jedda*. Up until then,
white actors on stage and screen took a cue from their overseas
neighbors and donned black face paint instead of hiring Aboriginal

---

* I do not use the word *Ab*rigine* unless it's part of a direct quote or the
  title of some legislation. It's considered offensive for a non-Aboriginal
  person to use.

actors. Whereas shoe polish and grease paint were popular in the antebellum South, Australian actors typically used burnt corks to discolor their faces. This had a particular significance: in Australia's Northern Territory, between the years 1910 and 1940, a white man who had fathered a Black child with an Aboriginal woman would be "presented with a burnt cork" to symbolize how he had "charred his character."[14] With this knowledge, it's clear that the weaponization of blackface serves two purposes: one, it becomes the clear manifestation of the shame that white people inflict upon other white people for falling outside the norms of acceptable white behavior, and two, that shame is projected onto Aboriginal people as further dehumanization.

Whereas minstrelsy in the United States is *now* widely considered to be deplorable, it continues to have a foothold in Australian media representations of Black people. *Larrikinism* is a word commonly used to describe Australian comedy that employs humor characterized as defiant, ironic, or self-deprecating; many comedic stunts are known to aggressively target anything seen as politically correct, including an objection to the use of blackface.[15]

I saw this firsthand in 2009, on an episode of *Hey Hey It's Saturday*, a popular variety show on Australian television. After a nearly twenty-year hiatus, Channel Nine announced a reunion show, and one of the acts featured a rendition of the famous American boy group the Jackson 5—reimagined by five men, renamed the Jackson Jive. Four of the men, who were white, wore black face paint, curly black wigs, and crude zoot suits. The fifth man, who was Sri Lankan, played Michael Jackson in white face paint and a sparkly red jacket and spoke in an absolutely cringeworthy falsetto to mimic the late pop star. They jumped around onstage, hugging one another, gyrating, smiling, and laughing—demonstrating just how enjoyable it was to put their ignorance and lack of rhythm on display for national television. Their performance was rated on a scale of zero to ten by three judges, two local Australian TV personalities and one American, Harry Connick Jr. One judge gave them a seven and a half. Another asked the audience, which responded with a resounding, "Ten!" before giving them a solid one. Connick gave them an emphatic zero—citing that if that performance had been done in the United States, the show would have been canceled.

The ensuing media storm was unlike anything I had ever seen. Within days, newspapers published a series of caustic op-eds taking aim at the American actor and musician. One commentor on the Murdoch-owned *Herald Sun* website wrote, "This has been blown totally out of proportion. It's a tribute. They had done this before and they weren't mocking any race or disrespecting mj . . . I would also like to point out that there was a white painted face as well. Is that being racist too?"

Another commentor wrote on a different Murdoch-owned site, news.com.au:

> Man I love double standards. Making fun of any thing but white people is bad, but once it's racism towards white people then bam! It's a-okay. Racism is a matter of perspective and opinion, if people stopped taking everything so seriously when it wasn't necessary (i.e., comedy) then there would be no racism.

But the most unhinged comment appeared on a blog by *The Age*—a left-wing paper, which completely erases the country's love of minstrel performances:

> Black face minstrels were never part of our culture. Yes this 'art form' did belittle Afro Ameri-

cans and is not acceptable now or then but I do
not see this act as a minstrels act. It is just white
guys doing a cover of an act by Afro Americans.
Lousy music but not racist. If black Australians
did Abba would we white guys be offended. No,
I suggest not.[16]

It's interesting that the only thing people can point to as a
defense from accusations of racism is the borders they illegally
crossed to establish a so-called republic on land where Indigenous
inhabitants were slaughtered so that it could be created. And I
might just be one person, but that feels *very* American to me. If
African Americans are the only demographic who have the right
to be offended by blackface, and if the performance was obviously
parodying a well-known African American pop group, then clearly
I have the right to determine if it's offensive. And if *I* am the arbiter
of how offensive this performance is, then I can determine if it's
offensive to me simply because I'm American, or if it's offensive
because it's racist. For the record, I choose the latter. Of course,
that's not what they meant. That would make too much sense.
These commentors mean that *they're* the arbiters of what is and is
not racist. As the white dominant population, *they* have the right
to adjudicate the entire national discourse, and "Others" like me
are tolerated as long as they don't shine a light on that hypocrisy or
gross imbalance of power.[17]

While these commentors patted themselves on the back for
their expert analysis, the public also weighed in. News.com.au
held an online poll a few weeks after the episode aired asking the
public if they thought the Jackson Jive was a racist performance.
Around thirty thousand people voted, and more than fifteen hundred people left comments. The Murdoch-owned *Courier Mail* and

*PerthNow** reported that 53 and 81 percent of participants, respectively, voted that the performance was not racist.[18] If the *Courier Mail* results are accurate, then that means there is enough dissenting opinion for a wider conversation. If the *PerthNow* results are accurate, then that need becomes a state of emergency. Either way, since both titles were owned by News Corp at the time, the results didn't come as a surprise to anyone.

What *did* surprise me was the response of everyone else that showed me the kind of fresh new horror I had found myself living in. I spoke to Matteo at length about how the national conversation had infuriated me, and being the calm, objective man he was, he responded by defending it as a demonstration of reverence, how much the men in that group loved Michael Jackson, and how it couldn't possibly be racist if one of the members was also a person of color. I told him that colorism is just one more imaginative way in which whiteness is replicated among people who are not white. He rolled his eyes and laughed.

"Don't be silly, Jenn," he said before parroting the same trope that has stalked me around the globe like minstrel fanfare does with colonizers.

"This isn't America."

TECHNICALLY TRUE. WHAT a revelation. But it doesn't take into account how blackface and minstrelsy has also harmed and mocked First Nations Australians. Blackface has been an issue battled by Aboriginal, Torres Strait Islander, and Pacific Islander people in Australia for decades. Here is a non-exhaustive list of those incidents:

In 1834, Henry Melville's play *The Bushrangers* (or *Norwood Vale*) was performed on Australian stages, featuring an

---

* *PerthNow* was sold to Seven West Media in 2016.

Aboriginal character called Native, played by a white Australian actor in blackface.[19] The story is based on the life of Tasmanian bushranger Matthew Brady. Aboriginal characters in the play are portrayed as both addicts and hopeless beggars who covet Western comforts like bread and tea, creating a dissonant image of a people that is both inferior and sinister.[20] Historian Margaret Williams described the Aboriginal characters depicted in the film as "crudely drawn 'Sambo' figures."[21] The Bushrangers is widely considered to be the first Australian play written and performed in the country, heralding in a new era of Australian storytelling on the stage.[22]

In 1928, the Australian silent film Trooper O'Brien used white actors in blackface to depict Aboriginal men as a hazard to white women.[23]

Boney was a very popular show that aired on Australian television during the 1970s, based on a series of books by the same name, that centered around a police detective who was half-Aboriginal and half-white. The producers claimed that they couldn't find a suitable Aboriginal actor, so they hired a non-Aboriginal actor from New Zealand, James Laurenson, who played the character for two seasons in blackface. In 1973, this role saw him awarded a Logie—Australia's most prestigious television award—for Best Single Performance by an Actor.[24]

In 1992, two police officers attended a charity ball dressed in blackface with nooses around their necks as two dead Aboriginal men, Lloyd Boney and David Gundy. Both had died in police custody: Boney in a cell in rural New South Wales; Gundy was shot dead in Sydney after being misidentified as someone else. The latter incident came with video footage that aired on national television, supposedly shocking a nation—but not the police officers who cruelly mocked him. This is especially callous considering that Aboriginal people make up just over 3 percent of Australia's total population, yet constitute 33 percent of the country's prison population.[25]

In 2007, Australian comedian Chris Lilley created the character Jonah Takalua for his globally syndicated comedy show *Summer Heights High*, wearing brownface and a curly black afro to depict a character of Tongan descent who struggled with authority in schools and bullied other kids. He later reprised the role when it was given its own show in 2014, *Jonah from Tonga*. Lilley then went on create a third program in 2011 called *Angry Boys*, where he donned blackface to play an African American teenager named S.mouse, a wannabe rapper and troublemaker, who drops the N-word repeatedly and raps about his "big black balls."

In 2016, two men from the small Victorian town of Ballarat decided to impersonate the Aboriginal community for an Aussie-icons party. They painted their faces and whole bodies black, drew fake dot paintings on their arms, and wore woolly wigs. The post was proudly uploaded onto social media by the host of the party, who said these two men had "the best costume" and called them "legends." First Nations people expressed outrage, including curse-laden commentary from Koori* rapper Briggs, who called them "dumb, redneck scumbags." Indigenous singer Thelma Plum echoed his sentiments, calling the two men "disgusting little boys." The response on social media was the usual backlash from racist commenters, where both Briggs and Plum were accused of taking from the country and not giving anything back.[26]

These examples underscore a shared philosophy between the United States and Australia: white authors, white viewers, white audiences, and white actors assume a "position of control" over both real and imagined non-white people.[27] Blackface echoes the

---

* An Aboriginal peoples from southern New South Wales and northern Victoria.

entitlement and discriminatory attitudes held by white people that are implemented in countless other nonfictional dynamics, even if it's done so by means of theatrical fictions. Australia is not the United States. But if my nationality can be used to discredit my efforts to point out the racist history of blackface, then what reasoning can be used to discredit the same comments from First Nations Australians?

Unless—shock and awe—nationality has *nothing* to do with it at all.

During my time in Australia, I saw many more instances of blackface, once even in person. While talking down Chapel Street in the southeastern Melbourne district of Prahran late one night in 2013, I passed a club that had closed for a private party. A sign on the window said, 40s AND FABULOUS, as in a 1940s-themed party to celebrate someone's fortieth birthday. Some people stood outside smoking, including a white man dressed in a bright-yellow zoot suit, donning a full face of black shoe polish, with two women in wigs and flapper dresses on either side of him. My heart instantly sped up, and my feet slowed to a halt. My jaw dropped. When he saw me staring at him, he asked me if I was his sister. I kind of gaped and asked if I could take a picture of them, and the three posed—smiling proudly one next to one another. I needed a record of that monstrosity before I cursed them out. I walked away shaking.

DURING THEIR EARLY development, minstrel shows were known to feature adult themes including lewd acts of sex, drunkenness, and debauchery—not very suitable for people under a certain age. Black people were depicted as lazy, hypersexual, ignorant, and prone to criminal behavior. Golliwogs provided children with an age-appropriate entry to racist ideology. Virtually identical to the white actors in blackface that entertained their parents on stages, these dolls had oversize red lips, unkempt frizzy black hair, patched clown pants, and striped shirts with colorful bow ties. Upton described her own dolls as "ugly" and said that she used them as a "target for rubber balls."[28] This isn't uncommon behavior for little white girls. Robin Bernstein, a Harvard professor and cultural historian, most notably detailed the connection of racist toys to racist attitudes that develop in children in her seminal 2011 text, *Racial Innocence: Performing American Childhood from Slavery to Civil Rights*. One of the pillars of the framework used in her study was sweeping archival and historical performances, imagery, and books from the mid-nineteenth century to the early twentieth century, where she examined the "histories of oppressed peoples" in the messages relayed by these objects and scripts. This landmark study asserted that "racial innocence" is developed in childhood, covertly influenced by children's toys, including dolls, books, play etiquette, and bodily autonomy—or lack thereof.[29] Bernstein also drew connections not just between these seemingly "innocent" childhood pastimes and adult racist attitudes, she asserted that these childhood pastimes prompted "meaningful bodily behaviors," meaning physical reactions to color and race. White dolls were treated tenderly, and Black dolls were abused. By extension, white children were "tender angels" who could feel pain, whereas Black children were "insensate pickaninnies."[30] We see this, of course, in Upton's work.

Upton drew her golliwogs with paws instead of hands or feet—giving the characters a "distorted, animalistic, or frightening appearance."[31] In *The Adventures of Two Dutch Dolls and a "Golliwogg,"* the accompanying Dutch dolls, Peggy and Sarah Jane, are by comparison tall, thin, and pretty with rosy cheeks. Upton went on to create twelve more books—with titles like *Golliwogg in the African Jungle* and *"Golliwogg" at the North Pole, a Happy Christmas*. Without a copyright on the character, it went on to be reproduced by English toy manufacturer Merrythought and Dean's as well as German companies like Steiff, Shuco, and Levin.[32] Merrythought was the first to mass-produce the doll, and Dean's is still in operation today—shipping to fifty countries around the world.

Given their popularity, some of the children who grew up on Upton's golliwog books grew up to become authors themselves, like Enid Blyton. In Blyton's 1944 book *The Three Golliwogs*, the three titular characters named Golly, Woggie, and Nigger get into all kinds of playful shenanigans, which can be observed from the following excerpt:[33]

Once the three bold golliwogs, Golly, Woggie, and Nigger, decided to go for a walk to Bumble-Bee Common. Golly wasn't quite ready so Woggie and Nigger said they would start off without him, and Golly would catch them up as soon as he could. So off went Woggie and Nigger, arm-in-arm, singing merrily their favourite song—which, as you may guess, was *Ten Little Nigger Boys*.[34]

"Ten Little Nigger Boys" is the name of a children's nursery rhyme that rejoices over the deaths of ten Black children.[35/*] The first verse begins thus:

Ten little nigger boys went out to dine;
One choked his little self, and then there were nine.[36/†]

---

* This nursery rhyme also appeared in English writer Agatha Christie's 1939 book, *Ten Little Niggers*. The title was later changed to *And Then There Were None* when the U.S. edition was released in 1940. The title *Ten Little Indians* was also used at one point in the 1960s for several decades. The book is a mystery novel about ten people tricked into going to an island. Each person finds the nursery rhyme tacked to their room door, and each guest is murdered one by one. The book has sold more than 100 million copies worldwide and is one of the most successful bestsellers of all time.

† It was later adapted to become a song, probably written by Franklin Green and most likely in 1869.

If it sounds familiar, that's because there is another version called "Ten Little Indians," whose characters meet a similar fate:

> Seven little Indians cuttin' up their tricks,
> One broke his neck and then there were six.[*]

Blyton's book was also a major commercial success. Her follow-up 1945 book *Five Go to Smuggler's Top* featured a "very very dark boy" named Sooty—as in the soot from a fireplace, with a yellow-haired sister, whom he describes as "the beauty" to his "beast."[37] And in Blyton's 1965 book *The Little Black Doll*, the main character, Sambo, is a little boy who hates his appearance and is only accepted by the other characters in the book once his "ugly black face" is washed pink and clean by the rain.[38] Throughout the series, the golliwogs are depicted as mischievous or troublesome characters, sometimes even broaching the role of villain—a common trope when dark skin intersects with the white gaze.

Critical responses to the golliwogs have become more vocal and been reported more widely in recent years. Part of this is due to the name of the doll itself. While Upton may have coined the term *golliwog*, *wog* is a common racist epithet used in Australia to describe someone with darker skin. During the White Australia policy, this applied mostly to immigrants from southern European countries like Italy and Greece. Now, its usage extends to people from the Middle East or the African continent. Some people claim that it's a word that can be reclaimed and used by the people it's meant to deride, similar to the N-word. A 2019 comedy show called *Wild Wogs 2*, featuring comedians of Sri Lankan, Syrian, Italian, and Greek descent, sold out across Melbourne.

The root of the word is subject to some debate. In an

---

[*] Also referenced in the same Agatha Christie novel.

investigation led by misinformation fact-checking website *Snopes*, historian James Whidden said the term may originate from British colonial Egypt when *wog*, or "workers on government service," was a racist insult used by British authorities to refer to Egyptian workers who worked subordinate to them.[39] Whereas journalist David Wilton says that the word is most likely an abridged version of Upton's *golliwog* itself—meaning that the epithet originated from the doll and not the other way around.[40] Whatever the original etymology, the timeline puts its genesis around the same time Upton's first book was published, making a link between the word and its racist connotations pretty clear.

The Egyptian-origins theory is especially curious because that has somehow spread as an acceptable mythology used to sanitize the doll's racist origins—one that persists without any evidence. I've seen golliwogs in several shops around Melbourne—specifically a toy shop in Bourke Street Mall in the central business district (CBD), a very fancy heritage building in the middle of the city filled with expensive boutiques and artisanal foods shops. The window of the toy store is filled with little black golliwog dolls in striped clown pants with bow ties and polka-dot dresses. In the same window, there's a sign attempting to explain how the dolls themselves are not racist, but just a beloved children's toy that had come from Egypt in the late nineteenth century—when the country was invaded and pillaged by British colonizers.[41]

It's pretty wild to me how they became associated with the British occupation of Egypt in 1882. It seems Egypt has been victimized a second time by an Australian toy-shop manager who decided to make it the scapegoat for the proliferation of racist imagery that clearly originated from the English-speaking world, all the while overlooking how the British also waged a violent colonial campaign that gave birth to the nation now known as Australia. But displacing colonial guilt onto another brutalized people is nothing new. In fact, I'd call it a hallmark of white settler colonialism.

Not only did this Egyptian origin myth rewrite the racist history of the golliwog, but it sanitized the crimes of theft and murder committed by the British Empire on both the African and Australian continents. It also operates under a bizarre assumption that imagery featuring bow ties, tailcoats, and striped clown pants is native to Egypt when—if they were indeed present in that country at that time—they would have been introduced by the English. By spreading these fictions, Australia's own colonial British roots are reinforced, and this is at the heart of so much of the country's own racist history that still permeates its present-day political landscape.

I didn't go into the Bourke Street shop with the golliwogs, but I spotted the shopkeeper tidying up the window display, looking equal parts nervous and angry. She made a show of straightening the slumping dolls while happy shoppers walked out with large bags and smiles on their faces. I could only look on in disgust. It made me reexamine why Emilia was so resistant toward having her beloved books characterized as racist. She was kind of right, in the sense that children aren't born racist—but just because children can't conceptualize racist structures doesn't mean depictions of Black people aren't relevant to early-childhood development.[42]

It's racist symbols like the golliwog that teach children what Donna Varga and Rhoda Zuk called in their 2013 paper "Golliwogs and Teddy Bears: Embodied Racism in Children's Popular Culture" the "associated meanings and values of racism."[43] In Emilia's mind, critiquing her beloved books, however racist they were, might feel akin to an assault on her childhood. But then why would it be more important to preserve the innocence of her childhood than it was to acknowledge the tears I had shed during my own? If she didn't believe a child could be racist, could she at least see how racist *adults* were made? Could she understand why her two-year-old son proudly declared one day that he didn't like Auntie Jenn "because she's Black"? It didn't appear so. If she had always wanted a sister, then that was a sneak peek into how the new relationship would look. Her denial would be prioritized over my emotional security, and the results would always leave me feeling shattered—like I was being used for target practice by a mercurial, reckless child wielding a rubber ball.

Golliwogs are still around in Australia. Sadly, I don't think they're going anywhere anytime soon. Australian food maker Arnott's finally decided to change the name of its popular chocolate cookie in the mid-1990s from Golliwog Biscuits to Scalliwag— but the snack retained its signature blackface figure, with frizzy afro hair, large clown lips, and bow tie until they were discontinued in the late '90s. In 2016, Aboriginal author and activist Stephen Hagan called Toowoomba the "most racist city in Australia," when he saw a display of nine golliwog dolls in the shop window of TerryWhite Chemmart in Clifford Greens with a sign that invited shoppers to "experience a white Christmas."[44] And just a reminder, Australia celebrates Christmas during the summer months. A soft-toy contest came under fire at the 2018 Royal Adelaide Show when the first, second, and third place all went to golliwog dolls. And in northern Queensland, again in 2018, that debate was reignited when a tourist named Soyla Echeverria saw those same dolls in a shop window.[45] The dolls are produced by Australian toy manufacturer Elka, which sells hundreds of thousands of their dolls every year all over Australia.[46] And when reached for comment, national sales manager Jan Johnco described the dolls as "benevolent and beautiful," adding that they have a "very honourable past" that had nothing to do with any "sick connotations of racism."[47] When asked about the complaints, like those raised by Echeverria and several Aboriginal activists who have been longtime critics of the dolls, she dismissed them as part of a vocal minority.

Later that year, the news program *Today Tonight* launched an online poll asking viewers if they thought golliwogs were racist. The number of participants was much smaller than with the blackface poll, with just under thirteen hundred ballots cast—and 98 percent voted no.

So, sadly, Johnco appears to be right.

My own discomfort with these racist attitudes was exacerbated the more I noticed my inability to discuss these things with Matteo—who listened and nodded empathetically, but then concluded the conversation with calls for me to take things less seriously, and to "be aware" that discussing these things with people would "make" me a "target to some pretty strong reactions."

"And you should be prepared for that."

I wish I could go back to tell my young self not to take his dismissals so personally. To not feel so deeply wounded and devalued by them. To not spend countless nights with knots in my stomach, feeling as if I were fashioning myself into the target I was becoming by pointing out the rabid racism I saw all around me. I wish I could have told myself that these were his moral failings, that these conversations were indicative of his emotional and intellectual inadequacies. That he wasn't offering me a "friendly piece of advice," but a thinly cloaked warning that calling out racism would make me a target even more—and that every time he told me to "prepare" for that, he was really saying: "You're on your own."

13.

Always Was, Always Will Be

AFTER COMPLETING A FEW TEST SHIFTS AT RESTAU-
rants where the staff paid me in small coins and threw little bits of food into my afro to demonstrate how little they
wanted me there, I was finally offered a server position at a restaurant on Acland Street. This is a part of St Kilda known for a trendy
strip of clubs, bars, and eateries that catered to the ultrarich and
the destitute alike. I was relieved because it meant I had an excuse
to duck Emilia.

St Kilda looked and felt very similar to Venice Beach, California. It was a short walk from the water and its affixed outdoor
gyms, where Rollerbladers and muscle enthusiasts spent most of
their time when the weather was warm. It has a popular beach,
known not only for swimming but small bags of white powder and
used needles left in the sand. The nearby tourist attraction, Luna
Park Melbourne, operated as an STI testing center during World
War II, where soldiers returning on leave were treated for syphilis and gonorrhea. And sex workers still operated in narrow alleys
between the bars and their attached grocery stores, stopping into

the friendlier restaurants early in the morning for chin-wags and strong cups of coffee in between jobs, heels dangling from their wrists by sequined straps, heads in hands, cigarettes burning to the nubs between their chipped fingernails.

The restaurant paid me about half of the Australian minimum wage in cash under the table. Matteo and Hazel agreed to pay the rent and bills so that I could save for my visa application, which cost three thousand dollars at the time. I worked twelve-hour shifts serving burgers, fries, Halloumi, bubble and squeak,* risotto, and pastas, with a thirty-minute break, which was just long enough to notice the blisters forming on my heels. I cleaned up after drunk tradesmen, washed vomit down the sidewalk from their sick dogs, and learned the inner magical workings of every single item on the menu so as not to accidentally poison someone with celiac disease or accidentally offend a vegan customer with a splash of honey in their chai latte (which *did* happen once, by mistake, I swear). Then, I limped home to Matteo smelling like bacon fat and grilled jaffles.

I pulled my weight at home by cooking, particularly for Hazel—who had nothing to gain by letting me live with them. I made her chocolate chip cookies and sticky date pudding when she was hungover, which was often. Matteo had quit his corporate lawyer job to take up training as a physiotherapist—which he had described as his dream—and I used what little money I could spare to buy groceries and make dinner for him. Because I didn't drink, I took my knock-off-shift beers home to Matteo and quizzed him on the body's different muscle groups while he rubbed my feet back to life. I tried my best to make myself seem useful while feeling, in

---

* A savory British breakfast food, made from potatoes and cabbage, mixed together and fried. Sometimes it appears like a large pancake, other times like a hush puppy.

fact, quite useless without prospects for a better-paying job on the horizon. I reasoned that everything would change once we lodged our de-facto-spouse application at the Department of Immigration and Citizenship, as soon as I had saved up enough money.

Sometimes, Matteo came to the restaurant after his physio classes, occasionally even bringing his friends, who were all curious about me. Some were nice and asked me about Chicago and Florida, and how my family felt about me living so far away. Others tried to show off their knowledge of the U.S. Civil Rights Movement, presumably trying to impress me, while relaying their deep love for Obama and voicing how they wished local Aboriginal people could "learn from his example." Kieran, an immigrant from Belfast who had become an Australian citizen, could talk at length about his admiration for Malcolm X but did not know a single thing about the Aboriginal men and women who established the Aboriginal Black Power movement—inspired in large part *by* the writings of Malcolm X. Matteo's friends were familiar with the American ecosystem of racism, so much so that most believed it to be an *exclusively* American problem. But it wasn't just them. It was many of the people around me. The red-headed Kiwi servers I worked with who sneered at Asian customers when they left the restaurant—pulling at their eyelids to make racist gestures behind their backs. It was the dinner guests who praised African Americana while deriding the influx of Sudanese refugees on Australian shores. It was the racist anti-Black epithets football fans shouted at the television when Australian rules football legend Adam Goodes strode onto the green of the MCG to play against their favorite teams. Most of them were white, with a couple of Brown folks who believed that reverse racism was the real bogeyman, and that the issue of racism itself was only a problem "if you look for it."

It seemed that I had, by proxy to my spouse,* been elevated to a level above what was deemed *Black* in Australia—which I began to notice was a term white Australians used to describe Aboriginal people. It took me a bit of time to recognize how that came paired with a bizarre desire to segregate *me* from the word, from the color Black—which has been my racial classification since birth. By detaching me from that word, they gave themselves permission to openly display vitriol and ignorance with pride—and became a thinly veiled threat that said, "We'll do the same to you if you step out of line." A racist country doesn't need laws to enforce a racist ideology when its residents are fervent supporters of the white order.

Whenever I stumbled into the trap of trying to make someone see the error of their ways, I was promptly crushed by any number of copy-and-paste platitudes that ranged from dismissive to downright hostile. I was told how much I did not understand about Australia. I was told that I was bringing my American discourse to a place where it did not apply. "This is Australia," Matteo's friends said back to me.

"This is Australia," other servers said back to me.

"This is Australia," customers said back to me.

Yes, exactly. And white Australia has a Black history.

For all their attempts to divorce being an African American Black person from an Aboriginal Black person, they overlooked the parallel histories of oppression and resilience that have existed between our two communities since the 1960s. When I wrote my Blaxit column for *The Root* about the city of Melbourne, I made a conscious decision to limit interviews to people of African descent who had migrated to Australia because that column focused

* In Australia, de facto spousal relationships carry the same significance, tax credits, and legal recognition as marriage. In fact, de facto spousal relationships are considered common-law marriages.

entirely on Black migratory experiences. But it would be disingen-
uous of me to reexamine the life I had in Australia without pointing
out how learning about the experiences of Aboriginal Australians
expanded not just my own ideas of Blackness, but my ideas of community as an act of defiance. Because those ideas are just as migratory as the racist institutions and structures that Black people
of every ethnicity seem to be battling across the diaspora. What I
learned there has changed the way I think of "better" and "worse"
countries because it comes down to the people you keep around
you and ways we combat the lies we hear about ourselves.

Despite African Americans originating from Africa and Aboriginal Australians being a dispossessed group indigenous to
Australia with their own unique belief systems that connect them
to the land, there have long existed undeniable parallels between
the challenges that the two groups have faced. This common
struggle still serves as the foundation for the solidarity between
us today. In the United States, the 1960s is synonymous with the
Civil Rights Movement—but I think discussions on that subject
are sometimes limited exclusively to the United States. The fight
for civil rights is a global phenomenon, and many other countries
around the world were waging their own battles in the fight for
equality. In 1960 alone, seventeen African nations gained independence from their European colonizers, including the Democratic Republic of the Congo (from Belgium); Senegal and Togo
(from France); and Nigeria, Somalia, and Cameroon (from Great
Britain and France).* The Black Liberation movement also gained

---

* On January 1, 1960, French Cameroon (Cameroun) gained indepen-
  dence. In February 1961, a plebiscite saw the southern part of British
  Cameroon joined with the Republic of Cameroon. The Federal Repub-
  lic of Cameroon was created on October 1, 1961. The northern part of
  British Cameroon joined Nigeria. Previously, Cameroon had also been a
  German colony, known as Kamerun.

a foothold in Redfern, a suburb of Sydney, now known as a historic hotbed for Australian Aboriginal activism during the 1960s.

In the earlier years of the Civil Rights Movement in the United States, Freedom Rides, or road trips where Black and white political protesters campaigned against segregation, were used to raise awareness and support for desegregated travel. This began in 1946 after the U.S. Supreme Court banned segregation on interstate bus travel—which did absolutely nothing to stop bus operators from enforcing segregation anyway. The next year, the Congress of Racial Equality (CORE) staged the Journey of Reconciliation, the country's first Freedom Ride of white and Black activists who rode through the Deep South to test the effectiveness of the ruling. For Bayard Rustin, one of the main organizers and CORE's treasurer at the time, it was a personal endeavor. Four years earlier, he had refused to give up his second-row seat and move to the back of a bus traveling from Louisville to Nashville. Despite severe intimidation, he remained in his seat and arrived at his final destination, where he was subsequently beaten and arrested.[1] This is a common story; activists who participated in the Freedom Rides were taunted and harassed and had guns pointed at their heads by police officers. Thurgood Marshall, then a member of the NAACP Legal Defense Fund, questioned the effectiveness of the protest, claiming that it would lead to "wholesale slaughter with no good achieved."[2] This is why white activists were so important—not just to demonstrate what integration looked like, but to keep potential casualties to a minimum. Out of twenty-six bus rides, six resulted in arrests. And in Chapel Hill, North Carolina, a mob of angry white men with sticks and rocks made national headlines and served as a boon to the ideology of nonviolent protest.[3]

The most famous Freedom Rides took place in 1961—a joint effort between CORE and the Student Nonviolent Coordinating Committee (SNCC). Like the 1947 Journey of Reconciliation, the

1961 protests were also a response to a U.S. Supreme Court decision, one that further expanded the 1946 ruling to desegregate
terminals, restrooms, and other interstate travel facilities. These
demonstrations were organized all over the South to test the ruling, where they were met with violent acts of retaliation. Buses were
vandalized and firebombed, and protesters were harassed, arrested,
and beaten with metal pipes.[4] The violence was so swift and brutal
that the Riders couldn't find bus drivers willing to finish the demonstrations. When newspapers published images of burning buses and
bleeding activists, U.S. attorney general Robert Kennedy stepped
in to negotiate with Alabama governor John Patterson to secure a
new driver and state protection so that one bus could finish.[5] Once
again, nonviolence proved effective in raising national awareness of
America's insidious racism. But it did something else—it showed
how legislation in and of itself is essentially useless without proper
enforcement, without strategic implementation, and without white
people willing to put their own lives on the line.

Inspired by what they saw in the southern United States, Australian Aboriginal activists conducted their own Freedom Rides
to protest segregation in 1965. Charles Perkins, an Aboriginal activist and soccer player, and Reverend Ted Noffs, a white activist
and founder of the Wayside Chapel, organized a Freedom Ride
with thirty white students from the Student Action for Aborigines
(SAFA) group at the University of Sydney.[6] As one of only two
Aboriginal students at the university, Perkins was appointed the
first president of SAFA. Together, they rode through some of New
South Wales's most "notoriously racist towns," including Walgett,
Kempsey, Gulargambone, Bowraville, and Moree.[7] Activists were
taunted, harassed—in some cases, the bus was run off the road.[8]
In Moree, they attempted to desegregate a swimming pool that
only allowed Aboriginal children access during certain times and
required them to shower before entering.[9] The protesters were

"pelted with eggs and rotten fruit," and the violence eventually escalated to the point that their bus driver abandoned them mid-tour.[10] But by then, the Australian Freedom Rides had made international headlines, reaching as far as *The New York Times*. White Australia was confronted with racism in a way that had never been displayed in media before.[11]

Nonviolence worked, but it was far from perfect. In 1967, Australia held a referendum to change the Australian Constitution, and the public was tasked with voting on whether it should be altered to include Aboriginal and Torres Strait Islander people as part of the Australian population. The original 1901 constitution stated that the Commonwealth could not make decisions on Aboriginal Australians because they were not to be counted in the national census, effectively stating that they weren't Australian.[12] This meant that the individual states and territories devised their own policies, resulting in many Aboriginal children being removed from their families and homes.

The referendum passed with a resounding 90.77 percent majority. Changing the constitution was a gigantic leap in the right direction, but many younger Aboriginal activists felt that it did not address the daily injustices and inequities that they faced—many of which are woefully familiar to the African American experience. Census statistics from 1966 show that Aboriginal children were "disproportionately represented among the low achievers" and that, in a nation of full employment, unemployment within the Aboriginal community was around 7 percent.[13] For people who did enter the workforce, 67 percent of those jobs belonged to the manual-labor market. And despite amending the Australian constitution, which theoretically granted them the same rights as white citizens, it was not uncommon afterward to see places where there were signs strictly forbidding Aboriginal people from sitting down for a meal, getting a haircut, joining a club, or enjoying

a drink at a bar.[14] There was absolutely no legal basis for this behavior, but white communities proved to be what Kathy Lothian,
author of the 2005 paper "Seizing the Time: Australian Aborigines and the Influence of the Black Panther Party, 1969–1972"
described as "effective enforcers of social segregation as legalized
Apartheid."[15] In her paper, she highlights how the similarities of
structural racism endured by African Americans and Aboriginal
Australians nurtured the perfect breeding ground to embrace
Black, and Blak, Power.

It's critical to note that, even though inspiration was drawn
from the African American and the Pan-African movements,
Aboriginal Australians had been campaigning on the topic of returning land since the 1860s.[16] This is a crucial point of distinction
because it demonstrates the importance of the subject of Indige-
neity in discussing this history, as it would be important if I were
discussing the Māori people of New Zealand or the First Nations
people of North America. Land is regarded not only by the Aboriginal Nations of Australia as a major source of economic and spiritual well-being, but by Indigenous peoples of colonized countries
around the world.[17] This did not apply to the African American
Civil Rights Movement.

Heather Goodall, professor at the University of Technology
Sydney, described land as "a central factor in [Aboriginal peoples']
experience of colonialism," one that encompassed a sense of "invasion, and dispossession" that had been "at the core" of Aboriginal
concerns and protests for more than century.[18]/*

Aboriginal activism expanded even more at the same time as
the U.S. Civil Rights Movement—to tackle issues of police brutality and harassment.[19] Amending the constitution was a significant milestone, one that had been nearly a decade in the making,

---

* More on this in the Further Reading section at the end of the book.

but many Aboriginal activists had little faith that it would lead to actionable change. Gary Foley, a vocal Aboriginal activist, playwright, and actor, was a young man when the referendum was passed, and he too wrote about the sense of "betrayal and cynicism" he felt when he saw the promises of elected officials go unfulfilled; he issued a call for "more effective" means to be considered.[20] In agreement with Foley, many younger Aboriginal activists were angry and felt disillusioned by the calls of older activists for patience and diplomacy, which they saw as centering white comfort and interests. More "militant" Aboriginal activist groups rejected the idea of integration altogether and campaigned on the idea that Aboriginal platforms should be addressed by Aboriginal people, without the involvement of white Australia.[21]

I can't help but think of the Civil Rights Act of 1964, a watershed piece of legislation that made discrimination based on race or ethnicity, including segregation, illegal in the United States. It was not simply adopted by all Black leaders. In fact, it was debated among different factions of African American activists, because—as the Freedom Rides had already demonstrated—laws do not enforce themselves, and a piece of paper is not a golden ticket that just hands over rights. Just as the Emancipation Proclamation did not actually grant enslaved people freedom, nor Juneteenth the safety they needed to embrace it. And even when a paper does, like the Voting Rights Act of 1965, there is no guarantee that those rights won't be taken away, like voting protections were when the act was gutted less than fifty years later in 2013. People in the United States *today* are still fighting for the rights that were guaranteed to us almost sixty years ago. No amount of paper seems able to change that.

Black activists had similar criticisms for nonviolence, the protesting method made famous by Dr. Martin Luther King Jr. Rejecting the militancy of his peers like Malcolm X, Dr. King was still closely monitored by FBI director J. Edgar Hoover, who kept a

COINTELPRO* dossier on King. Hoover feared that he could become a "messiah" who could unite the Black nationalist groups if he chose to "abandon his supposed 'obedience' to 'white liberal doctrines' (nonviolence) and embrace black nationalism."[22] Hoover recognized the threat of Dr. King's methodologies, even though they were firmly rooted in peaceful resistance, while Malcolm X saw civil disobedience as a weakness—and he was steadfast in those criticisms. While a member of the Nation of Islam, X referred to Dr. King as a "fool" and an "Uncle Tom" and described nonviolence as Dr. King "teach[ing] the Negroes to be defenseless."[23]

But after leaving the Nation of Islam and founding Muslim Mosque, Inc., X changed his approach toward collaboration and became more conciliatory toward Dr. King and other Civil Rights leaders. In March 1964, four months before the Civil Rights Act was passed, Malcolm X was in the Senate gallery during late-stage debates of the measures listed in the legislation. When asked for his thoughts about the bill, Malcolm X stated that he wanted the bill passed "exactly as it was," but that it would not solve the "Negro problem" because he believed that "goodwill" could not be solved by legislation, that "only education" could do that.[24] He maintained this position until the end of his life. With the assassinations of X in 1965 and Dr. King in 1968, many Black activist groups in the United States abandoned the ideology of nonviolence altogether and turned to more radical, militant means of demonstrating—leading to the rise of Black Power. And Australian Aboriginal activists, who underwent a similar shift in their approach to activism, were paying attention.[25]

In 1969, Aboriginal activist Bruce McGuinness, then director

---

* An illegal counterintelligence program run by the FBI that infiltrated, discredited, and disrupted American activist organizations between 1956 and 1971.

of the Aboriginal Advancement League,* urged other Aboriginal peoples to buy a copy of *Black Power*. This seminal text was written by Trinidadian American activist Kwame Ture (born Stokely Carmichael) and Charles V. Hamilton, who were two original members of the Black Panther Party for Self-Defense in the United States.[26] McGuinness declared that the book "should be a prized possession among every Aborigine" and stressed that "the content of the book about American Negroes runs almost identical lines [to that] of the Australian Aborigine."[27] In fact, a number of books by African American Black Panther Party members were circulated—including *Soul on Ice* by Eldridge Cleaver and *Seize the Time* by Black Panther Party cofounder Bobby Seale.[28] But it was *The Autobiography of Malcolm X* that seemed to captivate the minds and hearts of young Aboriginal activists the most—including Gary Foley, who said that X's book "transformed" him and "blew [his] mind."[29]

McGuiness's calls for Black ownership and agency and the rejection of white involvement struck the hearts of people like Gary Foley, and they worked together to further define what that would look like in Australia. Self-determination lay at the foundation of the developing Aboriginal Black Power movement, and chants from the American Black Power movement were adopted during protests in Australia. Between 1969 and 1972, it was not uncommon to hear slogans like "Black is beautiful" and "power to the people" alongside "land rights"† shouted on Australian streets alongside insults directed at police officers who became "pigs" when they harassed activists. Protesters wore black berets, clenched their fists, and styled their hair into afros, drawing a strong visual comparison with the U.S. movement.[30]

---

* At the time, it was known as the Victorian Aborigines Advancement League.
† "Land rights" is still shouted during protests led by Aboriginal people.

Black and Caribbean activists were invited to Australia by the Victorian Aborigines Advancement League. Roosevelt Brown, a Bermudian activist and chairman of the Caribbean and Latin American Continuation Central Planning Committee of the Black Power Movement* and member of parliament for the Progressive Labour Party in Bermuda, met with Aboriginal leaders in Melbourne in 1968.[31]/[†] His critical stance toward the White Australia policy made local government officials incredibly nervous, and some papers printed statements like "Black power not wanted" while the Victorian minister for Aborigines, a white man of Irish heritage named Edmond Raymond Meagher, said "I am sure I speak for Victoria's Aboriginals when I say that we are happy to forget Mr. Brown."[32]

You can't make this up.

Many in the Australian Aboriginal-activist space were influenced by Brown's visit—especially Denis Walker, an Aboriginal activist from southern Queensland. As the son of another Aboriginal activist, Oodgeroo Noonuccal—who had also been an early adopter of the Black Power movement—Denis had grown up surrounded by ideas of self-determination. But his attraction to more militant methods led him to break away from his mother when he declared himself the cofounder and minister of defense for the Australian Black Panther Party in 1971.[33] Joining him were other Aboriginal activists like Paul Coe, Billy Craigie, and Gary Foley—who had been mentored by Bruce McGuinness. Denis advocated

---

* It hasn't been uncommon for me to come across titles or committee names that are difficult to substantiate. This title belongs in that category. Though Brown's activities in the Caribbean Black Power movement are well documented, I can't confirm his title at the time. I include it because it has been pulled directly from the cited source.

† Foley's paper says that Brown was invited in 1968, whereas Lothian's paper states 1969.

alignment to the African American Black Panther Party's platforms of self-determinism and militant self-defense to eventually
"overthrow" the Australian government. They adopted a similar
discipline, including reading two hours of radical literature every
day and political education courses for all general members. New
recruits were given texts by Malcolm X, Bobby Seale, and Eldridge
Cleaver to read.[34] Black was beautiful, Black was powerful, Black
was determined, and Black was self-governing. Right on.

Both the Australian and American parties demanded "land,
bread, housing, education, clothing, justice, and peace" alongside
an "immediate end to police brutality" and education that taught
the real history of both nations.[35] The Australian chapter also made
amendments to the American platform—namely the U.S. Black
Panther Party's ten-point program, a list of demands that operated
as a de facto manifesto. Point seven demanded an end to police
brutality, and Aboriginal activists amended it to include an end to
rape, one of the terrors that Aboriginal women had been subjected
to since the colonial invasion began.[36]

A number of community initiatives addressing hunger, education, and police brutality were also incorporated into the Australian
Black Panther Party. Gary Foley recounted an evening when he was
confronted by a white police officer who forced him to admit to having sexual relations with a white Australian woman in 1968. The police officer beat the confession out of him, then beat the woman for
keeping his company, despite Foley not even knowing her name.[37]
This type of police harassment was commonplace in Redfern at the
time. There was even an unofficial curfew, where locals widely understood that staying out past ten o'clock at night came with heightened potential for violent encounters with the local police.[38]

Paul Coe, one of the party's cofounders and a recent law
school graduate, took it upon himself to tackle this state violence
head-on. In 1970, he set up the Aboriginal Legal Aid Service of

New South Wales. It was the first organization of its kind founded, managed, and controlled by Aboriginal people. Soon after, white lawyers began to volunteer their services, and federal funding was secured to allow the employment of a secretary and a field officer. Not only did this drastically change the behavior of the police officers who harassed Aboriginal people in New South Wales, but the Redfern curfew was dropped altogether.[39] The success of the legal aid initiative inspired other Aboriginal groups, and similar organizations emerged in South Australia in 1971, as well as Victoria, Queensland, and Western Australia in 1972. By 1974, an Aboriginal legal aid office existed in every Australian state and territory.

While the Aboriginal Legal Aid Service was a response to the police brutality that the Aboriginal community faced, the Aboriginal Medical Service was a response to the institutional racism that Aboriginal people faced in the Australian health-care system. In 1971, stories circulated of an Aboriginal man being refused care at a hospital or refusing to even go to the hospital for fear of being "treated like scum" by white medical staff; though versions vary somewhat, it's a story inextricably linked to the everyday reality of Aboriginal people seeking health care. Within a few weeks of the story's circulation, Gordon Briscoe, a founding member of the Aboriginal legal defense group, held meetings with health-care providers to found the Aboriginal Medical Service in Redfern. It provided basic health care and educational initiatives on malnutrition to combat respiratory infections, eye diseases, parasites, and anemia—which affected Aboriginal children in particular.[40]

The Australian Black Panther Party also adopted the U.S. Black Panther Party's most dangerous initiative—one that grabbed the attention of FBI director J. Edgar Hoover himself, who turned feral over the party's free-breakfast-for-children program.[41] In an internal FBI memo, Hoover said this:

The [Program] represents the best and most influential activity going for the BPP and, as such, is potentially the greatest threat to efforts by authorities to neutralize the BPP and destroy what it stands for.[42]

Aboriginal Black Panthers distributed free fruits and vegetables to families around Sydney and worked with a local church to create the Free Breakfast Program. By 1974, these programs had also spread to Western Australia and Victoria.

For all the ways in which Black Power aligned itself between two countries divided by an ocean, Australia took the tenets of Black Liberation and made them their own. The most significant example that I encountered centered on the enduring subject of land rights, which emphasized not only the moral element of returning land, but also meant acknowledging the Aboriginal community as the rightful Indigenous custodians of the continent.[43] In the 1960s, Aboriginal activist groups from all parts of the political spectrum were petitioning the government to return land. In January 1972, prime minister William McMahon gave a devastating response: Ignoring the recommendations from the Office (now Department) of Aboriginal Affairs, McMahon denied Aboriginal land rights, setting up instead a special leasing system available to Aboriginal people—contingent upon their "intention and ability to make reasonable economic and social use of the land."[44] It was a decisive blow to the movement.

The Aboriginal response was the 1972 Tent Embassy, established on Australia Day—the national holiday that commemorates when the First Fleet landed in Sydney Cove in 1788 and raised the Union Flag.[45] Many Aboriginal people refer to it as Invasion Day, and to "celebrate," organizers set up tents all over the lawn of Parliament House in Canberra. The tents were green, white, and orange, some with multicolored flags—including a red-black-and-green flag to showcase solidarity with the Pan-African movement and a brown-and-black flag overlaid with a white spear to represent

Aboriginal people and the land they fought to reclaim.[46] The message was a simple one, as relayed by Ghillar Michael Anderson, a Euahlayi activist from New South Wales: "The land was taken from us by force—we shouldn't have to lease it." The activists who set up the Tent Embassy released a five-point program that same month, demanding ownership of all Australian reserves and settlements, the preservation of sacred lands, ownership of certain Australian cities and the entire Northern Territory, legal title and mining rights to areas in and around Australian capital cities, as well as six billion Australian dollars in restitution with a yearly portion of the country's economic gross on top.[47] Anderson and his fellow activists refused to leave the Tent Embassy until the government reconsidered its statement, swearing to stay for as long as it took for that to happen. Denis Walker was known to survey the area in his Black Panther jacket while waving the Aboriginal flag. Activists from the legal aid and medical services in Redfern, including Gary Foley, Paul Coe, and Cheryl Buchanan, defended their tents.

At the time, it was unlike any demonstration the government had seen before. The minister for the environment, Aborigines, and the arts Peter Howson described his concern over calling the area an embassy, as he felt it implied the assertion of an independent, sovereign state—which it did. Eventually, minister for the interior Ralph Hunt passed an ordinance that made it illegal to camp on parliamentary grounds; the police tried several times to forcibly remove the activists, resulting in clashes with protesters who were beaten and hospitalized.[48] Ultimately, Parliament passed a law stating that tents on government grounds were illegal, and they were removed nearly nine months later in September 1972, but Tent Embassy remains a permanent fixture on the parliamentary lawns. I visited the Tent Embassy in 2014. It was an overcast afternoon, no tents, but a nearby truck painted in the colors of the Aboriginal flag, and the word *sovereignty* was spelled out on the grass in large white letters. An Aboriginal flag hung above it. It is the longest continuous protest for Indigenous land rights in history, anywhere in the world. I took pictures of the area, but I didn't step onto the grass because, after all, that is their embassy. And all of Australia is still their land—always was, always will be. Whether the government recognizes it or not.

I met a lot of white Australians who gave me unsolicited commentary on how they viewed my proximity to Blackness. But they were all noticeably absent from events and protests where I wasn't the only Black person present. Demonstrations in Melbourne had a tendency to start off as protests against conservative policy and absorb other politically aligned causes along the way. When I attended a protest against a conservative government, I was not surprised to see people raising awareness of the impending climate collapse, Israel's occupation of Palestine, Australia's involvement in the war in Afghanistan, or calls for a treaty between the Aboriginal Nations and the Australian government. As the demonstration marched on, an Aboriginal woman holding a sign on the sidelines looked down at me, and I looked up at her, and we both smiled at the exact same time. She had a bob hairstyle and wore a black T-shirt with the Aboriginal flag on front.

"Hey, sister," she said.

"Hey, sis," I said back, more slowly. We both laughed. She hopped down from the curb and began to walk with me, waving her sign overhead. We chatted about the crowd and the weather, pointed at the sneering bystanders who were clearly not part of the demonstration and sneered back at them. When the crowd gathered at Melbourne Parliament, we pushed toward the front of the crowd to hear the speakers make their announcements and demands.

"Can I ask you a question, and you can tell me to get stuffed if you like?" I asked her, leaning in close.

She nodded her head to say *Go for it.*

"So, I'm Black . . . and you're Black too . . . Right?"

Her face took on this expression that seemed to say *Get on with it.*

"So why do some white Australians insist that I'm . . . not?"

She laughed so loudly some people stopped to turn around and stare at us. Totally unencumbered, bent over, belly laughing. When she stood up, she placed her hand on my shoulder, leaning against it.

"Who says that? Friends of yours?" She eyed me with what seemed like pity.

"Not mine . . . Not exactly," I replied.

"Right. Well, get new friends."

I chuckled, then nodded wordlessly and replayed that conversation in my head all the way home. It was such a simple piece of advice that I returned to often. Every time I called myself Black and Matteo's friends "corrected" me by saying I was "not Black" but "African American," they gave the latter word an air of superiority that felt like an expletive when it passed through their lips.

I began to notice the difference between his friends and mine. I thought about the people from Foodies International in Chicago, and how we had created a diverse group of greedy eaters from almost every corner of the world in just one year's time. Matteo had had an entire lifetime, and twelve years on top of mine, to do the same in a city he had characterized as *European* and *multicultural.* These ended up sounding like euphemisms for *colonial* and *racist* to me. Our group pictures looked like the diversity ad campaigns from universities—featuring that one Black person with poor personal boundaries who can't say no to anyone.

Matteo's friends were also all much older than me, and I was not yet mature enough to accept that, beyond a certain age, all racism is willful and intentional. There were many days when I should have just walked away from conversations that clearly weren't going anywhere. Once, I was on a shift at the restaurant, bringing a round of drinks to Matteo and his friends at a table outside when he introduced me to Billy, a friend originally from South Africa who currently lived in the United States. He patiently listened while I explained how ridiculous it was that he and several others insisted that I was African American and not Black. He responded by saying, "You know, I'm more African American than you. I was born in South Africa, and I migrated to the United States." His blue eyes smiled back mischievously, and the entire table erupted in applause—including Matteo, who clapped his hands and said "Ha ha! In your face!" Without any room for me to respond, I went back into the restaurant, humiliated and furious.

*

When I had managed to finally save up enough money for my de-facto-spouse application, Matteo and I went to the Department of Immigration and Citizenship with a binder full of documents containing evidence of our shared bills, bank account statements, copies of heavily redacted emails, photos of our vacation to Tasmania, and certified testimonies from our friends and families authenticating our relationship.

When it was time to pay the fee, I asked the agent behind the desk if it was still three thousand dollars.

"No, oh no." She looked at me wearily. "It's now three thousand four hundred and twenty-five."

My heart sank. It was all the money I had.

Matteo saw my face drop and whipped out his credit card. I felt my heart skip a beat, and relief wash over me. He leaned in close and whispered in my ear, "You can pay me back later."

14.

Fear of a Brown Continent*

LODGED MY DE-FACTO-SPOUSE APPLICATION IN SEPTEMBER 2009. The following month, a boat carrying seventy-eight Tamil asylum seekers from Sri Lanka to Australia was in danger of capsizing in the waters around Indonesia. After speaking with Indonesian officials, prime minister Kevin Rudd dispensed the *Oceanic Viking* to rescue the passengers and return them to Indonesia, where they would be deported back to Sri Lanka. But they refused to disembark the boat and reenter Indonesia. Negotiations with Australian maritime authorities were recorded, showing that the passengers would have rather died by mass suicide than return. According to the United Nations High Commissioner for Refugees, all seventy-eight passengers were refugees.[1] This standoff lasted for four weeks, creating a diplomatic nightmare for Australian and Indonesian authorities, until the Australian federal

---

*   This chapter title is a reference to the phenomenal talents of the Australian comedy duo Fear of a Brown Planet, Aamer Rahman and Nazeem Hussain, who appear to have borrowed their name from the iconic 1990 hip-hop album *Fear of a Black Planet* by Public Enemy.

government managed to strike a deal with the passengers to eventually resettle all of them in several different countries around the region. The incident sparked a national debate on the country's asylum-seeker policy—and the newspapers had a field day, especially conservative pundits on the Murdoch-owned media that churned out absolutely feral articles. Everyone around me seemed to debate whether or not these people were "queue jumpers" and "boat people," and asylum seekers were turned into an existential threat for Australia.

I couldn't understand how a country of twenty-two million people—most of whom were descended from immigrants themselves—couldn't fit seventy-eight additional people. Then I saw an awful black-and-white video from 1962 produced by the Australian Broadcasting Corporation (ABC). In it, a journalist with a strong transatlantic accent interviews Australians about the White Australia policy. The interviewer wanted to see how white Australians felt about growing interest in ending the policy, and he does an excellent job of capturing the mass hysteria that underlies the country's obsession with border protection:

"I think it's good, and they should really have it and keep out the colored races." [2]

"Migration is a very good thing. We should stick more to British migrants."[3]

One man who heard the interviewer speaking to someone else interjected off camera, saying that immigrants should be treated like the Aboriginal people had been in Queensland. When the interviewer turned to him, he added, "Keep 'em out! Keep all the niggers out! … Japs and everybody!"[4] Some of the people had strong European and North American accents. One woman from New York said that people of color and white people live side by side where she came from, only to follow up with, "And I wouldn't care to have them living in the same house as me."[5]

But the most interesting response was from a white Australian man who appeared to be a police officer: "When you consider what's happening overseas and South Africa and all those places . . . We seem to be very well off here."[6]

He didn't seem to understand that the White Australian policy had borrowed heavily from racist South African immigration law.

When transportation of British convicts to Australia ended in 1840, it created a labor shortage that was met by Asian immigrants, who began arriving toward the end of the nineteenth century. These were mostly indentured laborers from China who came predominantly from present-day Guangdong and Fujian, where rebellion, flood, and famine were tremendous sources of socioeconomic hardship.* When they arrived, infrastructure jobs were readily available to usher Australia into a modern country: clearing dangerous bush, digging wells and irrigation ditches, and shepherding livestock.

Despite the enormous contributions of Chinese immigrants, many white Australians were not pleased to have them in the country—and the White Australia policy became the legislative response to "the Asiatic question."[7] In 1901, the Immigration Restriction Act became the first piece of federal legislation around immigration, drafted by then attorney general Alfred Deakin and passed by then prime minister Edmund Barton. This law instilled immigration officers with sweeping powers to deny entry to anyone deemed undesirable. However, the British Crown considered explicit racial discrimination unsavory, knowing that any law that denied people based on their country of origin could cause unrest throughout the Commonwealth, which extended throughout

---

* Some were also kidnapped from their homes and sold into slavery in Australia—a practice that was pejoratively referred to as "the sale of pigs."

Asia; so, the law was denied by the Colonial Office in London.[8] Undeterred, Australian immigration authorities introduced a dictation test instead: An immigration officer would ask the new arrival to write fifty words in a European language of the agent's choosing—Italian or French, for example—targeting people from Asia specifically. When a new arrival failed the test, they were deported, achieving racial discrimination without even mentioning the word *race*—which received the royal stamp of approval from the Colonial Office.

Despite being called the White Australia policy, the scheme is Australian only in name. In practice, it was a strategy that migrated from one colonized country to the next with the aim of restricting the immigration of non-white people *after* benefiting from their cost-effective labor. Located in present-day South Africa, Natal was a British colony founded in 1843. A growing need for affordable food manufactured in the industrial hubs of Europe and the United States led to a surge in demand for sugar at a low cost.[9] Sugar consumption in the United Kingdom alone more than tripled from 1830 to 1890, and new labor was required to meet the agricultural demands of sugar harvesting.[10] Several new sugarcane-producing countries and territories emerged as a result, and one of them was Natal—which was experiencing a labor shortage because they were unable to recruit Zulu workers. In the 1860s, colonial authorities decided to import Indian indentured laborers from what was then the British Raj.[11] Nonlaborers or "passenger Indians," who had paid for their own passage, also arrived in Natal and set up businesses, markets, and shops.[12] As they became successful, local white Natali merchants began to feel threatened, and violent reprisals against Indian business owners were documented. In 1894, the Natali colonial parliament passed a measure to exclude Indians from settling, but the British Crown didn't sign off because the measure was a blatant violation of antidiscriminatory measures in the colonial charter; if it had been allowed to pass, it could have caused negative repercussions in other colonies, like the British Raj.[13]

So, a series of other measures were passed targeting free Indians instead. The 1897 Immigration Restriction Act included stringent quarantine measures and a requirement for licensed retailers to keep all financial records in English. The bill borrowed language from the U.S. Immigration Act of 1891, which had introduced the term *aliens* to describe immigrants and excluded people from the following: "All idiots, insane persons, Paupers or persons likely to become a public charge, Persons suffering from a loathsome or a dangerous contagious disease, Persons who have been convicted of a felony or other infamous crime or misdemeanor involving moral turpitude."[14]

Natal incorporated the same vocabulary, nearly word for word, into the definition of *prohibited immigrant* in its own act, but the defining feature of their legislation was the dictation test, which stated that anyone "who when asked to do so by an officer appointed under this Act shall fail to himself write out and sign in the characters of any language of Europe an application to the Colonial Secretary' be prohibited from entering the colony."[15]

Because a specific European language wasn't identified, immigration officials were allowed to deploy whichever one they felt the applicant was most likely to fail, accomplishing two things: it restricted Indian immigration without once referring to race specifically, and as a result, it earned the seal of approval from the Colonial Office in London—which, it's pretty clear at this point, was fine with discriminatory laws.

The colony of Natal and Australia fed off the legislative learnings of each other, improving on the verbiage and restrictions in ways that would address the failures of the other's approach. The architects of these respective anti-immigration bills that swept across the colonies during the turn of the century wrote to one another while drafting their laws. Harry Escombe, the attorney general for the London Colonial Office from 1893 until 1897, assured the Natal Assembly that the government would be "perfectly content" to replace their bill with the Australian restriction if it proved to be successful, just as he stated that it would be taken "as a compliment" if the other colonies were to follow the Natali example.[16] To compound this, the Natal Legislative Assembly Bill was passed in 1894, depriving all Indians of the right to vote—a law that formed part of the earliest policies of what went on to become South African apartheid law.

The origins of the dictation test are hard to pin down, but the language used in the policies of Australia and Natal has some basis in an immigration bill debated by the United States Congress in 1896, which sought to ban anyone "who cannot read and write the language of their native country or some other language," the latter of which was also never specified. And this bill would have been a federal expansion of literacy laws that were passed in the Southern U.S. states *after* the Fifteenth Amendment gave African American men the right to vote.[17] Many Southern U.S. states were unhappy with the amendment of their mighty constitution and drafted their own pieces of paper that introduced voter suppression to circumvent federal law. In 1890, twenty years after the Fifteenth Amendment was ratified, the Mississippi state convention introduced a new constitution that included a literacy test and a poll tax for anyone to be considered eligible to vote. It required potential voters to read an unspecified section of the Mississippi constitution, or to interpret a section of the constitution when read to them. James Vardaman, then a member of the Mississippi House of Representatives, made the reason for this law quite plain: "In Mississippi we have in our constitution legislated against the racial peculiarities of the Negro . . . When that device fails, we will resort to something else."[18]

All these laws were debated and/or passed only years apart from one another—sweeping from state, to colony, to country. And though their genesis seemingly originates from anti-Black racism in the American South, the aim with each "new" legislation was to maintain a stronghold on colonized land for the exclusive use of white settlers.[19]

Though the White Australia policy is far from distant history, it seemed largely excluded from contemporary conversations on asylum-seeker policy in 2009, a social amnesia that Australian historian Marilyn Lake described as a "tyranny of the national narrative of Australian history."[20] The country's memory seemed purged of this racist history, or how it had served to benefit one group of immigrants at the expense of others—resulting in a fragile national identity that, by sanitizing its own history, was only eroding itself.

National histories are typically presented as individual creation myths. Our national identities *depend* on governments telling their citizens that their way of life can't be replicated anywhere else. But these creation myths have a lot in common—and one of the commonalities that unites Western nations is their shared love of racist immigration policy. This bond creates the "geographies of connection" that differentiates countries that steal and hoard the wealth from countries that have been pillaged.[21] These connections are also about the linkage between systems of oppression and how they're used to compound the hardships of exploited ethnic minorities—turning the people who were once a solution to an economic or labor problem into a social question that must then be answered by white supremacy.

As the grainy black-and-white ABC video demonstrates, the White Australia policy received widespread support well into the second half of the twentieth century. There is a great irony to the Australian police officer raising concerns about "problems" happening in South Africa, as it was clear that the biggest problem of all—racism—had been imbedded in Australian immigration policy for years. And it is still alive and well in the twenty-first-century treatment of asylum seekers.

The Immigration Act of 1901 was replaced by the Migration Act of 1958, which no longer contained the dictation test. But it wasn't until prime minister Gough Whitlam passed the federal Racial Discrimination Act of 1975, making any form of racial discrimination illegal, that the White Australia policy officially came to an end. The second, not the first, is the only reason why someone like me was able to settle there at all.

My own application process for my de-facto-spouse visa was stressful but manageable. English is my native language, and I came bearing an American passport, which put me at a considerable advantage over someone from an African or Southeast Asian country, for example.

The entire process took nine months and cost me close to thirty-five hundred Australian dollars, which seemed like a fortune to me at the time (and still kind of does).* But with enough twelve-hour shifts cleaning up after drunken corporate predators, and a loan from the partner I had moved there to be with, I was able to pay it.

Still, it's difficult for me to look back on the process without seeing the relics of colonial thinking. It's difficult for me to look at the HIV test as something that doesn't target people from central African countries. I can't look past the fact that test results are mailed to applicants with explicit instructions that state any attempt to open the letter renders the report, and therefore the immigrant's entire application, invalid. It's difficult for me not to see

---

* That was in 2009. The application fee now is in excess of ten thousand Australian dollars.

the tuberculosis-X-ray requirement as something that targets people from Southeast Asia, particularly India, which, according to a 2022 report by the World Health Organization, had the highest number of cases globally between 2019 and 2020.[22] As of 2023, the X-ray is still a requirement for people planning on staying in the country for longer than six months. These application requirements didn't explicitly mention anyone from African or Southeast Asian countries on the Department of Immigration and Citizenship's website—but neither did the dictation test.

I rewatched that video from 1962 again recently. Every time I do, I notice something new. At first, it was hatred. That's all I saw: people who hated anyone who wasn't white. Then, I saw the absurdity of cognitive dissonance and entitlement met with the amnesia of their own unwelcome place in Indigenous Aboriginal society. This time, it was fear. More than that, it was terror. When I watch the video now, they all seem deeply aware of exactly what they were saying and why. They seem deeply aware of the consequences of being so terrible—terrified of reckoning with the brutal reality of what they had said and done. That, if they didn't close their borders, one day they would have to reckon with the dire consequences of what they had allowed to happen. It's almost as if they had an irrational fear of migrants forcing their way onto their land to convert *them* to a foreign religion, force *them* to speak a new language and pay taxes to a bureaucratic body that will always treat *them* like second-class citizens. I recognized it because of how many times I had seen those same expressions on people's faces myself, while pouring them drinks on Acland Street, and hearing them tell me just how non-Black I "really" was.

15.

Anatomy of a Nice Guy

I AM FORTUNATE ENOUGH TO HAVE SOME AMAZING stories about my grandpa—who didn't seem afraid of anyone or anything, only the idea of someone harming his family. He was protective of his sisters, of his son, and of his grandchildren. Growing up, Dad used to tell me stories of him standing up to bullies, murderers, white foremen in the citrus orchards who feared his tall, robust build, and deep bravado. I mine these stories when I want to be reminded that I too can be brave. Because, if a Black man can tell a white man to go to hell in 1950s central Florida, I really have no excuse. He had a moral compass that always seemed firmly attuned to doing the right thing, no matter what. And that's something I'd like to think I've also inherited. But he also tended to stick around in relationships that weren't exactly healthy for him.

My grandparents divorced when my dad was a little boy—an event that apparently broke my grandpa's heart, even though I can say objectively they were absolutely no good for each other. He eventually shacked up with another woman, who was incredibly jealous. Someone told me a story in which she stormed into the bathroom while my grandpa was taking a bath—holding a loaded shotgun that she began to fire in all directions. None of the bullets hit him, and she immediately burst into tears apologizing. My grandpa didn't leave her just then. Instead, he went to comfort her. And that relationship lasted for a while longer yet.

I know it's a jarring story, but sometimes—when I think about my own relationship choices—it makes me feel a little bit better.

✳

In the beginning, being in love with Matteo felt like a matter of life or death—because I believed it was such a rare thing, this love. Unique and glowing and frail, like embers in a dying fire that someone blows on to keep a dark room lit. If I didn't nurture it, it would dissolve, and I'd never get another opportunity to love again. Because it was my first adult relationship, I felt like loving someone else required endless sacrifice. Not just moving across the world. That part was easy compared to everything that came after. The main sacrifice—and by far the most difficult—was my internal compass, my true north that told me when to stay and when to leave. It was broken. Day by day, I felt the magnetic field around my heart eroded by the things Matteo's family said about me, until their words wrote the script of my core monologue. And I began to believe, as I had heard from him, his cousin, and his mother time and again, that I *did* speak up too much. That I did have a chip on my shoulder. That *I* was the problem. That *I* was combative. That I was *creating* dysfunction where previously there had been none.

The people around me, even the ones who saw the writing on the wall, knew that they couldn't interfere—it was a defining event. I would only learn by doing. I would only learn, after convincing myself that I *had* to demonstrate my lovability, that I had nothing to prove to anyone. It could not have been easy for them to watch as I curled inside myself, an ocean between me and the life I had given up. Fighting for a relationship with someone who I had begun to feel didn't love me, so much as managed to keep a peace that felt, to me, like war.

For all my clashing with Emilia, Matteo's mum and stepdad proved to be the final obstacle, and breaking point, around whom I found no means to navigate. Many afternoons in their house ended with fights that spilled over into emails where I countered passive aggression with full-on threats to shepherd my biracial family off to the United States, where there were no statues of Al Jolson, no dinner conversations where Sudanese refugees were referred to as mongrels, and a *lot* more Black people whom I could dial in for backup like my personal calvary. I needed an army of Blackcoats to pull me out from that siege. Matteo removed himself from these exchanges, offering neutral platitudes from the shadows like courtside affirmations to run-down athletes. And I was playing that game all by myself, which is why it's so easy for me to pinpoint the exact moment when my relationship with Matteo self-destructed.

We were having evening tea at Maria's house, when her husband Michele initiated a heated conversation about Israel and Palestine. He was known for instigating arguments with people to the point of exhaustion, which Matteo described as a "talent for starting shit." Michele had brought out a neighborhood paper, upset about an article that claimed President Obama had made then Israeli prime minister Benjamin Netanyahu walk through the back door of the White House.* I pointed out that this particular paper wasn't exactly renowned for its objectivity or hard-hitting reports—it was essentially a gossip magazine made by a small

---

* As of the writing of this book, Benjamin Netanyahu is once again prime minister of Israel.

subgroup of hard-line conservatives. Michele pursed his lips and folded the paper in his hands.

"Well, I think that Barack Obama is a closeted Muslim." He went on, punctuating his next sentence with added spite. "I think he's an Arab. Leader. Arse-licker."

He glared at me as he said his words, directing them specifically at me.

Barack Obama didn't need me to stand up for him. For that matter, neither did the almost two billion Muslims of the world. This was less than one year into his first term, before the bombing of Libya or the bombing of Syria, his expanded drone-strike campaign, or the U.S. air strikes that leveled a Médicins Sans Frontières hospital in Afghanistan, killing forty-two people.

Maria joined the discussion, unapologetic and angry. She seemed personally offended by "that man" holding office halfway across the world. I stared at her, aghast as she continued ranting. And, perhaps in response to the look of shock on my face, she returned to the subject of Palestine, giving a fevered lecture about how "these women blew up their own children, and didn't care about themselves or their families." I pointed out that Palestine had been illegally occupied for decades, and stories like that were manufactured to justify that occupation. She leaned across the table and pointed her finger at my face.

"They are animals."

The house became deathly quiet. I could hear the sound of the heater switching on and humming from the panels installed in the wall. I wrapped my hands around my mug of tea and sat still, crawling inside of myself. I didn't know whether to scream or storm out of the house. Matteo sat quietly through the entire thing, without so much as a change in facial expression.

Maria tried to move on, asking about dinner of all things, but I gave only monosyllabic replies. I looked over at Matteo with an expression that begged him for an exit strategy. All he did was smile—at me, at her, at Michele.

Maria asked me if something was wrong, and I scoffed, like *no fucking shit, lady.*

She asked me to explain.

"Well, you obviously don't have much respect for human life or for me, my thoughts and comments. You've been so rude that I don't see the point in speaking anymore, so I don't want to," I said through clenched teeth.

She burst into tears. Maria stood up from the table, turned to Matteo, and began to shout at Matteo. She stormed off to her bedroom, and Michele sat there as embedded in his seat as a yeast infection, saying, "What happened?" in the calmest tone anyone had used all night.

I hesitated, paralyzed by a lifetime of people-pleasing that left me bewildered about what I should do or where I should be. I felt like throwing up, but I went to the bedroom where Maria was sitting on the end of a mattress, dry heaving, and sat next to her. I flinched as I placed my hand on her shoulder, steeling every single nerve in my body from recoiling. Deep down, I knew exactly what she was doing, but I attempted to comfort her anyway—drawing on the same platitudes Matteo had used with me. I didn't know what else to say.

She stood up suddenly, and I looked at her creased face—as dry as the sands of Egypt.

"I don't need counseling," she sneered. She stormed out of the room again.

I MENTALLY CALCULATED the cost of a flight home, knowing that I could barely afford anything on my under-the-table salary of cash in hand and tips. I contemplated booking passage on a cargo ship, earning my place by washing dishes. I contemplated jumping into the ocean and swimming. I contemplated committing a crime to be extradited on the government's dime.

Then, I thought about what my family would say. But I remembered the accusations of desperation I had endured when declaring my intent to move to Australia; I knew they would be even more feral if I returned to the United States. And I knew that I would take them this time around because of the shame that made me feel like those accusations were true. Forcing a resolution with Matteo felt easier. I was young enough to put a price on my self-respect, which was the first thing I surrendered when I decided to stay and try to make the relationship work after that night.

After a week of radio silence, Maria and Michele invited us to an African café to talk things through—which seemed targeted. Matteo and I planned to express how unacceptable their behavior and comments had been, and to establish clear boundaries about how they could and could not speak to me.

Maria and Michele were calm. They didn't interrupt us as we outlined our feelings and how the argument had affected us. When we finished, I felt like we had actually accomplished something. I felt proud of myself for not running away again.

Maria sipped her coffee quietly.

"Now that you've spoken, I'd like to get something off of my chest. I think you should apologize for what you said to Michele."

Matteo and I looked at each other and both replied at the same time, "What do you mean?"

"When you called him white trash. I apologized for what I said to my son, and now you have to apologize to us."

My mouth dropped. All my words—every single letter in the alphabet—evaporated. She leaned in with a smug smile that showed off her teeth.

"You see, Jennifer, when I look at you—I don't see color."

Michele nodded by her side before chiming in.

"But then," he continued, "when I asked Maria if she had heard the same thing, she said yes, so that's why we're bringing it up. Because I may be a lot of things, but racist isn't one of them. And I'm surprised that you, Jennifer, would resort to racist insults simply because of an opinion you don't agree with."

My words returned.

"I didn't say that. I *never* said that." I was emphatic, turning to Matteo. "I never said that!!"

He responded, "Mum, I didn't hear her say that."

"What do you mean, you 'didn't hear'? I didn't!" I shouted, almost standing up from the table. I felt shrill, furious, insane. I could have combusted. Maria's smile widened.

"It's okay, Jennifer, really. We forgive you. But we just want you know that that was totally uncalled for."

"*I didn't say that!!!*"

Matteo, worried about an encore performance that our relationship wouldn't survive a second time, decided to—rather than affirm me—make it worse. "She probably said something like 'what trash,' and that's just what Michele heard."

"No! I didn't! *I didn't say anything like that!*" I shouted again. "I tried to *comfort* you!" I said in a voice that didn't even sound like me.

Maria looked up and smiled, while Michele calmly shrugged his shoulders. "Well, that's what we heard."

I stormed out of the café, waiting for Matteo so we could drive home. I had to give it to them. As much as we had prepared for the meeting, they had thrown a magnificent curveball and, together, rewritten the events that had nearly broken us up—drafting a new script that was guaranteed to tear us apart for good.

IN THE YEARS that followed, I cried a lot more. I stopped reading, shutting myself off from new information that might affirm the feeling in my gut. Sometimes, I lay on the couch for an endless marathon of old television series, taking comfort in the predictability of their endings, which in turn allowed me to disassociate. Matteo couldn't reach me when I was in that place. I may as well have been passed out on a kitchen floor on the other side of the world. It wasn't just my relationship. It was my place in that world. It was the frustration I felt in having chosen it, while knowing deep down that I didn't want it anymore.

I couldn't control these depressions. They pulled me down like an anchor, and I felt physically pinned to the sofa, lost in a nebulous fog that I couldn't see through. It wrapped around me like a cold hug. Matteo didn't understand. He told me to exercise more, suggesting walks around the block to lift my spirits. Sometimes I did and ended up crying on a park bench. Then I came home and acted like it had been the best advice I'd ever received—why on earth had I not thought to do it sooner? When I sank, I could still hear the fervent tapping of his fingers on computer games somewhere in the distance, telling me that he was at least nearby. At least he was there. And when I pulled myself out with sheer willpower long enough to eat something or laugh with him, he seemed relieved.

"There she is," he'd say.

Here I am, I thought. *And here I go.*

Maria stopped coming to our home. By then, our encounters had become so venomous that the home I shared with Matteo became the only place I felt truly safe. When I sank into my depressions, I problematized an entire future that, I decided, would not look any different. I resigned myself to this in all ways but one: children. When I asked Matteo about what kind of father he would be to Black children, he insisted that things would be different—because *children change things*. More than that: they change people! Like magic—"magic" in air quotes. If a relationship with a person, or their in-laws, isn't working, throw a child at it—that'll fix it. That'll fix everything—the parents, the cousins, and the Middle East.

I had heard this fiction repeated many times over the years—but never paired with a real-life example that proved its efficacy. Almost all the weddings I went to in my twenties had ended in divorce. Some with kids. And the same problems that existed before those marriages became exacerbated when dependents were introduced, tiny people who relied on dysfunctional adults to protect them. I was afraid of being drawn into a cycle where I would replicate the mistakes I had seen others make. I was wary of joining the not-so-exclusive club where tiny humans become the masks that disguised the cracks in a relationship that should have ended. The idea of calling that love would change even my relationship to that word—making it strange and terrible.

Sometimes, I brought up the phone call we'd had in Chicago after my first visit.

"Do you remember the promise you made me? The one we spoke about when I was still in Chicago?"

He always acknowledged that he did, but then added nothing else—as if the memory of that conversation was enough to secure my trust that it was being fulfilled.

This went on for several years.

In 2012, I had my first laparoscopic surgery for endometriosis. The pain became so abysmal that going under the knife was the only option. Another incentive that pushed me over the edge was discussions with Matteo about starting a family. My gynecologist told me that the best time to try would be after the surgery. But the surgery was extensive; the damage caused by the disease was greater than anticipated, and it took me six weeks to fully recover. The more I healed, the more I hesitated. I found legitimate reasons: it wasn't the best time for me personally to have a child—I had just quit my job and was looking for new employment. But those reasons were countered with my youth and access to socialized health care, so Matteo and I decided to go on a trip to New Zealand to see if it felt right, knowing that we could be returning as a party of two and a half.

When we landed, we immediately went to the car-rental service to pick up our reservation. Matteo was so happy to be back in New Zealand that he chatted up the agent across the table from us, a woman who smiled back politely—probably used to the joy of people embarking on a new holiday. Picking up my accent, the woman asked where I was from. I told her that I was from the United States but had lived in Australia for four years, giving her an abridged version of our relationship's story.

Everyone loves a good love story.

"She just got her permanent residency," he said, reaching for my hand. "And she's still with me. So it must mean it's for real."

They chuckled together and completed the paperwork.

I read a book once about someone who ended a serious relationship while on vacation in New Zealand. It was the snow-capped mountains and drinkable spring water, the dazzling vistas around every curvy stretch of highway that marry coastal beaches with jagged cliffside. The sweet air that you can taste from the car even with the windows rolled up. The overwhelming beauty in every direction was the problem that compelled me to inject something ugly, restoring a wretched balance.

My timing was far from ideal, but it hadn't felt so deeply necessary until that moment. Matteo and I romped around all the most scenic spots of the South Island: a ferry through the enigmatic fog of Milford Sound; tramping (or hiking) around Lake Te Anau in search of hidden bushels of magenta flowers and herds of sheep; glacier climbing on Franz Josef, devouring cone after cone of soft serve mixed with berries, enjoying freshly baked meat pies, finding the most inappropriate times to cite obscure *Lord of the Rings* references, melding our love of nature with our appreciation for nerd culture. And with every new adventure, every tasty frozen treat, every quoted line, I thought to myself: *I can leave you.*

The conversation with the car-rental agent planted the seed in my mind that sprouted beneath the Kiwi sun like a weed. Before, it had not even seemed possible. Suddenly, it seemed so simple. Liberating. Urgent. I wanted to roll around in the snow and scream at the sea air—*I can leave him!*

We arrived to Cardrona for snowboarding. Matteo left to shred the advanced slopes at full speed while I carefully talked myself through heel-side-to-toe-side turning with toddlers and teens. I hit a snow mound and tumbled, hitting my head hard enough against the mountain to see stars. At the medical station down the slope, a doctor diagnosed me with a mild concussion, and I waited for Matteo to figure out where I was—all the while whispering more gently to my shaken brain, "I can leave him." It was a secret that became more powerful the more I said it to myself—until I realized that I would have to tell *Matteo* at some point as well.

We found a bed-and-breakfast near Hanmer Springs, a thermal spa in the northern part of the island. Steam rose off the warm baths and turned into crystals in the frigid air that I tried to eat while a Māori couple gave us tips on the best local restaurants. After we changed, we went to one of their recommendations and sat in part of the restaurant where the setting sun reflected off the snow-capped mountains and turned the deep brown of Matteo's eyes into little fires. Matteo reached for my hand, saying how happy he was to be there with me. I squeezed it back, winced, and told him that I didn't think the relationship was working.

*

I moved out of the flat I shared with Matteo on my thirtieth birthday, three months after we returned from New Zealand. We were together for five years, four of which were spent together in Australia. If those words read like an obituary, it's only because the love for him I once held had long expired, and when it ended, it was like seeing, breathing, and hearing for the first time. I was resurrected—and felt no cause to grieve because I had already done that through the course of our relationship's extended deterioration.

When I look back, I can see that our relationship was political—regardless of our intentions when it began. Race had not been a factor for us when we fell in love, but it was still something we had to navigate in the world. When we decided to be together, we were engaging in a radical act. But people cannot love as equals in a world where inequality is the foundation upon which that love is forced to exist. "Love is all you need" is an aspiration. It's the goal. As it currently stands, interracial love requires the assistance of intensive anti-racist education within the relationship, and a talented constitutional lawyer outside of it.

And that sounded a lot more like a job than a partnership. So I quit.

16.

Mythologizing the Mixed Baby

FOR A BRIEF PERIOD AFTER THE BREAKUP, I CONSID-
ered moving back to the United States. I considered cities like
San Francisco, Chicago, and New York, where I had friendships and established networks. It was around this time that I was
also diving deep into my family history. I found a drawing of my
great-great-grandfather from what I believe is sometime around
the 1860s, but nothing about my grandpa. I couldn't even find
his parents' birth certificates, and there didn't appear to be any
consensus on when they were born. Sometimes, our last name
was spelled differently. Our family tree sprouts all over the place:
Northern Ireland, the Highlands of Scotland, all along the west
coast of Africa, Indigenous America, the Caribbean, South America, and almost every Southern U.S. state.

Through some overlap in our online ancestry research, a distant cousin named Brenda in Atlanta reached out. Her father
and my grandpa had been brothers. He had never mentioned any
brothers to me—only sisters. I spoke to her on the phone once,
and she recommended I add Georgia to the list of possible new
homes. I was moved by the idea of intergenerational reconciliation

and considered it. Later, on a phone call with my dad, I mused over what my grandpa may have thought about the life I had created. My dad said that he would have wanted me to come home—period. I paused to consider why he was throwing that in there, recognizing his own sentiments disguised as a dead man's.

"I'm not so sure that's true," I replied.

He was resolute, insisting that Grandpa would have thought that me being so far away was borderline unnatural and that I "belonged back home."

I pushed back. I reminded him of when I invited Grandpa to join us for Thanksgiving in a letter I wrote when I was about nine or ten. He drove two hours to join us for dinner, and instead of staying the night—as we had all planned—he drove right back. When dad suggested that he stay, Grandpa became annoyed. "Boy, I got my own life," he told my dad, who couldn't hide his disappointment. Then he took off in his Chevy truck. True, he was a stubborn old man—but that didn't mean he was wrong. On another occasion, we visited him in Haines City, and my dad suggested that he move in with us. Grandpa said, "You're supposed to leave home. Not come back." I told my dad this on the phone—pointing out how his needs from Grandpa were different from my own.

I explained that Grandpa had never moved back to *his* home in Woodland. He would have thought of himself as a failure if he had. He prided himself on making a life in a different part of the world. He wanted the same for my dad. He would have wanted the same for me. And he would have been proud of me for doing exactly that. When I finished my retort, there was a moment of silence on the other side of the phone.

"Oh, shut up," he mumbled.

✳

There are fresh starts and there are so-fresh-and-so-clean starts. I wanted the latter. After I moved out, I enrolled in a full-time master's program for communications and media studies at Monash University and started a full-time job at IBM. I also decided to give dating another shot, but the dating scene had changed remarkably during the five years I had spent with Matteo. Myspace had been surpassed by Facebook, and everyone's favorite first friend Tom had been replaced by personal-data pimp Mark Zuckerberg. Profiles went from being expressions of creativity to polemicist rants about politics and conspiracy theories.

Tinder had also shaken up the tech industry as the world's first swipable dating app. And *everyone* was using it. My massage therapist. My BodyPump instructor. My divorced (and married) colleagues at IBM. Even my osteopath told me that, if she were single, she would "give it a go."* After finding her now husband on Tinder, my friend Miranda wouldn't rest until she had convinced all her girlfriends to download the app. I did. And my first thought was, "This feels... odd." No theme music? No favorite-books section? No HTML-customized background with a gnarly digital design that expressed my idiosyncratic personality? How was anyone supposed to know if they wanted to date me without first inspecting the online street cred of my carefully curated top-eight friends? Rest in peace to the OG of social networking.

I didn't have the same experiences as my white peers on Tinder. For one, I dated women and men, which, while increasing the potential encounters, also quadrupled my experiences with fetishization. For another, I stayed and studied in the more affordable southeastern suburbs and worked in the central business district, so most of the people I encountered were white. But not just white. They were white

---

* When I began to tell her about my encounters on the app, she changed her tune to "Thank God I got married before all of this happened."

people whose entire social circles were white and who consumed only literature by other white people—if they consumed literature at all. People whose perceptions of the world were shaped by the hate speech of far-right Murdoch-baptized pundits like Andrew Bolt.

People I matched with were quick to steer the conversation to their love of hip-hop, dancehall music, Oprah Winfrey, Barack Obama, and Eddie Murphy stand-up specials—proof of their cultural acumen. They waxed lyrical about mythological mixed-race babies with dark skin and blue eyes I didn't even want as the "magic solution"* to eradicate racism the world over. When my rebuttals referenced the colorist, classist, and strict caste systems of countries with heavily mixed populations like Brazil, South Africa, and India, my matches responded by describing these countries as happy, vibrant amusement parks that taught them the virtues of "gratitude" and the pleasures of the "simple things in life." Then they talked up their brand-new BMWs or Audis.

On the rare occasions that I actually went on dates, they quickly devolved into white lectures on racial "preferences" that I challenged as the by-products of harmful stereotypes, leading the other person to deploy some sexist or racist defense mechanism in hopes of restoring a power balance that, up until then, they would have denied ever existed. Things like, "Hold on there, Oprah. Don't burn your bra just yet."

The alternate reality I had first experienced with Matteo's friends years before wasn't unique to them; rather, they were part of a larger ecosystem where I continuously found myself speaking a different language about a different experience in a different world where anything I said would be deemed irrelevant because of my American accent. I knew that I had to find some way to make peace with this because I couldn't change a country's racist history or culture.

---

* All the air quotes. Every single one of them.

And, as a newly single woman, I didn't want to make the same mistakes that I had made in my recently dissolved common-law marriage. I decided the best way to manage my frustration was to look at my encounters with sexual fetishization as an anthropological curiosity. I wondered how a mindset so obviously warped by colonial degradation could become the standardized approach to dating. I ended up writing my thesis on racial exclusion categories and social-exchange theory in online dating. When I approached Tinder from that perspective, I stopped looking for romance and began to see the people I matched with for what they were: test subjects. Objects whose time I could waste for my own personal enrichment.

. . . Finally introducing some modicum of equality to our interactions.

People I interviewed were surprisingly forthcoming—proud, even—about how their infatuation with Black women had been influenced by entertainment. Serena Williams was a huge factor for a lot of men *and* women. Beyoncé, whom I could not seem to escape no matter how far I traveled, was another one. A comparison to either was couched as complimentary because both of these women are extremely talented and beautiful—ignoring the fact that I look nothing like them. But having even the *faintest* proximity to these physical comparisons—which, to be clear, were based on skin color alone—didn't translate into respect or even basic human decency. I was groped on a number of first dates; when I recoiled with anger, I was met by surprise by people who had seen Black women's bodies handled roughly in some music video, movie, or problematic porn. I was told to feel complimented by such hostility, or flattered by how someone's previous encounter with a Black woman made me desirable by extension of our sameness.

It wasn't that these people didn't understand that their desire was deeply offensive, it's that they didn't care about the fact that *I* *felt* offended by the methods of their desire. Critical theorist Homi

K. Bhabha describes this contradiction as "splitting" beliefs of colonial discourse—where ethnic minorities are categorized into fixed and knowable stereotypes resulting in the othered person being both idolized and demonized for the qualities that distinguish them from whiteness.[1] The people I met were attracted to me because of a skin color that also made it easier to stereotype, disrespect, and discard me.

The anecdotal experiences were useful enough for my thesis, but I was missing the historical context needed to understand why the fetishization of African Americans played such an extensive role in Australian dating. I didn't find much outside of the firsthand accounts I read about and interviewed people on, until I learned about the country's history of anti-miscegenation laws—specifically how they policed the bodies of Aboriginal women. Then, it all made sense.

IN THE LATE nineteenth century, around the time when dictation tests were being introduced across the Commonwealth to address the "Asiatic question," Australian authorities also debated how best to address the "Aboriginal question." The two identifiable solutions seemed to be: assimilation into white Australian society through education, or the gradual erosion of Indigenous features through interracial relationships—referred to at the time as the initiative to "civilize" through "biological absorption."[2]

The basis of this belief system, firmly rooted in eugenics theory, had begun infiltrating Australia in the 1890s and increased in popularity during the interwar years.* Local politicians began

---

* It's also important to note that eugenics is firmly rooted in ableism. For the purposes of this book, I do not go into detail about this subject matter—but it is a crucial component to an intersectional approach. I will include sources in the Suggested Reading section that explain this history in more detail.

adopting ideas about who was and who was not "fit to breed" in order to both write immigration policy *and* complete the "necessary" task of disappearing the physical attributes and characteristics of Aboriginal people.[3] Absorption was identified as the approach with the most potential. One enthusiastic eugenics supporter named A. O. Neville, who served as the Chief Protector of Aborigines from 1915 to 1936, heavily promoted this policy—causing even the most ardent white proponents to feel a little nervous. After all, there is no shortage of contradiction to be found in an *interracial* breeding ideology meant to promote a pure race, even if it's intended to eliminate one of the races involved.[4]

Neville's goal of biological absorption was the eradication of the Aboriginal race within three generations: a "half-blood" union between a white Australian man and an Aboriginal woman, followed by a "quadroon daughter," and an "octaroon" grandchild who would be, for all intents and purposes, indistinguishable from a white Anglo-Saxon Australian person.[5] In Neville's 1947 book, *Australia's Coloured Minority*, illustrations are included—showing an Aboriginal woman, whose features are gradually anglicized next to two progressively lighter relatives.[6] These same terms were also used in the United States throughout the pre–Civil War era, when U.S. states made their own laws for how to classify someone as Black. For example, Virginia passed a statute in 1705 that defined a Black person as "the child [mulatto] the grand child [quadroon] or the great grandchild [octoroon] of a negro."[7] Utah law used those terms directly, referring to all "mulattos, octoroons, and quadroons" as Black people and, therefore, forbidden from engaging in interracial marriages.

Typically, the words *mulatto* and *negro* sufficed, but after the U.S. Civil War, these more granular racial "enumerators" began to appear in census reports. In 1870, the word *mulatto* included a subcategorical definition of "quadroons, octoroons, and any person having any perceptible trace of African blood."[8] By 1890, these census enumerators had become their own racial classification— all based purely on visual inspection. Clearly, this was far from an exact science. Even the U.S. Census Bureau recognized how difficult it was to determine how mixed someone's ethnicity was just by eyeballing it. So, in 1920, the Fourteenth Census of the United States formally adopted the "one-drop" rule instead, a legal racial classification that defined any person with a traceable amount of African blood to be Black.[9]

These terms were used, in large part, to restrict miscegenation—but only between Black men and white women. Black women were routinely raped by white slavers, who suffered little to no social ramifications for doing so. Even at slave auctions in the United States, quadroon slave women took a higher price because slavers saw them as preferable sexual objects, finding dark skin generally more repulsive.[10] Australia operated under very similar principles. White women were strictly forbidden from engaging in relationships with Aboriginal men because they were legally considered the property of white men. But white men, on the other hand, engaged in the widespread violent rape of Aboriginal women across Australia.

Though white bushmen took savage liberties with the bodies of Aboriginal women, the resulting offspring were loathed.[11] The children from these attacks raised alarm among colonial officials. And in 1905, Walter Roth, the Protector of Indigenous Peoples of Northern Queensland, presented a Royal Commission report to British Parliament conveying deep concern and disgust over the "roving sexual habits" of white Australian men, calling the prevalence of interracial relationships between white men and Aboriginal women "rife."[12]

The response was the Aborigines Act of 1905, which limited sexual encounters between whites and Aboriginal people by forcing the latter group of people onto reserves, transferring guardianship of mixed-race children to white parents, removing them from the homes of their mothers and putting them under state supervision in government institutions; it also subjected all interracial marriages between Aboriginal people and whites to the approval of a designated Chief Protector—to limit the number of mixed-race births between white men and Aboriginal women.[13/*]

I cannot overstate the extent of the violence inflicted by white Australia.

In his book *With the White People* historian Henry Reynolds describes the situation leading up to the 1905 act thus:

> On pastoral stations Aboriginal women were preyed on by any and every white man whose whim it was to have a piece of "black velvet" wherever and whenever they pleased ... [A pastoralist] had known stations where every hand on the place had a gin, even down to boys of 15 years of age.[14]

The term *g*n* is an extremely racist epithet derived from the Dharuk word diyin, meaning "wife." It was commonly used by bushmen at the time to reference the sexual exploitation of Aboriginal women. Terms like this, along with *black velvet*, come inherently paired with the assumption of sexual availability that legitimize the rape and abuse of Aboriginal women—which was extensive.[15] According to professor of Indigenous policy Boni Robertson, these kinds of "discursive meaning systems" gave white men the language and tools to disparage, dehumanize, and

---

* The 1905 act was repealed by the Native Welfare Act, which was implemented in 1964.

disempower Aboriginal women.[16] Not only did this rationalize the violence on Aboriginal women's bodies, but it made that violence their fault and burden—rationale that was commonly deployed on the rare occasion a case of rape was brought before a white judge, many of whom were "quick to accept claims of devalued Aboriginal womens' sexuality" that "lowered the standards applied when determining consent."[17]

The result was unmitigated rape of epic proportions. And not just in the distant past.

In 2006, two years before I moved to Australia, a ten-year-old Aboriginal girl was gang-raped in an Aurukun settlement located in northern Queensland by no less than nine males.[18] Judge Sarah Bradley determined that the young girl had "probably agreed" to have sex with the males, and the prosecutor responsible for trying the case described the crime as something "naughty" and merely "a form of childish experimentation."[19] Six of the males were given probation and three more suspended sentences. Even though the prosecutor and the judge stepped down after national and international backlash—including from then soon-to-be-elected prime minister Kevin Rudd—neither of them ever faced any form of discipline.

Even as a survivor, it's difficult for me to comprehend the depth of such injustice—or the wounds it creates, despite having many of my own. But reading about this story reminded me of an incident with Matteo, during one of the more tumultuous periods of our relationship. We had been wrestling around for fun, as we often did. It often began with tickling (me as the primary instigator) and, because we were both physically strong people, we could go for hours without hurting each other—always knowing when to pull back and when we were both exhausted. Silliness was one of the things that I had loved about our relationship. When I had him pinned, I began tickling him like mad until he begged me to stop.

We were both breathless and smiling, then we went back into the living room. He laughed as he spoke before bringing up something I had told him in confidence early in our relationship.

"How could anyone have raped you? You're so strong!"

I still feel the shame from that moment—the fleeting thought that I should have done something to defend myself first when I was assaulted, and then when my partner very subtly said that he did not believe I had been.

WHEN I WONDERED about how this kind of institutional barbarity has affected Aboriginal women, I found sobering insights in the poetry some have written—where verse operates as both a stark reflection of the brutality of White Australia and the reclamation of agency.

Romaine Moreton, an Aboriginal poet whose work explores themes of racialization of Indigenous peoples, interrogates the body as a weapon of cultural debasement and colonial ownership. In her poem "Mamillates and Tresses," Moreton uses the body as a record of the violence wrought against Aboriginal women and land.[20]

Aileen Corpus, another Aboriginal poet, examines the colonial attitudes that have facilitated such gross miscarriages of justice as the one that took place in Aurukun.[21] In her 1975 poem "Taxi Conversation," Corpus relays a seemingly mundane conversation between a Black woman and a driver, who openly fetishizes her by playing on tropes that tie the color of one's skin to their sexual nature.[22]

Something that sticks out to me about the second poem is how it uses a conversation that I have endured more times than I can count applied to poetic verse—with little embellishment. The mundanity of the conversation becomes its own kind of poetic performance, where the punctuation emphasizes and interrogates the absurdity of its content. The first poem captures the way the conversation from the second poem has always made me feel: as if I am terrain to be explored, discovered, and owned. In both, it's the use of the same language that was so central in the oppression they faced that has become a mirror and a testimony to their survival.

The experiences of Black women in the United States and Black women in Australia both appear to complete the cycle of racial fetishization as outlined by Homi K. Bhabha. The bodies of Black women become the subject of desire; they suffer through the commodification of the white gaze, stripped of their sexual autonomy and physiological subjectivity; and then they become subjects to be addressed, questions to be answered, and problems to be solved. In this contradiction, I see both the appetite for Black bodies as well as the compulsion to punish them for being Black as a defining trait of white supremacy, which seems so confused by its own will to dominate others that it can't even recognize this behavior as an extension of its own idiocy. Or, perhaps more fittingly, people who were

> Idiots, insane persons . . . Persons suffering from
> a loathsome or a dangerous contagious disease,
> Persons who have been convicted of a felony or
> other infamous crime or misdemeanor involving
> moral turpitude.[23]

—To use their own language.

Learning more about how Black Aboriginal women were treated, I was able to better understand the fetishization I experienced in Australia—and to visualize it as an extension of the entitlement that colonized the country. There was historical context to having my skin color compared to the color of chocolate, or berries, or licorice. I was African American when white people needed to manufacture a distance from Aboriginal history that allowed them to sanitize or forget it, but I was *always* Black when they tried to coerce an act of intimacy that would have degraded me in the same way.

Much of the poetry I read connected the experiences of sexual exploitation on the Australian "frontier" to the repugnant stereotypes that continue to influence how Aboriginal women are treated today. In being denied the right to subjectivity (which seems reserved for white women) Black women become objects that can be used, traded, collected, owned, then discarded. Like land. Like property. Like dolls.

The exact figure of Aboriginal Australian deaths caused by colonialism is difficult to know because the exact number of Aboriginal inhabitants who originally resided in Australia isn't known. Estimates range from 300,000 to over one million, and the rate of deaths that were a result of the violence of colonialism range from 80 percent to 96 percent of the population from the time the First Fleet landed in 1788—though these figures are disputed among historians and anthropologists.[24] But one of the most sinister ways in which Aboriginal women died was from sexual abuse—including venereal disease and sexual violence.[25] Around 1847, two-thirds of the Aboriginal population around Port Phillip died of sexually transmitted diseases—mostly young women.[26] Aboriginal girls were the most vulnerable, with victims as young as eight being rendered infertile by venereal disease, if not dying altogether. In an 1845 survey, magistrates of the Dungog district attributed a shocking decline in births to the sexual abuse by white men perpetrated against young girls at a "tender age." Between the years 1839 and 1845, only one Aboriginal child was born in the Port Phillip area, and the number of Aboriginal residents in the area decreased from 207 to 152. By 1859, there were only fifty-six.[27]

In the 1860s, Aboriginal people were being forcibly removed from their traditional lands and moved onto missions, reserves, and stations. This was done under the pretense of protection, but these locations expressly forbid the practicing of their language, ceremonies, or culture.[28] The solution to the "Aboriginal question" was first "breeding" them out, then a hysterical counterreaction to quarantine them from white people altogether—demonstrating the exact insanity that authorities seemed terrified of inheriting from the nebulous other in early immigration-legislation verbiage. It's still the first thing that I think of whenever I encounter someone cooing over the possibility of having a mixed baby with a Black person: that impulse to consume the qualities of another person because they think *their* racial genetics will somehow improve my own and become the building blocks of an anti-racist utopia in which only white people and their light-skinned kin exist.

I don't need the assistance of poetry to know that this isn't a post-racial paradise—because it's more like hell.

The words of Aileen Corpus and Romaine Moreton are not about me—they are not about my people. African American culture and that of the different Aboriginal nations are two very different experiences, not to be conflated or compared. In understanding the ways in which white supremacy has replicated its strategies, inflicting them on both of us—along with so many other peoples—I see the deeply unimaginative ways in which we have all been harmed. I can see how the regurgitated tools of oppression have been ridden on horseback around the world under cover of night. I see the devils that chased my family across the South, that gave me an Irish surname and a Scottish family tree. They are the exact same ones that sailed into Australia's eastern seaboard in the 1700s, claimed it for the British Crown, and renamed it New South Wales. They held the same lit torches. They were cut from the same pointed white sheet. That's why I know, that sticking with the ones I know didn't make a lick of difference. Because they are everywhere.

Especially on Tinder.

17.

Problematizing Patriotism

WHEN I WAS THIRTEEN YEARS OLD, DAD TOOK US on a road trip to Washington, D.C. We usually went on more accessible holidays during the two weeks a year he took off from work—the Florida Keys or Sanibel Island, for example. Once, we went back to North Carolina—though I was only six, and my memories of the trip are marred by the smells wafting from the portable toilet he had installed in the back seat of the van to save time. Dad wasn't too keen on new places or big cities. He liked to talk about all the places he wanted to visit but seemed afraid of them at the same time—and was more comfortable with the secondhand accounts I brought back after being dispatched to the far-flung corners of the world. I don't know what possessed him to take a fourteen-hour car trip from Tallahassee to D.C. But I listened to Garbage's debut album over and over on my Discman until the CD scratched, reading *The Vampire Lestat* by Anne Rice while vibing out to Shirley Manson. My brother was equally as lost in his own world. Mom was lost in hers. Miles of highway looked the same, but the trees that lined our path changed from palm trees to holly and beech in Georgia. I knew we were crossing into North

Carolina before I saw the sign because the smell of pine seeped in through the air vents. I hadn't been there in years, but I somehow still remembered that scent.

Washington, D.C., felt as vast and consuming as Disney World—which should say something about my perspective back then. The walk from monument to monument seemed endless. My mom hated it. My brother and I just kinda did what we were told. We gazed upon the Lincoln and Jefferson memorials and saw the Constitution up close. We looked upon the White House—but never discussed who had built it. I could sense the mythos that had constructed these objects and structures and written our national anthem. I could easily see how our national identity acted as a unifying force against an external threat—which I later observed as a college freshman at Florida State during the events surrounding September 11, 2001. Being American suddenly became an ambiguous battle between us against a shadowy them—with the distinguishing factor being how ardently one side supported the war in a country that had nothing to do with the terrorist attacks. It's much easier for us to measure the strength of our national identity by the way it responds to external threats somewhere in a faceless country than it is to face the internal threats that have been ripping the country apart since it was founded. The United States I know, and the one I left, cloaks those internal threats as patriotism, founding principles—fathers.

I sat next to my dad on the steps of the Lincoln Memorial, staring out toward the surrounding lawns. The Korean War Veterans Memorial lay to my right, the Vietnam Women's Memorial to my left, and directly opposite the reflecting pool in front of us, the World War II Memorial straight ahead. My father, a Black man born poor and in the Jim Crow South, who was part of the first generation of integrated students after the ruling of *Brown v. Board of Education*, who has worked since he was eight years old, and who has been told his entire life where he belongs and where he doesn't by people far less than him simply because of his skin color, gazed out in front of us and said to me, "This is the greatest country on Earth."

And he meant it. Just as fervently as he believed that the history of heroes who fought bravely in World War II had been whitewashed to remove the contributions of African Americans like my grandpa—*his* dad—he believed that the country they fought for is the greatest one on Earth.

I did not feel the same way. I feel even less so now.

*

I used to only associate words like *nation* and *patriotism* with the United States. But I don't *feel* patriotic about American history, most of which is dedicated to securing the freedoms of white men exclusively. Whatever pride I felt in being American stemmed from our so-called greatest hour—World War II—because of my grandpa. He was my personal connection to a sliver of that American mythos, and he embodied the best of that nation while fighting fascism in Europe. White people in both places have the privilege of feeling proud of their entire history, but that's not something Black people have ever had. I would argue it's something we still don't. We're proud of one another, we're proud of ourselves—and that's separate from a nation. Having grown up on intensive Holocaust education, I felt deep pride in knowing that my grandpa had been part of something to end one of the worst genocides in history.

World War II is responsible for creating the alliance that exists between Australia and the United States today. It's also a major source of my problematic feelings regarding my relationship to both nation-states.

Britain was stretched thin battling Hitler in Europe and quickly exhausting its resources to supply Russia with equipment while managing supply channels across the Atlantic Ocean. So, Winston Churchill made the decision to preserve its forces by cutting off resources to Australia, putting the country in a very precarious position.[1] Australian prime minister John Curtin made a decision that became a defining moment for both nations. In December 1941, he penned an essay in the Melbourne *Herald* that was followed by a speech in March 1942, where he boldly declared that Australia "look[ed] to America" for support against Japanese aggression.[2] It is impossible to overstate the importance of this moment. Many older Australians were shocked because of the country's strong history with and allegiance to England. But it was a logical call to make, and Curtin rightfully pointed out that if Australia fell to Imperial Japan, then there was nothing to stop it from moving on to the Americas next.

After that speech, U.S. president Roosevelt dispatched General Douglas MacArthur to the Pacific to lead the Allies into battle against Japan—and the deployment of American troops began soon thereafter. While this was the outcome that Australia wanted, a 1941 meeting between U.S. forces and the Australian War Cabinet made it very clear that they were emphatically opposed to the inclusion of African American GIs because of their commitment to maintaining the integrity of the White Australia policy.[3] While the legislation had originally been drafted to target Asian immigrants, it was in effect meant to halt the arrival of anyone who wasn't white. General MacArthur gave assurances that they would only be stationed in remote locations or around—but not in—the country, but keeping that promise proved impossible because it meant isolating Black troops from the army's supply chain of food and ammunition, which would have impaired their ability to fight.

The first African American soldiers arrived in Melbourne in January 1942—which seems to indicate that they had left the

United States even before any consulting procedures had been decided, perhaps even during the promises that MacArthur would
soon have to break. By August 1942, 7,285 African American soldiers were stationed around Australia—making up more than a
third of American resident depot personnel.[4] As they began arriving, there was general confusion among the larger Australian public over how to receive them. On the one hand, they were Black, and
the country had clearly defined attitudes toward people with dark
skin. On the other hand, they were sent there to defend Australia
from probable Japanese occupation, presenting a moral conun-
drum: be racist or be colonized. What seems like an easy decision
proved to be an existential crisis for a country that had formed its
core identity around who was white and who wasn't. Ultimately,
Australian military leaders made the decision to accept soldiers of
every background, though the local Queensland and Commonwealth governments established "a complex, interlinking pattern
of segregation."[5] Meanwhile, white GIs brought U.S. segregation
laws with them to maintain the racist hierarchy emblematic of the
United States at the time. This put African American soldiers at
the mercy of two structurally racist systems: Jim Crow and White
Australia.

It's difficult to know which brand of discrimination drove the
other, but U.S. military officials certainly commended Australia's racist policy. In 1942, the U.S. naval attaché in Melbourne,
L. D. Causey, openly praised the "doctrines of racial superiority"
in Australia, and the Office of Strategic Services wrote in 1943 of
how impressed they were that Aboriginal people "had no status in
Australian society . . . Their existence is scarcely recognized."[6]

In fact, the treatment of Aboriginal people in Australia and the
treatment of African Americans was so comparable that Black GIs
were instructed to claim Aboriginal identities so that white Australians could understand how to treat them—because introducing a

new kind of Black person would have been confusing. White U.S. soldiers exploited Australia's horrific attitudes toward what U.S. military officials called the "Australian Negro," to shape white Australia's attitudes toward African American soldiers.[7] As private Travis Dixon of the United States Army wrote to his father in in 1943, he had been instructed to "act like the Abbo"* to avoid offending the local white population.[8]

White Australia brought African American GIs into its policy using a three-phase strategy: First, they would be confined to remote rural areas; secondly, because it was inevitable that Black soldiers would be stationed in large city centers like Brisbane, Queensland, their movements would be restricted by areas designated as "colored only" by U.S. troops; and lastly, their exposure to white Australian women would be controlled using segregated recreational activities.[9]

By mid-May 1942, the first platform began its rollout: 3,500 Black GIs were stationed in northwest Queensland—the Australian state most renowned for how it had formalized its entrenched attitudes about segregation—to construct a road. With Aboriginal people still legally restricted to living on reserves and missions, Queensland was indisputably the most racist state in Australia. Once they were in place, the second phase was rolled out, and U.S. troops began to designate which areas were "white only" and which areas were for "colored" troops—leading to serious conflicts between Black soldiers and white ones. In Wacol, 150 Black soldiers got into a fight with white soldiers who had "invaded" on their territory.[10]

In Brisbane, Black soldiers were relegated to areas south and east of the riverbank—where only non-whites lived. These parts of town were cheap and run-down, where brothels operated and

---

* *Ab*o* or *A*o* are more racist epithets.

worked by Aboriginal women were common. When white soldiers from the more affluent northern and western parts of the area crossed into "Black territory," brawls often ensued.[11] At the same time, there were stories of white Australian soldiers developing a sense of camaraderie with African American troops—until an Australian provost-corps sergeant sent a letter in April 1942, claiming that such fraternization threatened the safety of the city.[12] This letter prompted all commanders based in Queensland to send directives to cease any and all recreational relationships with Black soldiers.

So afraid were they that the rules of engagement of global war could erode the racist policy of a country in need of Black soldiers to stave off a potential occupation.

Private Travis Dixon's letter also described how he and his fellow Black soldiers initially moved around freely going wherever they pleased, but it wasn't long before signs began to appear labeling places as being "off limits" to Negro soldiers.[13]

On May 26, 1942, the general director of the state directors of security made this statement at a conference:

> The only way to deal with them [Black soldiers] according to Americans, is to keep them in their proper place. I think you should give consideration to making it an offence for any Australian member of the forces to procure for or supply to any coloured member of the American forces any liquor. The Americans don't want it and they have put the hotels out of bounds to the Negroes.[14]

The worst treatment African American soldiers received, however, was from their own military police, who were used in large part to restrict the movements of Black GIs. In November 1942, a fight broke out in southern Brisbane where Black soldiers threatened white ones with knives. Local Australian police acted with such restraint that several were recommended for major commendations; whereas U.S. military police used batons to beat the Black soldiers back in line.[15]

All of this proved as effective in Australia as it was in the United States. Save for the third phase of this strategy: access to white Australian women. White American soldiers spread appalling rumors about the licentious Black troops and their "animalistic" sexual appetites along with claims that they were infected with STIs like syphilis, which was likely meant to dissuade white women. But these rumors seemed to have had the opposite effect, heightening their curiosity to investigate the gossip themselves. Upon a visit to a "Colored Service Club," Lieutenant Colonel Pelzeman remarked on how amazing it was to see "white girls dancing and loving up the darkies" whereas white sergeant John F. Line, based on an air force base in southwest Sydney, described the sight of Black soldiers "necking" with white girls as "disgusting as heck."[16] At the end of the war, an estimated fifty white Australian women traveled to the United States as the wives of African American soldiers.[17]

Some were less fortunate. Dorothy Beatty was a white Australian woman who married Reuben Franklin Beatty, an African American soldier, in 1946. One week after their wedding, he was nearly deported—but because Dorothy was sick, he refused to leave her side. On May 9, 1946, Australian Customs and Immigration Officials threw him in prison for violating the White Australia policy.[18] On the last Sunday of that month, Reuben was boarded on a boat bound for New York without being allowed to say goodbye. When Dorothy applied for a visa to join him in the United States, she was denied on account of a previous criminal charge.[19]

Perhaps this part of our shared history is less known because of the word *American* in African American, which allows the racism of the United States to be used as the standard against which all other forms of racism against African Americans is measured. But historian Kay Saunders described the racist treatment of Black soldiers by white Australians and white Americans as "dual and interlocking systems of segregation" that ultimately reinforced the "resilience" of White Australia. And while many Black soldiers seemed to experience "less" racism than what they endured in the United States, it's widely regarded to be a "matter of degree."[20] I find it difficult to rejoice in varying degrees of inequality, especially if Jim Crow is the base unit of measurement. The results look exactly the same. And I find it difficult to honor calls for patriotism from two countries who created such elaborate systems of horror to preserve their claims to land—the same land that had been stripped from Aboriginal people, the same land that African Americans weren't welcome to live on after defending it.

I can't help but think of my grandpa while reflecting on all of this. I wonder about how he was treated in France. I know he was in a segregated unit in the army, but how was he treated by the locals? Did they complain to Allied officials about having Black soldiers protect them from the Nazis? Did someone invite him to their house for tea? I hope so. At the same time, if he was invited into people's homes—I wonder how he ever found the stomach to return to the United States. I wonder how he managed to spend the rest of his life there. But I also wonder, if he had been stationed in the Pacific—Australia in particular—would he have been able to have any life there either?

These questions deeply impact my ability to feel patriotic, even though citizenship and the nation-state demand that we do. And placing the onus on me to perform patriotism with hats, flags, and the policing of dissenting opinion only absolves nations from creating an environment that we all *can* feel proud of. As long as individuals are shamed into being patriotic, then nations avoid the shame *they* should confront in admitting that they've failed to create a better country for everyone.

I am emotionally pulled to the ideas and cultures that make up American and Australian identity, but that's completely separate from the concept of the nations themselves. Culture is about a people, a shared way of existing, and a way of life; the nation-state serves the objectives of a governing body. A culture is a shifting, fluid concept that can change and grow to include others; whereas the nation is a rigid, immovable entity that demands blind loyalty. Western nation-states rely on expansion and preserve their global positioning through intervention and oppression. British race theoretician Paul Gilroy described "the nation" as "a neat, symmetrical accumulation of family units . . . secured in part by sustained exposure to national history in the classroom."[21] Which sounds like a brilliant way to describe the mafia—perhaps one with an entire military at its disposal? And time has shown me that the nation is just as neurotic and fragile as the central egos that govern any dysfunctional family systems—including illicit criminal enterprises.

It's difficult to feel proud of any of that.

*

In 2015, I began the process of applying for Australian citizenship. Not for any reasons of pride or duty. The reason was simple: I didn't want to return to the United States. At that point, I had lived in Melbourne longer than I had lived in any other city. I wanted to vote. I wanted to be done with the bureaucracy of immigration. But I harbored concerns over the jingoistic rhetoric that seeped into the political discourse like a transpacific contagion. I was happy to be adopting a second nationality, but I was also wary of signing on to the absolutist rhetoric of a country's greatness after years of watching children play with golliwogs, hearing tone-deaf defenses of blackface, listening to politicians use reverse racism as a dog whistle, and consuming annual data reports on the continued systemic discrimination inflicted upon Aboriginal peoples. And I was wary of the national mythology that did not tell the side of its story that was most applicable to me—a history that isn't taught in Australia. I had chosen to live in a country where I could create some semblance of a life that was sustainable and safe, and I viewed being naturalized as an exchange of equitable goods: to take citizenship in a country whose laws I had been obeying and whose taxes I had been faithfully paying, without which I would have been ineligible.

My peers, my caseworker, and the proctors who administered my knowledge exam described it as a privilege, which, given the background of racist, ableist belief systems on which Australian immigration legislation is built, seemed to be the epitome of audacity. I certainly had privileges: being an American citizen with a U.S. passport and having reasonably good health being examples. I don't think that should bypass criticizing the *authority* that governing bodies possess and enforce by creating policies that determine which people, from which countries, will benefit from the "privilege" of citizenship the most—and which people, because they don't have them, will suffer the worst. That authority, that privilege, is the most sinister of them all.

My ceremony was on a summer evening in December that year. Warm days were turning to cool nights before morphing into the heat waves that sweep across bushland and scorch the sky with red clouds of smoke and ash. The friends and colleagues I had made over the past seven years—even Matteo—came to Glen Eira City Council for the ceremony. As I found my seat with the other immigrants in front of the stage, I was moved to find a room full of people of color. Men and women who were every different shade of Black and Brown, with hijab and kufi and without, with spouses and with children—elderly citizens holding their tiny mixed-race grandchildren in one hand and small plastic Australian flags in another.

I raised my hand, said my oath, walked across the stage—and the room where my support system sat erupted in applause.

"That must be for you!" the officiant said beaming, shaking my hand and passing along my naturalization certificate.

"Yes, sir," I squealed in delight.

It remains one of my most beautiful memories of Australia.

Several of us, including Matteo, went for ribs afterward. Friends who were immigrants from Ireland, Israel, and Russia, who had gone through the same process, shared their stories and gave me gifts. In that moment, I felt a shared understanding about the stress and exhaustion of the process. But deep down, I knew that solidarity hit a wall when it came to the subject of race. For all the inclusive language these fellow immigrants had used during my naturalization ceremony, I watched the same people post rants on Facebook calling for "a return of skinheads" to sort out the "African problem." *Immigrants* calling for violent racist reprisals against other immigrants. People who seemed excited by the prospect of distinguishing themselves and their respectability from the tarnished public image of a people with dark skin. And why wouldn't they? After all, the White Australia policy, despite having been over for almost fifty years, was designed to *help them*. Not anyone from Sudan. Not even an African American. Like the Black soldiers who went to Australia before me, I had fallen in through a loophole—caught somewhere between a rock and a hard place, happy to be there, but unsure if I really belonged.

PART 4

*

Berlin, Germany

August 1, 2016–Present Day

My Pisces Venus (Heart) in the Tenth House: They are so receptive and open to all possibilities that it is hard for them to commit to any one person, idea, or place. With Pisces representing the dueling fish, they have emotions that push and pull like the tides of the ocean and long for something that is hard to define and even harder to find. Borders and boundaries blur—leaving them susceptible to victimization and delusion. They are evasive, love unconditionally, and are prone to relationships of martyrdom and mercy. The more they align themselves with places and people who encourage their drive for creativity, the less susceptible they will be to the negative projections of others—the more comfortable they will become embodying their own multidimensionality. More than anything, this watery placement needs a piece of earth to call home, where it can grow—and thrive.

18.

A Graveyard of Streets

The Black victims of the Nazis have long not been considered—neither by academic research nor by memorial politics. But in a town like Berlin, a Black community in the 1920s and 1930s did exist, all of whom were at first harassed and later more often than not murdered during Nazi rule. It is our aim to uncover their stories and make them present again, late as it is.

—SOPHIA SCHMITZ, STOLPERSTEINE BERLIN

T HE SOUND OF THE AMBULANCES CHARGING THROUGH the streets was the first difference I noticed about Berlin. Their bloated sirens were like curse words berating cars and pedestrians, expressing how morally offended they felt sharing the same roads. It was an attitude I frequently encountered from elderly people judging me when I jaywalked to the inscrutable grocery store cashier with the asymmetrical haircut, known as Frau Netto, who scanned my items and then hurled them at warp speed down the pass where I stuffed them frantically into a tattered tote bag. It was all new, but I was most fascinated with the ambulance siren. In the United Kingdom, emergency service vehicles use the Klaxon horn. In the United States and Australia, it's the wail. In Japan, I personally never heard an ambulance. In Germany, they use the Martin-Horn—which is *by far* the most obnoxious of them all.

At least once a week, an ambulance sneaks up on me while I'm spaced out on a stroll, and its siren scares the piss out of me. More than once, I've caught the driver grinning deviously through the driver's side window while speeding past—my nerves completely rattled out of place.

That loud dissonant sound of people being rushed to the hospital from accidentally overdosing at the quarterly queer rave at KitKat Club is the musical score to my brand-new life, I thought to myself.* But when I first arrived, it was music to my ears!

When I first moved to Berlin, I spent most of my time walking between places, in part because I lived in Neukölln off the U8, a city train line with a reputation for illicit drugs and violence. As the district struggles with spiking levels of addiction, poverty, and homelessness, stations like Hermannstraße have turned into makeshift shelters for people turned away from other housing. Drug use and mental health crises have become a defining characteristic of this train line, which is favored by heroin and meth dealers. Sometimes, I had to step around people splayed out on the steps with needles sticking out of their arms. More than once, a stampede was created in the train after someone high on bad product began to accost random strangers, their eyes bulging and bloody. After a close call around midnight, or the witching hour, when a topless man covered in what appeared to be Russian prison

---

* The quarterly queer party is called Gegen, which means "against" or "opposite," as in, attendees should expect to experience all things counterculture—and I do mean *all*.

tattoos crawled on the train floor yelling for Maria, I decided to find other ways to explore the city—by walking it. I liked discovering how *I* wanted to see Berlin, and how *it* chose to reveal itself to me.

As I walked north, in Mitte, I saw more start-up bros doing their best to dress down vast amounts of inherited wealth in distressed jeans by Tom Ford; farther north still, puritanical yoga moms aggressively pushed expensive baby strollers through crowds on Kollwitzstraße in Prenzlauer Berg. I turned back south toward Tempelhof, then veered farther east to Treptower Park, passing competing shisha bars whose owners stared at one another from across the street. I arrived at markets that carried stockpiles of ethnic foods. Freak sightings of unripe plantains on Maybachufer gave way to chance encounters with other Black and Brown people, who pointed at the mini green fruits and said, "Noch nicht."*

When I wandered east, I saw brutalist apartment buildings covered with graffiti tags that renewed themselves on building fronts each night like regenerating organs in the body of the city itself. Neo-Nazi bars in the old Eastern quarter of Marzahn are easy to identify by the abundant Weimar Republic flags hanging outside their front doors. When I went west to Charlottenburg, I saw the clear divide between a Berlin untouched by Stasi rule and a Berlin still recovering from it. How one side thrived under Western patronage during the Cold War, acquiring the wealth and affluence described as "decadence" by my friends who grew up in the communist East, who I saw sneer at their fancy boutiques and preserved neoclassical architecture. The Berlin Wall came down in 1989, but the East and West are still palms rubbing against each other—creating friction. And that is just the information I receive from looking *up* at the city's buildings and signage—reimagining

---

* "Not yet," as in, "not ripe yet."

the city's urban-geographic evolution over time. When I look *down*, I see the multivocal blocks of a country's attempts at atonement. Street names have become the battleground for remembering an extremely racist past. And the sidewalk has become an ever-growing memorial to many of the lives lost by unsilencing their extraordinary histories. That dark, evil history is all around me—painting a more comprehensive picture of German history that some would still like to pretend never happened.

Before moving to Germany, I was only tangentially aware that a local Black community existed here before World War I, due to the fact that the transatlantic slave trade left virtually no Western country unaffected. My perception of Blackness in Germany was restricted to African Americans like Josephine Baker, who gathered intelligence for the French resistance by performing for the Nazis, and Jesse Owens, who won four gold medals at the 1936 Berlin Olympics. Twice, I've visited the street named for him near Olympiastadion (the Olympic stadium) where his athletic talents humiliated Hitler's ideas of the master race. As a child, my Americanness was the only lens through which I could perceive Blackness. That expanded with every trip to the Caribbean, Africa, and Australia I took during, between, and then after college. I saw for myself how Blackness is much more dynamic and vibrant than I ever knew. The same can be said for Black life in Berlin—which is still teaching me something new almost every day.

A Black presence has existed in Germany since at least the thirteenth century.[1] During the reign of Emperor Henry VI and then Emperor Frederick II (1220–1250) Muslims of Black African ancestry began to appear in countries dominated by German-speaking people after claiming dominion over Sicily. Frederick even established an Islamic colony at Lucera in Apulia, taking Black people as royal retainers (attendants) to convey his prestige and legitimize his rule in the area.[2] His family was apparently very fond of their Black servants, who were bestowed with important responsibilities like guarding the royal treasury and playing chamberlain to the emperor himself.[3] These positions were considered to be an honor, and this is reflected by a rich collection of art that depicts Black Muslims as proud characters alongside members of the royal family—which are still displayed all over Europe.[4] In *Liber ad honorem Augusti* by Pietro da Eboli, for example, Henry VI is depicted making his triumphant entrance into Palermo, led by "an identical set of turbaned black trumpeters," to showcase his familiarity with the customs of his new dominion.[5/*]

In the centuries that followed, Germany expanded its influence and rule over the African continent during a precolonial and then colonial period. While it may not have had as many colonies or subjects as Britain and France, Germany did participate in the trade, ownership, and genocide of enslaved people.[†] During the precolonial period, Groß Friedrichsburg was a Brandenburg-Prussian trading post based in the Gold Coast of Ghana where nearly thirty thousand enslaved people were shipped to the Americas before the site was sold to the Dutch West India Company in 1717.[6] And later, when the Berlin Conference of 1884–1885 initiated the "scramble for Africa," Germany established colonies on the African continent in present-day Namibia, Tanzania, Togo, and Cameroon, as well as other Pacific and Asian countries.[‡] More people came to Germany from these African territories, and this is when Black communities really began to form. Germany's colonial legacy is often overshadowed by the horrors committed against

* This text can be seen at the Burgerbibliothek in Bern.
† In 1914, Germany had the largest African colonies after Britain and France.
‡ Samoa, Nauru, Papua New Guinea, the Marshall Islands, Palau, the Caroline Islands, and the Northern Mariana Islands in the Pacific and Jiaozhou in China.

European Jews during World War II, but the Holocaust and the country's African campaigns are directly linked. And the memories of these injustices feed off one another, demanding that we discuss both atrocities together, in a noncompetitive manner, to create a "multidirectional" memory.[7]

One of the most violent and systemic exertions of Germany's colonial power was the first genocide of the twentieth century, which took place in Namibia, formerly known as German Southwest Africa.[8] From 1904 to 1908, an estimated seventy-five thousand Herero and Nama people (along with other social groups like Dagara and San) were shot, starved, tortured, and killed. Between one thousand and three thousand perished in the world's first death camp, located on Shark Island. By the end of the gruesome campaign, German colonial forces exterminated 80 percent and 50 percent of those ethnic groups, respectively. It was an atrocity for which the German government initially offered ten million euros in compensation in 2020, while also announcing a six-hundred-million-euro expenditure to reconstruct the palace of Kaiser Wilhelm II, the Prussian imperial leader ultimately responsible for the genocide. In 2021, the government's offer to Namibian descendants was increased to 1.1 billion euros—but it noticeably lacked the words *reparations* and *compensation*.[9]

When I began tracing Berlin's Black history by foot, I took an anti-colonial tour with a historian who pointed out the deep level of continuity between the Herero and Nama Genocide and the Holocaust, noting specifically how many of the grizzly punishments and tortures performed on Namibian people during their imprisonment on Shark Island were later applied toward European Jews in the Holocaust. I cannot name my tour guide because he cited concerns about attracting negative attention from German funding bodies, which could impact his work, so I called him Bill in my article. But his comments about continuity made me think about people like Eugen Fischer, a Nazi anthropologist, who went to Namibia in the early 1900s to study phrenology—the pseudo-science that drew conclusions about intellect, health, and physi-ological superiority based on the measurement of skulls—which was later applied to eugenicist theories that shaped the antisemitic policy to murder European Jews.[10] More than three thousand Her-ero and Nama skulls were sent to Germany to be studied. Many of them were prepared, boiled, and cleaned out by Herero and Nama peoples. A lot of the skulls have since "disappeared." When I asked my tour guide where they went, he kind of sighed and said that it wasn't uncommon to hear stories of kids cleaning out Grandpa's attic after he died and for one of them to pop up.

Considering the atrocities committed under German colonial rule, it feels especially malicious to name streets after the archi-tects for this murderous chapter in the country's history. And my feelings on this, which are shared by most Black Germans, re-quired major societal transformation before they were viewed as a relevant perspective—because these figures are celebrated in German history. And yet, these colonial monsters were once com-memorated in areas of Berlin populated mostly by people of color. The northern Berlin district of Wedding, known as the African Quarter, has a higher concentration of Black residents than other parts of the city. There, Lüderitzstraße was once named for Franz Adolf Eduard Lüderitz, the founder of German Southwest Africa. Nachtigalplatz was once named for Gustav Nachtigal, the founder of German colonies in Togo and Cameroon. Petersallee was once named for German imperial high commissioner Carl Peters.[11] A twenty-six-page document compiled by AfricAvenir International, a Berlin-based nonprofit, reveals dozens more colonial tributes all over Berlin, including Wissmannstraße, named after colonial administrator Hermann Wissmann in Neukölln; Otto von Bis-marck Platz, Otto-von-Bismarck-Allee, and Bismarckstraße; and

Takustraße, which commemorates Germany's even-lesser-known colonial expeditions in Asia. And in central Berlin, Mohrenstraße (which I will here on abbreviate to M-Straße, because the M-word is an anti-Black slur) was the name of a street and still is the name of a train station.

To me, these names felt like a smug reminder of the roles between colonizer and colonized—and a longing for the days when one country ruled by force over foreign territories and their peoples. That sense of entitlement and arrogance could be seen as one kind of continuity, a representation of ongoing feelings and political tensions that exist within German society today, along with the ignorance of how colonial brutality underpinned an era that Germans romanticize as heroic. That continuity can also be seen in the treatment of Black Germans during World War II, under National Socialist rule, for the critical role the Namibian genocide played in the Holocaust. It's impossible to fully comprehend the horrors of these events. But one memorial is doing the very difficult job of trying.

Conceived by the German artist Gunter Demnig, the Stolpersteine, or stumbling stones, are small four-by-four brass stones embedded in the sidewalk at the last known residential or working address of someone who was murdered by the Nazi regime. There are more than seventy-five thousand throughout Europe, making them the largest decentralized memorial of its kind in the world. Each stone is engraved with the name of the person memorialized; their dates of birth and death, if known; and their place of death— primarily concentration camps. The idea is that these lustrous stones would compel people to stop, pause, and consider—for a moment—the memory of these individuals. Six million Jewish, Roma, Sinti, disabled, and queer people were murdered during the Holocaust. Most of the stones in place so far are dedicated to victims from those communities. I've seen these stones as far north as Oslo and as far east as Prague, but Berlin is the epicenter, with more than five thousand stones inlayed into the footpaths of buildings now turned into movie theaters, shopping plazas, offices, and renovated apartments that house people from around the world—including me. I must have walked over these stones a thousand times before looking down to read one for the first time. Their ubiquity is the point—there is no place in Berlin, Germany, or Europe untouched by the genocide committed by the Nazis. In Berlin, there are also *Stolpersteine* dedicated to Afro-Germans who were murdered by the Nazis in death camps.* The first three are dedicated to the memories of Martha Ndumbe, Ferdinand Allen, and Mahjub bin Adam Mohamed.†

In the early twentieth century, many of the Black people who came to Germany were from the upper echelons of African society. Many African aristocrats sent their children to Germany to strengthen diplomatic relations, as servants for missionaries and colonial traders, or as language teachers. And before World War I, many African immigrants also came to Germany as performers in the Völkerschauen, or massive ethnological exhibitions where Africans were displayed in tribal dress that reinforced racist stereotypes catering to a German supremacist mindset. According to Robbie Aitken, historian and author of *Black Germany: The Making and Unmaking of a Diaspora Community, 1884–1960*, there were approximately four hundred of these "human zoos," with several thousand performers, up until 1930. Originally from present-day Cameroon, Martha Ndumbe's father, Jacob, performed in the First German Colonial Exhibition in 1896. He stayed on afterward and

---

* The Further Reading section at the end will include three new names. As of November 2023, there are now fourteen in total located in Berlin and fifteen in Germany. More will undoubtedly continue to emerge.

† There is also a Stolperstein dedicated to Hagar Martin Brown located at Marburger Straße 9 in the city of Frankfurt.

started a family with Dorothea Grunwaldt, a German woman from Hamburg. Martha was born in 1902 and had a difficult life from a young age. According to the Stolpersteine office, her brother, Alfred, died in infancy, and her family struggled financially, causing them to move several times. Jacob's application for German citizenship was rejected, and he eventually separated from Dorothea in 1910.[12] Dorothea moved back to Hamburg, and Jacob, unable to care for Martha, sent her to live with family friends—the Steidels. Later, Jacob's physical and mental health began to decline, and he was forcibly committed to Dalldorf Psychiatric Hospital in 1918.[13] At the time, it was Berlin's main institution for treating people then referred to as "lunatics" and the "insane" or people with mental and developmental disabilities.[14] When it opened in 1880, many health professionals were hopeful that the hospital would become a new blueprint for how to treat people as patients instead of prisoners—forgoing common treatments like straitjackets and bed restraints—which was considered a radical approach at the time. But the hospital was plagued by problems from the start. Dalldorf had the capacity for six hundred people, and six months after opening, one thousand people had been admitted. Overcrowding was an immediate issue.

During World War I, around the time when Jacob was admitted, Germany's food supply became blocked, and mass starvation hit all Germany's hospitals and clinics—including Dalldorf.* The circumstances of Jacob's death are unclear, but he passed away in the hospital in 1919, when Martha was only sixteen years old.[15]

---

* In 1933, Dalldorf was taken over by the Nazis, and the hospital became a medical torture chamber. According to the 1940 study by Karl Bonhoeffer, *A History of Psychiatry at the Charité in the 19th century*, "scientists" performed horrific experiments on patients—featuring the use of spraying machines, plunge baths, forced sitting and standing, and putting patients into centrifuges.

World War I's impact on Black residents was far-reaching because it turned Germany's transient Black population into a fixed one. Black performers from the Völkerschauen could no longer move about freely, and many performers settled down, got married, and started families.[16] When the war ended, Germany lost its African colonies in the Treaty of Versailles, and economic growth came practically to a halt. Resentment from hyperinflation and economic hardship made the Black community a target for racist abuse and discrimination.

In the 1920s, twenty-five thousand soldiers from the then French colonies of Algeria, Morocco, and Tunisia occupied Germany west of the Rhine River. Approximately six to eight hundred children were fathered with white German women—introducing a new generation of Afro-Germans at an extremely dangerous time to be different. These children, derogatorily referred to as the *Rheinlandbastarde* (the Rhineland Bastards, whom I will from here on out refer to as Rhineland Children) came to represent the shame that Germans felt living under French rule, precipitating the rise of violently racist Schwarze Schmach (Black Shame/Black Horror) propaganda that sought to discourage white Germans from socializing with Afro-Germans and to discredit the treaty. This materialized as horrific claims of sexual crimes committed by the African soldiers, depicting them as savages and "barbarians" who ravaged pure, innocent German women.[17] One example can be found in a May 1920 edition of the German magazine *Kladderadatsch*, which features an illustration of a large black primate in a kepi, or French military hat, carrying an unconscious white woman. The title of the piece reads, "Der Schwarze Terror in Deutschen Landen," or "the Black terror in German lands." These types of images circulated throughout the German media, and their moral persuasion can, at least to some degree, be considered part of the political violence and tactics that later informed Nazi ideology, as well as the Nuremberg Laws.[18] It was the proliferation of these kinds of images and messaging that made conditions for Black Germans like Martha Ndumbe increasingly hostile.

Like her father before her, she was unable to find work. Sometimes, she worked as a seamstress, but ultimately, Martha resorted to petty crime and sex work for survival in the mid-1920s—the latter profession was labeled as "Asoziale" (or antisocial) by the Nazis.[19] It was presumably around this time that she met the man who eventually became her husband and pimp, Kurt Borck. They married in 1932, but their union was violent and unhappy; he frequently sent her out to work in the streets while controlling the money she brought home. Martha filed a police report against Kurt in 1937, and he was sent to prison, and they formally divorced a year later. By then, Martha had gained attention from the Nazis, who had become increasingly hostile toward people they considered "antisocial" and "racial outsiders."[20] She was imprisoned at several institutions before being sent to Ravensbrück concentration camp, where she died on February 5, 1945. Martha Ndumbe's Stolperstein rests at Max-Beer-Straße 24 in the Berlin district of Mitte.

While the Nuremberg Laws initially applied to the Jewish community, they were later expanded to include Black people and other marginalized groups. While drafting this legislation, German lawmakers frequently referenced and mined inspiration from American Jim Crow laws.[21] Though the Nazis admired America's racist mandates, and President Roosevelt, they concluded that the one-drop rule was too severe to be applied to the German landscape, as it was impossible to enforce: How could anyone tell if someone had a single ounce of Jewish blood just by looking at them?[22] In his 1936 book-length pamphlet *Blood and Race: A Tour through the History of Peoples*, Johann von Leers, a notorious antisemite and Nazi lawyer, dedicated twenty-three pages to the

Fourteenth Amendment and Jim Crow laws, as well as thirteen
pages to immigration statistics regarding each racial minority.[23] In
particular, he was intrigued by the Cable Act of 1922, which outlined that American women who married "noncitizen Asian men"
were stripped of their citizenship as well.[24] Just like the United
States and Australia, the Nazi obsession with miscegenation was
based on those familiar tenets upon which twentieth-century immigration law in anglophone countries was predicated: citizenship and marriage.[25]

This directly affected Mahjub bin Adam Mohamed. Born
in 1904 in modern-day Dar es Salaam, what was then known as
German East Africa, Mohamed joined his Sudanese father in the
German colonial army in 1914—at the age of ten. He was a signal
giver during World War I. Following the war, Mohamed worked
odd jobs, including as a waiter for German shipping company Woermann until 1929.[26/*] He eventually married a German woman
from Sudetenland (present day Czechia) and settled in Berlin.
According to the Stolpersteine office, locals often referred to him
as Bayume Mohamed Hussein or simply Husen. German historian Marianne Bechhaus-Gerst, a professor of African studies at
the University of Cologne, believed that—since he had spent most
of his life in Germany—Mohamed saw himself as a German man
more than an East African man.[27] He became involved in the neo-
colonial movement to get Germany to reclaim its former African
colonies, and he applied for German military decorations twice,
both of which were denied.[28] Mohamed even tried to enlist in the

---

* Woermann traded in West Africa beginning in 1837, dealing in rubber,
  ivory, coconut, bananas, and palm oil—the business of which they controlled in northeast Cameroon. This is one of the main reasons why the
  country was colonized and its Native inhabitants were driven from the
  land.

German army at the breakout of World War II, which was also denied.

When the Nazis rose to power, finding work became more difficult. To make ends meet, Mohamed taught Swahili at Friedrich Wilhelm University (now Humboldt University of Berlin) and worked as a waiter in a brothel called Haus Vaterland.[29] He also had several starring roles in Nazi propaganda films, including *Die Reiter von Deutsch-Ostafrika* (The Riders of German East Africa) in 1934 and *Carl Peters* in 1941—a movie based on a "founder" of German East Africa, whose name once graced a street in Wedding. Known for taking young girls as concubines, razing whole African villages, and hanging locals for rebelling, Carl Peters's reputation is one of the most notorious of all German colonizers. When his violent tactics were made public in an 1896 report, he was dishonorably discharged—not for what he had done, but for his personal behavior while doing it.[30] In this film based on his life, Mohamed played the role of Peters's guide.

At some point, Mohamed began engaging in extramarital affairs with other German women, fathering a child with his wife as well as another woman—within six weeks of each other. Bechhaus-Gerst says that this led to him being accused of "racial defilement," or breaking the German Rassenschande law that restricted sexual relationships and marriage between non-Germans and Germans, which, despite having served in the German colonial army, he was not considered to be. He was deported to Sachsenhausen concentration camp, where he was murdered in 1944. Mahjub bin Adam Mohamed's Stolperstein rests at Brunnenstraße 193 in the Berlin district of Mitte.

Learning about Mohamed's life in 2019 while writing an article about Afro-Germans who were murdered by the Nazis, I was once again confronted with how the horrors of British colonialism and American race law had been referenced and applied abroad—another kind of continuity. Even though British poly-math Sir Francis Galton's 1883 book *Inquiries into Human Fertility and Its Development* established him as the father of eugenics, his teachings found an enthusiastic audience in the United States. In the vile, racist 1916 book *The Passing of the Great Race; Or, The Racial Basis of European History,* American lawyer and author Madison Grant's writing emphasized the importance of sterilizing people with mental illness and the exclusion of immigrants who were considered to be genetically inferior.[31] He was a fierce advocate for restricting immigration to the United States from southern and eastern European countries and halting immigration from Asia altogether. He promoted selective breeding and provided racial data that was used in the U.S. 1924 Immigration Act to set quotas for immigrants from certain countries.[32] To Adolf Hitler, America's use of eugenics in the construction of immigration law elevated the country to that of a worthy associate, and he praised the country's commitment to disenfranchising minorities, stating:

> There is currently one state in which one can observe at least weak beginnings of a better conception. This is of course not our exemplar German Republic, but the American Union, in which an effort is being made to consider the dictates of reason to at least some extent. The American Union categorically refuses the immigration of physically unhealthy elements, and simply excludes the immigration of certain races.[33]

Grant's theories were eventually applied to the "Afro-German problem" introduced by the Rhineland Children who were fathered by the colonial French occupying forces after World War I. In 1937, Nazi officials ordered all of them to be sterilized—

a heinous fate inflicted upon many Afro-German people who lived with various forms of illness at the time. Ferdinand James Allen was born in 1898 to a Black British father, a musician named James Cornelius Allen, and a white German mother, Lina Panzer. James and Lina moved their six children to several different residences located in Berlin's Mitte district. According to the Stolpersteine office, Allen also endured tremendous hardship in his youth, facing multiple tragedies and health concerns. Because his father, James, was most likely of Caribbean heritage, this made him a British subject living in a country that was at war with Great Britain.[34] James was thrown into a "zivile feindliche Ausländer" (or civilian enemy aliens) prison camp in Ruhleben, on the western edge of Berlin, followed by his sons Ferdinand and Robert. Most of the one hundred other Black British men there descended from West Africa or the Caribbean.[35] When the war ended, the prisoners were freed in November 1918. Ferdinand and Robert returned home to their siblings and mother, Lina, possibly without their father, who may have died from a heart attack around 1918 or 1919.[36]

This was around the time when Ferdinand claimed that he began to have seizures, though other reports indicate that he experienced epilepsy throughout his life. In 1920, Ferdinand was admitted to the Municipal Institute for Epileptics at Wuhlgarten,* located in outer Berlin.[37] He remained there for nearly twenty years, where he was targeted for racist attacks and became involved in altercations with other patients. Like his father and brother, he developed an interest in music and began to take singing lessons in the 1930s, and he sometimes went home to visit his family, where he seemed to find some reprieve.

When Hitler rose to power, everything changed for Black

---

* Sometimes called the Wuhlgarten Municipal Institute for Epilepsy or the Municipal Health and Care Institute for Epileptics Wuhlgarten.

people living in Germany—beginning in 1935 with the introduction of the Nuremberg Race Laws, and then the outbreak of
World War II. Three of Ferdinand's siblings—Robert, Helen, and
Willi—fled the country to escape racist persecution. In 1935,
Ferdinand was sterilized under the Law for the Prevention of Offspring with Hereditary Diseases. In 1941, he was murdered at the
Bernberg Psychiatric Hospital under the Nazis T4 campaign, an
involuntary-euthanasia genocidal project that specifically targeted people living with physical and mental disabilities. Ferdi-
nand James Allen's Stolperstein rests at Torstraße 176/178 in the
Berlin district of Mitte.

IT'S DIFFICULT TO comprehend the extent of the evil that pro-
liferated with these ideas across the world in such a short period
of time, or how they've come to shape the world we're living in
now. Trying to wrap my head around it feels like trying to unlock
the fourth, fifth, and sixth dimensions simultaneously. The tragic
stories of Martha, Mahjub, and Ferdinand—among so many
others—have mutated around one another to become the mal-
adapted systems and institutions that rule the world today: immigration law, interventionist foreign policy, and disability advocacy.
The more I learn, the more I see that it's the *only* way to think of
history: not as singular, disjointed events, but as a linked chain
of horrors that led to more horrors. Only when I walk through
Berlin do I realize how vastly this multidirectional memory in-
fluences the global past and present—possibly, terrifyingly, even
the future. How overwhelmingly and unfathomably ubiquitous
it all is. Traversing the thousands of Stolpersteine, walking past
the Memorial to the Murdered Jews of Europe, the book-burning
memorial (known as *The Empty Library*) near Unter den Linden,
hiking all the way to the memorial to the Namibian genocide at
Columbiadamm in Tempelhof at the bottom of the city ring, it

begins to make sense. It's a history as connected to the present as the streets are to the monuments on top and the small brass stones laid into them. But to truly fathom the global impact, I'd have to keep walking until I reached the edge of Europe. I'd have to wash up on the shores of Liverpool and dive into the ocean and swim until I reached the coasts of Ghana and Namibia. I'd have to crawl on the ocean floor until my feet touched the wrecked ships off the coast of the Americas.

19.

Nazis on the Train

If the French are rightly proud of their emperor and the
Britons of Nelson and Churchill, we have the right to be proud
of the achievements of the German soldiers in two world wars.

—ALEXANDER GAULAND, COFOUNDER OF THE
ALTERNATIVE FÜR DEUTSCHLAND (AFD) PARTY

I N LATE AUGUST 2018, A LARGE FAR-RIGHT PROTEST
broke out in the eastern German town of Chemnitz. At the time,
there were reports that a German man, Daniel Hillig, had al-
legedly been killed by a Syrian refugee and an Iraqi man on the
previous Sunday, the twenty-sixth.* The response was thousands

---

* The Syrian man was identified in British media as Alaa Sheikhi, but in
German media he is only referred to as Alaa S., in keeping with German
privacy laws. Alaa was convicted of manslaughter and sentenced to nine
years and six months in prison a year later, in August 2019. His defense
team noted that the prosecution's case was weak, citing a lack of the defen-
dant's DNA on the weapon and contradictory eyewitness testimony from
someone who claimed to observe the attack from 150 meters away. One of
Alaa's lawyers, Ricarda Lang, is quoted as having said, "Someone needs to
be found guilty, so calm can return to Chemnitz." As of November 2023,
the Iraqi man, identified as Fahrad A., whose DNA was found on the murder weapon, is still being sought under an international arrest warrant.

of protesters, led by various neo-Nazi groups, taking to the streets flashing Hitler salutes and shouting xenophobic slurs and slogans. *The New York Times* reported that some chased dark-skinned by-standers. Then chancellor Angela Merkel described the protests as a push to "hunt down" foreigners, which was confirmed by Anas al-Nahlawie, a Syrian refugee, who watched in horror from a friend's apartment balcony. He described the mob as a pack "of wolves," that were looking for immigrants like him.[1] Fabian Eberhard shared video footage on Twitter of a similar incident. Various news outlets described the scene as unprecedented in the post–World War II era. Estimates say that their numbers were around eight thousand. While several hundred Neo-Nazis were identifiable, what shocked many Germans was the presence of so many "ordinary" citizens.

Counterprotests quickly sprung up around Germany. In Chemnitz, an estimated sixty-five thousand people showed up in force for a unity concert, shouting slogans like "Refugees welcome." German officials like then foreign minister Heiko Maas made very bold, very ardent pleas to the public to take a firm stand against any neo-Nazi demonstrations. Berlin also held a demonstration on August 30 in the district of Neukölln—which I attended. I was at a loss for what to write on my piece of posterboard, until an idea just came to me. I would call it inspired. MY BLACK-ASS GRAND-FATHER KILLED A BUNCH OF NAZIS IN FRANCE. Then in smaller letters beneath, in parentheses: I JUST WANTED YOU CUNTS TO KNOW THAT. Of course, I don't actually know if my grandfather killed a bunch of Nazis, or any Nazis at all. He could have dug trenches or driven a supply truck. It's not like he told me anything about the war. Or anyone else. In that silence, I've always just assumed the worst, which often lies dormant in the things we refuse to say. The point I was trying to make is this: He was some-one who stood up to Nazis. And so am I. I wanted to remind them that the people they hated the most had some role in their crushing defeat. That I, and everyone else who showed up that day, would remind them as many times as needed to crush them again.

My sign was a big hit at the protest. A lot of people asked if they could take a picture with me holding it. It was quite an Instagrammable moment, and I posted a picture of the sign on my profile—feeling very proud. Most of the comments were a delight. Someone called it the "sign of the year." Many positive emojis were deployed. I used the appropriate hashtags, and the post drew a crowd, including from one stranger, who posted a comment that said, "My NAZI-ASS grandfather killed a bunch of blacks in [sic] france. (I just want you cunts to know that.)"

*

In 2015, then chancellor Angela Merkel made the unprecedented decision to open Germany's borders to 1.5 million Syrian refugees. Like many morally sound decisions, it came with its fair share of political backlash: savage criticism from within her center-right party as well as her political opponents; European officials outside of Germany criticized her decision because, under the EU framework, they would also have to take in refugees; and the rise of a new far-right party—Alternative für Deutschland, or Alternative for Germany (AfD).

The AfD had campaigned on platforms like replacing the constitutional right to individual asylum hearings with the immediate deportation of rejected applicants to their countries of origin, regardless of whether or not those countries were deemed to be safe. When I arrived in Berlin on August 1, 2016, there was already a colorful display of AfD signs littered around Berlin, with captions like, BURKAS? NO THANKS, I PREFER BIKINIS! and NEW GERMANS? WE PREFER TO MAKE OUR OWN! The latter included a cropped photo of a pregnant woman lying down with the swooping AfD slogan, as blue as the eyes of the so-called master race.

Alexander Gauland, the party's cofounder, former leader, and (as of 2023) still-active member of German parliament, has gone so far as to say that Germans "should be proud of what the soldiers achieved" during both World Wars and that Germany should no longer be "reproached" for "what was done" during World War II.[2] The AfD also strongly opposed marriage equality, despite their current cochairwoman, Alice Weidel, being a lesbian herself.[3/*] The party has been described as anti-Islam, anti-immigration, Eurosceptic, and ultraconservative. Hungarian prime minister Viktor Orbán, who is often described as a dictator and autocrat, said that he was "forced to sacrifice relations with the AfD on the altar of good international relations."[4] Far-right Italian politician Matteo Salvini, whose leanings have been described as neofascist, said that he wouldn't continue a working relationship with the AfD because he was looking for "more centrist allies."[5] But Marine Le Pen, head of France's far-right National Rally party—who has been accused of supporting antisemitism and xenophobia—embraced the AfD from the beginning. I'd call it a real marriage of racist minds.

Germany became the epicenter of a changing continent reckoning with a dark past during a refugee crisis. And it forced the entire European Union to reckon with the effects of Western interventionism creating crises of humanity.[†] The various German amts, the government institutions that regulated immigration, were overwhelmed with processing refugees, creating a backlog that tested the very foundations of a country infamous for its

---

* Marriage equality passed in Germany in 2017.
† When refugees arrive to the EU, they must be taken in by the first EU country they land in. So, while Germany took in most, every other member nation was affected because rarely would someone arrive straight to Germany.

mind-boggling dependency on paperwork. The response from the German public was also heavily mixed. According to one report from *Politico*, the initial response was warm. Some Germans gathered at train stations to applaud people as they arrived, coining the term *Willkommenskultur*, or "welcome culture."[6] Some German families opened their homes, including two musicians from Röhrsdorf, Sarah and Stevi, who took out a mortgage on a former guest house to shelter a family.[7] But the general response appears to have soured in the years that followed. In a 2021 poll taken by state broadcaster *Deutsche Welle*, just over 30 percent of the two thousand people polled still supported the decision—whereas nearly 51 percent did not support it, and nearly 19 percent had no opinion.[8] That same year, Tareq Alaows, who had fled Syria in 2015, tried to make history as the first former refugee to be elected to the Bundestag, or German parliament, as a Green Party candidate representing Oberhausen in North Rhine-Westphalia. He withdrew from the race, citing "personal threats and security concerns," before removing himself from his local Green Party branch altogether to protect his privacy.[9]

When I arrived in Germany, I frequently interacted with and met people who were turning themselves inside out to create spaces for refugees, find them housing, and get them into integration courses. But hate crimes and attacks rose steeply around the country. In 2016, onlookers cheered when a building meant to house refugees in Bautzen was set on fire—they also tried to block firefighters from responding.[10] Many people I met in the Black community described increased encounters with rabid far-right racists. I also was forced to leave a sublet because of one who, when I called the police on him, proudly declared to the responding officers that "Germany was for Germans."

A 2016 report by Amnesty International titled *Living in insecurity: How Germany is failing victims of racist violence* stated that

hate crimes against asylum seekers increased sixteen times between 2013 and 2015, while crimes classified as racist and violent
against racial, ethnic, and religious minorities increased by 87 percent from 693 in 2013, to 1,295 in 2015.[11] In 2016 alone, nearly ten
attacks were made on immigrants every day in Germany.[12] Those
numbers are disturbing. But meeting a neo-Nazi face-to-face is
downright terrifying.

I had my first encounter with a German neo-Nazi a few days
before the 2016 U.S. general election. I was riding the S-Bahn
(suburban train system) on a Saturday from the gym between
Frankfurter Allee and Hermannstraße. At Ostkreuz station, in
the heart of former East Berlin, a large man sat down opposite. He
was maybe six four or six five with light-blond hair and blue eyes.
He wore a dark long-sleeved shirt and dark jeans, which, in and of
itself, is pretty normal. However, his overall physical presence was
imposing. He seemed to want to dominate not just the space where
I sat, but the space of the two people sitting next to us—one of
whom was Brown. The large white man shoved against the smaller,
Brown gentleman next to him, intimidating him with a forceful
look until the passenger looked away.

Then he stared at me. I didn't really know what to do, so I stared
back. I acted against my nature, as someone who often has trouble
making eye contact and tends to look around when making a point.
I was crawling out of my skin with discomfort, but I felt pinned by
his gaze. Several German men had given me a hilarious lecture on
why their intense urge to stare down a complete stranger qualified
as flirting, so I did wonder for a split second: *Does this man want to
fight or fuck?* A simple smile could disarm his stony gaze if it were
the latter. Women have all kinds of tricks to de-escalate when it
comes to the unwanted attention of men. Then, he made the subtlest movement—rolling up his sleeves to reveal the lightning-bolt
tattoos on his hand.

SS, or Schutzstaffel, was the major paramilitary organization within the Nazi Party—abbreviated and depicted then, as it is now, as a double lightning bolt. As far as the unofficial dress code is concerned, it's a favorite among neo-Nazis—right up there with combat boots, sunburns, and bad haircuts. The guy sitting next to him shook his head angrily and gave me the subtlest look of warning, which I interpreted as something like, *I'm just as uncomfortable as you are, and I don't want to be on this train either. But, for the love of God, DO. NOT. ENGAGE.*

I didn't. I couldn't move. Speaking up would've been ridiculous, especially with my nonexistent German at the time. What would I have said, anyway? "Hey, Hans, my Blackass grandfather killed a bunch of Nazis in France. I just wanted you to know that."

If I had, there's a good chance I would be *with* my grandpa right now. There was absolutely no way that would've been a fair fight, not even in my activewear. I stayed put, and Nazi McHitler got off at Neukölln S-Bahn—just one stop away from where I lived. When the train doors closed behind him, I felt myself exhale and begin to shake. The man across from me gave an empathetic smile, and we watched him stomp through the crowd while the train pulled away—presumably on his way to terrify more innocent Black and Brown bystanders. That was when I allowed myself to ask the question that had been strangling my brain during the whole trip: All those empty seats on the train, and he saw me, singled me out, and sat with *us*?

For ten or so minutes, I had been staring into the eyes of someone who hated me for no reason other than the color of my skin. He could have done literally anything else. Write a sonnet. Reread *Mein Kampf*. Get a manicure for his filthy fingernails. He could have had a V8! He *chose* to scare the shit out of me instead. He looked around the train, examined his options, and said, "This is the best use of my time today." What was worse, he was somewhere in Neukölln—working, partying, maybe even living. Which meant that there was a possibility I would run into him again—or someone much worse. If I did, what would he do next time? Or what would he do to someone who looked like me? What if no one else was around?

I got off at the next stop and quickly jogged home, extravigilant about my surroundings. I made three right turns and ran directly into a massive Turkish grocer, where I bought a week's supply of halvah, date paste, and chili peppers. The biggest appeal of the district for me was its diversity—and I had moved there reasoning that no moderately intelligent white supremacist* would bother living in an area like that—as if they follow any kind of logic when they decide to terrorize people. The areas in the United States with the biggest neo-Nazi contingents are also the most racially and ethnically diverse—like Florida, where groups like Stormfront, the Proud Boys, and the National Socialist Movement have enjoyed a sustained presence for years. As much as white supremacists love to preach about the "ethnic purity" of the so-called master race, they are pretty obsessed with being around Black and Brown people. They like to go where the action is. Or maybe, just where the food is seasoned. But unlike other white supremacists (running government institutions and banks, the police, and even people sitting next to you at work) neo-Nazis are usually pretty easy to identify by their ink.

While swastikas and other clearly identifiable Nazi signifiers are legally prohibited in Germany, countless other symbols have been adapted to work around these bans. The ancient Irish triskelion, for example, traditionally depicted as a pagan spiral of swirling lines, gets modified as a fixed series of straight, angular lines that resemble a broken swastika. The white power fist, which looks a lot

---

* Yes, that was an intentional oxymoron. You're welcome.

like the Black Power fist, gets reduced to a simple white outline on white skin. The number 8, which represents the eighth letter of the Roman alphabet, is repeated twice, and 88 becomes H.H. for "Heil Hitler." The number 14 is shorthand for the racist fourteen-word slogan coined by David Lane, founder of the American white supremacist organization the Order, which states, "We must secure the existence of our people and a future for white children." And these numbers are often paired together as either 14/88 or 1488. Fourteen is often paired with the number 28, which signifies BH or "Blood and Honor," a far-right network banned in Germany in 2000. Any of these numbers should make you sweat, run, or prepare to throw down. There are broken crosses with red or black coloring, Iron Crosses, bulldogs, and wolf heads. Skulls are associated with the SS Totenkopf (or "death's head"), an elite division of the Waffen-SS, and sometimes they even appear in triskelions, while crossed hammers are associated with the Hammerskins, a neo-Nazi group originally formed in the United States with affiliations around the world. I also keep my eyes peeled for Nordic-mythology tattoos, particularly anything with Viking helmets, bearded deities, references to Odin or Woden, Thor's hammer, and runes—*all* the runes. Neo-Nazis can be accused of a lot of things, but their obsession with appropriating otherwise innocuous pagan symbolism means that originality certainly isn't one of them.

I've seen just about every variety of these tattoos at one point or another in Berlin—especially during the pandemic. Right-wing hate groups joined forces with anti-vaxxer conspiracy theorists, or what we refer to as *die Querdenker*.* They demonstrated at Brandenburg Gate while I was taking socially distanced strolls through

---

* Translates to "queer thinker." Certified weirdos. Tinfoil hatters. Mad as a hatter. Teutonic love children of Marjorie Taylor-Greene and Anton LaVey. Avoid at all costs.

Tiergarten with my Black, Arab, and Jewish friends, course correcting at the speed of light toward Potsdamer Platz to avoid any
confrontations. When this happens, a Good Samaritan will send a
bulletin in one of the mutual WhatsApp or Facebook groups, which
gets passed around as an alert to anyone who might be tempted to
go near the area—at times, clearing out the entire city center of any
ethnic presence to let the Cracker Barrel Gang have their moment
in the sun, while we lounge about at home until normalcy returns to
the streets. Sadly, they're impossible to avoid all the time.

A friend of mine, who is Taiwanese, told me about a time when
she was on the tram with her dog, a scruffy little white Krom-
fohrländer named Brisket, when a German man covered in white
supremacist tattoos sat across from her. She froze, but this guy
saw this adorable puppy sitting on her lap, smiled ear to ear, and
reached out to scratch him on his neck. It's no secret that Germans
are mad about dogs—that's one thing we have in common. In fact,
if you truly want to integrate into German society and—like my
friend and me—you just so happen not to be white, I strongly recommend getting one. The social approval is instantaneous, and
you'll be inundated with affection from otherwise stoic German
pedestrians.* But *never have I ever* heard about a puppy being used
as white supremacist catnip. As she recalled this story, she pointed
towards her face and said, "Did he just not see this or what??"

The best time to spot a neo-Nazi in the wild is when
they're being countered by an even larger crowd of anti-fascist
counterprotesters—who faithfully appear at every white supremacist rally. Always. Just as there are people desperate to reinstate the

---

* In Germany, dogs are allowed in many restaurants, bars, even some
shops. The country has a long-standing love affair with dogs, especially
German breeds. Even Hitler's dog, a German shepherd named Blondi,
was used in a lot of Nazi propaganda.

Nuremberg Laws, there are also many, many people with a rabid dedication to stomping out the right. They feed off opportunities to scream "fuck off" at neo-Nazis, especially if techno music is involved, which, in Berlin, it always is. And, my God, there is something downright *magical* about seeing a neo-Nazi get punched in the face by a large, muscular butch queer in skintight black leather hot pants. It's what I imagine it felt like watching Muhammad Ali take down Sonny Liston. Certain forms of visual poetry defy language—and should be described as the transcendental experience of the soul levitating outside of the body.

These stories often remind me that Berlin is the epicenter for the *other* side of the history that Americans were taught in grade school. My grandfather fought the Nazis. The grandfathers of my colleagues, friends, and neighbors *were* the Nazis. And yet, I haven't met a single German person with a Nazi grandparent. I've met many people whose omas hid Jews in their basements.* I've worked with countless others whose opas bravely resisted Nazi rule by spitting in the face of this SS officer or that one (and miraculously survived to tell the tale). At parties, at clubs, and on dance floors, I've come across many revelers who bashfully cover their ink and use their mixed-race children as proof that the decisions of their youth didn't define them forever. But Nazis? Never heard of them. It reminds me of a particularly sardonic passage from Martha Gellhorn's book *The Face of War* where she describes conversations with European civilians as she moved with Allied troops across the Rhine into Germany: "No one is a Nazi. No one ever was."[13]

The war ended in 1945—but the legacy of that ideology lives on for many. In trains. In politics. In comments under Instagram posts. I don't live in Neukölln anymore. I live somewhere with a

---

* *Oma* is German for "grandma"; *opa* is German for "grandpa."

much lower concentration of neo-Nazi encounters but a higher concentration of people who may have been members of the original Nazi Party. Whenever I cross paths with someone who was old enough to have lived during that era and they do a quick double take that is just as likely to be about curiosity as it is about rabid xenophobia, I have to ask myself:

Were you part of that original generation?

AFTER MY FIRST Nazi scare, I took my time composing myself at home before heading to a party hosted by my Black in Berlin group. I needed to be somewhere safe, and I was thankful to be among people to whom I wouldn't need to explain the significance of that confrontation. First, I told Derek, who rocked up to stunt at the party in one of his signature thotty blazers. Then, one by one, people approached me to ask about this "crazy story" they had heard, wanting to confirm it from the source. Each time I shared, the person listening expressed equal amounts of shock and... well, not shock.

Someone mentioned that there had been a right-wing protest in the city earlier that evening—the man I eyeballed was likely on his way to or from the event.[14] Someone else mentioned that, earlier in the year, xenophobes had delivered a bloody "pig's head bearing an 'insulting inscription'" outside Angela Merkel's office.[15] Derek, in the signature deflated tone he uses when discussing the people who hate us, mentioned that right-wing protests had ramped up since their victories in the regional elections a few months prior. The Social Democrats (SPD), or center-left party, had come first with the highest number of votes in the northern German state of Mecklenburg-Vorpommern, a state Angela Merkel had once represented as a member of the Bundestag. But the AfD came away with nearly 22 percent of votes.[16] Angela Merkel's center-right party came in third, with only 19 percent of the votes—at the time, an all-time low for the party in the region. Germany uses a democratic and federal parliamentary system, which means that coalitions—or alliances between parties—form a majority government, locally and nationally. The more votes a party gains, the more seats it wins in the government. Majority governments are a constitutional requirement since the Nazis initially took power through a minority government.

When the results came through, Christian Democratic Union (CDU) candidate Lorenz Caffier blamed his party's disappointing performance on what he called "the refugee question."[17] The results were shocking to everyone. The key to the AfD's success lay in how well they had managed to disguise their rhetoric of hatred and bigotry as of narrative of reclaiming their country, just like any other nationalist movement. And just as the United Kingdom had learned with the Brexit referendum only a few months before, and as the United States was *about* to learn with Trump—it works. What I saw on that train was the living, breathing result of this trend in German politics. Neo-Nazis emboldened to step out into the world and proclaim their views openly, without fear, and without a shred of shame. They were becoming more brazen, bolder in expressing their hatred and enacting violence because they felt represented at the most senior levels of office. Which they were.

My friends and I partied late that night. But there was a general air of anxiety on the dance floor. It was the Saturday before the U.S. general election in November 2016, and we enjoyed the possibility that the first woman could take the Oval Office after the first Black man left it—but none of us were hopeful. The quiet desperation was palpable. I was deeply aware of just how dramatically the global landscape was about to change. Many of us were immigrants from white countries experiencing their own resurgence of right-wing movements—France, Denmark, Canada, the United Kingdom, Australia, and the United States—with roots in countries like Uganda, Ghana, Jamaica, Trinidad, Eritrea, Ethiopia, and Cameroon, places that had been colonized by Europe. Nobody was surprised by what happened next because, for us, white supremacy is where these roads met—and we were already well aware of where they led. But we had one another, and we hung on to that well into the early hours of the morning.

I wanted to shake off the interaction on the train with as much laughter and twerking as possible. Maybe that's why I left the party with a ton of new acquaintances—several of whom went on to become some of my closest friends. And over the years that followed, I would call on them, repeatedly, to vent about the state of my homeland—and the world at large—as we watched everything disintegrate from the safety of our more progressive Berlin.

It will always be a strange feeling to watch someone sporting a broken-swastika tattoo while they devour a kebab and a beer—while wondering if they've murdered someone. But it happens. They are *out* here. With their grocery bags. With their dogs. With their shaved heads, leather jackets, elaborate beards, and loving canine companions—recycling their beer bottles at the grocery store and suntanning at the lake just like everyone else.

Just look for the tattoos.

20.

Dance Your Fucking Tits Off, Bitch

AFTER A YEAR OF ON-AGAIN, OFF-AGAIN GERMAN lessons, a teacher encouraged me to find a text to use as motivation to learn the language. German classes involve reading dry paragraphs about Bismarckbrötchen,[*] Käsespätzle,[†] and Schweinebraten[‡] and answering questions on folk history about the origins of the lederhosen[§] or ten fun facts about Lübeck.[¶] None of the lessons touched on history that I found interesting, like the country's colonial campaigns in Africa and Asia, for example. German is a really tough language. Declension, or the way in which adjectives, articles, and even nouns change their

---

[*] A pickled-herring dish served on crusty bread that is said to have been beloved by the Iron Chancellor himself, Otto von Bismarck.

[†] Egg noodles topped with cheese and onions.

[‡] Roast pork, typically served with braised cabbage and dumplings. Very popular in Bavaria.

[§] Traditional dress common in the German-speaking world: leather breeches, typically worn by men. They used to be worn for performing manual farm labor, but now they're a common outfit at Oktoberfest.

[¶] The second-largest city on the German Baltic coast.

forms to reflect their role in a sentence, still brings me to my fucking knees.

I was also resistant to learn another language where vocabulary to describe issues pertaining to race, gender, and sexuality isn't available. For example, *Rasse* is the technical word for "race" in German, but it does not reflect the meaning of the English word; neither do *rassisch*, *rassialisiert*, and *rassenlos* ("racial," "racialized," "raceless").[1] None of these words are used in German when discussing race either. *Rasse* is actually used to speak about different "breeds," as in different breeds, or *Rassen*, of dogs. And if *rasse* can't be used to describe people, then how can *Rassismus* be used to describe racism?

That could be by design. If I were to use that word to refer to the race of a person today—rather than, say, 1940—I would be shunned. This causes confusion over whether the word is a legal concept or a Nazi term, and even today, there isn't a clear consensus. In Fatima El-Tayeb's book *European Others: Queering Ethnicity in Postnational Europe*,* she examines the "narrative of racelessness," meaning how the absence of a suitable word to describe the social construct described by the English equivalent conjures an image of a European continent where there is no race, no race problem, and no racism.[2]

But *Rasse* still appears in the German republic's most important democratic document: its Grundgesetz, or constitution, known as the Basic Law. Section 1, article 3, states:

> No person shall be favored or disfavored because
> of sex, parentage, race [Rasse], language, home-

---

* El-Tayeb wrote the book in English, then cotranslated it into German herself. A lot of Black authors in Germany do the same thing if their work centers on the subject of race.

land and origin, faith or religious or political opi-
nions. No person shall be disfavored because of
disability.[3]

The word *Ethnie* ("ethnicity") was introduced by W. E. Mühl-
mann in the 1960s to replace *Rasse*, but it's missing the colonial
history and context of race.[4] According to *poco.lit.* (short for post-
colonial literature), a Berlin-based organization dedicated to the
disambiguation of language to make both English and German
more accessible for everyone, *Ethnie* is usually used to refer to people who are not white as a means of "generaliz[ing]" and categorizing them. In my experience, this holds true in both German *and*
English, where *ethnicity* is generally applied to non-white people.
I do not recall having heard a person of Italian or Greek descent,
for example, referred to by their Ethnie or ethnicity; rather, the
ethnicity of a white person is actually used exclusively to describe
their nationality. As a translator myself, I use the word *race* and
italicize it while writing in German because a suitable equivalent
is not yet apparent.

German also assigns gender to all nouns, posing a number
of challenges. An author, in English, has no assigned gender. But
in German, a person is either an *Autor* (male author) or *Autorin*
(female author), which reinforces the gender binary while erasing
nonbinary and intersex people from the language.[5] The German
equivalent for *they/them* is also noticeably absent in the use of personal pronouns. Sometimes, the underscore is used to address this
as an *Genderunterstrich* or *Gendersternchen*. So, an author becomes
an Autor*in or and Autor_in, which still technically references a
"female author," but the underscore has a symbolic meaning that
disrupts the gendering of the word. That's the point. Growing use
of new words like *sif, sier,* or *xier* are becoming more common,
even if they have yet to be formally adopted into the German

language.* I have seen nonbinary German people use the English words *they/them* instead, italicized. As for transgender people, the German word *Transe* is considered derogatory and refers to the original German word *Transvestit*, or "transvestite." Historically, this wasn't just used as an insult to refer to transgender people, but many people who lived on the periphery of conventional gender roles.[6]

There are other challenges when searching for German translations of words like *disability, neurodivergent,* and *queer.* Some of these words are also problematic in English, and activists from these spaces have given us vocabulary in both languages to use, so it's not a lost cause. And Germanization of English words is typically accepted, though proper German translations for *person of color* and *Native American* are still a work in progress. But if you're a white, cisgender, heterosexual, able-bodied person—you'll be fine.

One key to changing this lies in the visibility of ethnic minorities (or, a more popular term gaining traction, *people of the global majority*). At present, Germany doesn't even collect race data, meaning that we don't actually *know* how many people of African (Asian, or Hispanic/Latinx) descent are living in this country. This can, in large part, be attributed to the country's Nazi history, when race data was used against people of Jewish, Roma, Sinti, and African ancestry. The country has been hesitant to revisit the conversation. But many advocacy groups today rightly argue that this continued policy makes the problems endured by Black people and other ethnic minorities invisible.

To make matters worse, during the 2020 global Black Lives Matter uprisings, several prominent German politicians from several different political parties proposed removing the term *race* from the constitution altogether.[7] Cochair of the Green

* As of August 2023, anyway.

Party Robert Habeck and party vice president for the state of
Schleswig-Holstein, Aminata Touré, penned a column in the
German daily newspaper *Die Tageszeitung* stating, "The word race
should be removed from the Basic Law [Germany's constitution],"
adding that "there is no such thing as race, there are only people."[8]
This sentiment was echoed by then justice minister and member of
the Social Democrats Christine Lambrecht. And Hendrik Cremer
from the Human Rights Institute in Germany called the word *race*
a Nazi concept, which might have given him some credibility had
he not followed it up with saying that the word "irritates people,
makes them speechless [and] is seen as hurtful." [9]

Because—*who* exactly is irritated by the word? People who are
victims of racism, or people who are racist?

The Basic Law doesn't mention race just for shits and giggles.
It uses the word to identify that discrimination *based on race* is
unconstitutional, which is a pretty important distinction to make
when discussing whether or not to remove it from the country's
defining document. Eliminating *race* from the constitution would
render the inviolability of human dignity, which is also listed as a
fundamental right in the German Basic Law, a much harder principle to uphold for visible ethnic minorities.[10] Removing the word
also offers some erasure of the horrors committed by the Nazis
and negates the ongoing inequality that still occurs, mirroring the
discriminatory ideologies that were initiated by the National So-
cialists. In critical race theory, *race* is a category of analysis used
to make the experiences of non-white people visible, just like *gender* is used in gender studies to have meaningful conversations
on sexism and misogyny.[11] While they're both social constructs,
removing the words does *not remove* the constructs themselves.
And—*stop me if you've heard this one before*—but erasing the word
race does not erase the lived experience of racism, it just removes
the language that impacted people living in Germany use to

describe it, and flattens out the entire population into a single, homogeneous legal subject that would be (in this case) white, male, and Christian by default.[12]

At the same time of this debate, the Afrozensus (or "Afro Census") tackled the issue of language and representation head-on. In an initiative spearheaded by the community-based education and empowerment project Each One Teach One, organizers conducted a massive grassroots campaign to get as many Black and diasporic people of African descent as possible to participate in the census. Karamba Diaby, who is to date one of four Black members of German parliament, and Pierrette Herzberger-Fofana, who is to date Germany's only Black member of European Parliament, wrote a forward praising the initiative when the results were published. They called it a vital step in understanding just how underrepresented Black people are in major German institutions and in combating anti-Black racism.

More than six thousand people took the census, which examined issues of personal and public safety, discrimination at work and in personal interactions and media representation, and the collected data was drilled down in reports to reflect differences based on sexuality and gender. Nearly a quarter of all participants cited an incident of discrimination with the police. While discrimination in health care was reported as the rifest, with nearly three in ten participants, or over 28 percent, reporting discrimination in that area—which was significantly higher among cisgender and trans-inclusive women than with cisgender heterosexual men. To reinforce this, I will not detail my first appointment at a white German gynecologist's office, which invoked feelings of being put on display like I was a prop in a human zoo—but you can use your imagination.

The Afro Census was a historic endeavor. Not only did it make Black people visible, but it expanded the use of language in this study by incorporating the words *Black, African,* and *Afro-Diasporic people.* This in itself was significant because it acknowledged the variation of experiences and backgrounds that make up what it means to be Black. This "cross-ethnic" exploration of European racialization should also be discussed alongside conversations on Blackness.[13] Immigration, war, and colonialism have created very distinct cultural and ethnic groups in North and West Africa, the Caribbean, and the Americas, which *is also* true for Europe, but the privilege of subjectivity and variability as it relates to these experiences is almost exclusively used to describe the white European experience.[14] And Blackness, while used to create a sense of cross-cultural solidarity among different Black diasporic groups, is also weaponized within the legal framework of immigration to separate what it means to be *white European* from what it means to be something else.[15] The Afro Census acknowledged that from beginning to end.

Now, there's data to show that we do exist, and under what conditions. But we need to continue expanding the language because most of the vocabulary used in the past has been downright racist. Black people who move to Germany, like me, are confronted with that reality very swiftly when they try to access the language. Afro-German people have been creating a vocabulary for themselves and pushing for new language to collectively describe their experiences in this country.

Early in my German studies, I met an Afro-German woman at an artist's talk. She was so cool that I ended up falling over myself, rambling on about the difficulty I was experiencing learning the language. I wished I had said something smoother. But Susanna suggested that we become tandem partners, so that I could practice my German and she could practice her English—which was flawless. After a few hangs, I realized she was just using this as an excuse. We were both nerds who both thought the other was too cool to hang. At some point, we got used to cooking each other dinner several times a week. I often complained about my Deutschkurs to her, describing how other people in my class had been using texts by Heidegger, Schopenhauer, and Nietzsche as references of interest to help with their reading comprehension.

"Great, the Nazi, the woman beater, and the humorless misanthrope," I said. "Where do I sign up?"

She asked me what *I* was interested in reading while she cut up some onions.

I told her that I wanted to learn more about her experience, and about Germany's Black history in general. She wrapped her arms around me while I rolled out the dough to a Flammekueche. It was her way of trying to get me to dance, which she did all the time—everywhere. Kitchens, bedrooms, train stations, balconies. Everything was a dance floor to her. Susanna was a kid when the Berlin Wall came down, and she spent her formative years in makeshift techno clubs that migrated from one abandoned building to the other in the city's east. It was far from the hip-hop and R&B of my own youth. Even further away from any kind of lap dances for Jesus. We were on the same page about politics, but not about rhythm.

"Did you know that dzee Flammekueche comes from Alsace?" I said in a stiff, rehearsed German accent. "A historic region in northeastern France on dzee border of Germany and Switzerland?"

She laughed.

"It's traditionally served mit Speck und Zwiebeln. Let's look at dzee history of this lecker tart."

Suddenly, a look came over her face and she disappeared from the room, returning a few minutes later with a book packed with scribbles and yellow-highlighted passages. "Have you read this?" she asked.

I dusted the flour from my hands onto my apron and picked

it up. "Farbe bekennen," I read out loud. She continued kneading small circles into my waist, and I read the authors' names: "Katharina Oguntoye, Dagmar Schultz, and May Opitz."

"May Ayim," she corrected me.

The name sounded familiar. I flipped through the book and gasped. "A forward by Audre Lorde???" She nodded and mm-hmmed affirmatively.

"Is this us? Is this the fairy tale of queer Black women coming together from across the Atlantic?"

"Eh . . ." She grimaced. "It's no fairy tale . . . But if you want to know about the Afro-German woman's experience, there's no better place for you to start"—she pressed her finger into the book's open pages—"than here."

I borrowed her book and bought an English translation as a companion to make sense of words I couldn't understand. I read like a toddler, sounding the sentences out loud, stumbling over the umlauts and groupings that made some words ten syllables or longer. It was the first German book I had read that discussed Blackness *in* German. In it, writers like May Ayim assemble the pieces of Germany's Black history—from the way that images of Africans changed in Germany before, during, and after colonialism, to the ways in which "psychic colonization" had traumatized the country's Afro-German community, which had been taught from an early age to aspire to be as German as possible—without the "Afro" part.[16] I was so moved by the stark, and stunning, analysis of the country's troubled relationship with race that I presented it in my language class with very rudimentary German—stumbling head over heels over my akkusativ and dativ conjugations.

I could feel the rumblings of another historic love affair blossoming, through kinship in shared experiences separated by decades. Shortly after, I began reading Ayim's poetry, which felt easier to grasp, thanks to the shorter form. But it was also very sad, interspersed with feelings of abandonment and isolation around her predominantly white upbringing so familiar I could have written them about my own childhood. Ayim had cut straight to the heart of Germany's racial denial—and cleaved it wide open with her pen, making herself radically vulnerable to showcase the human cost of using the white gaze to define Black existence. Every time I revisit her work, I'm reminded that rebalancing power dynamics within any relationship—whether it's between two people, or a group of people and the governing state—begins with the language. It's the backbone of oppression and the lifeblood of liberation.

Brigitte Sylvia Andler, nicknamed May, was born in Hamburg in 1960 to a white German mother, Ursula Andler, and a Ghanaian medical student, Emmanuel Ayim. Emmanuel wanted to take his daughter back to Ghana to be raised by his sister, but German law didn't afford biological fathers rights to their children at the time. Additionally, because May's parents weren't married, German law considered her illegitimate, and she became a ward of the state.[17] May was in foster care for the first eighteen months of her life before she was adopted by a white family by the name of Opitz—which she took as her surname. According to May, physical beatings and severe punishments were common. It seems that the Opitz parents wanted to make an example of May, as well as her parents. The strict foster family wanted May to play the role of a model minority so they could prove she was more than the by-product of an immoral woman and a wayward Ghanaian immigrant.[18] But the discipline they used caused May to live in fear, and she felt deeply misunderstood by her adoptive family. In her poem "mama," May describes this feeling in poignant verse, describing some of the physical abuse presumably inflicted by her adopted white mother; she also recounts her responses, which included wetting the bed and learning to be afraid from what sounds like a very tender age.[19]

There are many similarities between her words and the Aboriginal poetry I read in Australia. Ayim's poetry became the bridge that connected the facts and statistics of Germany's Black history to a more felt understanding of its impact. In this poem alone, I see the picture of someone who is lonely and afraid in the one place where she should feel safe from harm—and the disconnect between the two is heartbreaking.

The loss of her birth parents and the violence of her adopted home took a deep toll on May's mental health from a young age. She slept with a razor under her pillow and sometimes wrote about wanting to go to sleep and never wake up.[20] As May grew older, the fighting at home worsened. In 1979, when she was nineteen years old, May came home late one night and got into a fight with her parents that ended with them kicking May out of the house—an account they denied.[21]

Germany's use of problematic language continued after World War II. People like Opitz were described as a *Mischlingskind,* or "mixed-breed" or "mongrel child." Her parents were civilians, but many other M*schlingskinder were also Besatzungskinder ("children of the occupation"). The latter were mixed children of German women and American soldiers after World War II. White Besatzungskinder were readily accepted and easily assimilated into German culture and society, but the children of African American soldiers, of which there were approximately five thousand, presented a different "problem" while growing up in Germany during the late 1940s, '50s, and '60s.[22] To evade stigma from their communities, around 9 percent of white German mothers gave their Black children up for adoption.[23] Even as infants, these children endured horrific racism. One African American nurse in Germany at the time described the situation to the NAACP in 1949 thus: "These babies [of Black soldiers] need food. But the Germans have none for their own and easily tell these German girls that we make no provisions for 'nigger' babies."[24]

Not only were they a living reminder of the country's defeat in World War II, but they bore the burden of racist stereotypes and attitudes from the Schwarze Schmach and interwar colonial literature—including images that demonized dark skin and fixated on so-called savagery. Black children were sometimes taught more foreign languages than white children because there was a belief that they would eventually leave Germany and go somewhere they would be more accepted.[25] There was even an argument in the federal government that considered if they should be sent abroad because the German climate wasn't suitable for them.[26]

While white students went to the typical Gymnasium and Hochschule ("selection schools" and "secondary schools"), educators didn't know where to place Black German children—carting them off to "special schools." These were institutions reserved for children with behavioral challenges and intellectual disabilities where Rosemarie K. Lester, author of "Blacks in Germany and German Blacks: A Little-Known Aspect of Black History," wrote that "society [got] rid of its unwanted quite easily by sending all too many of the racially mixed children into the ghetto of the Sonderschulen [special schools]."[27] Pamphlets were printed and disseminated among teachers that addressed how to best deal with Black students' "behavioral issues," without addressing the discriminatory attitudes that had likely created them.

Maxi, unser Negerbub (Maxi, Our N*gger Boy)* was a pamphlet

---

* Some say that the word *Neger* means "Negro" in English, not "n*gger," but every time I or someone I've known has been called that word—it was definitely intended to be the latter.

published in 1952 and presented to the class whenever a Black child started school.[28] Likewise, the 1955 movie *Der dunkle Stern* (The Dark Star) advertised the impossibility of ever integrating Black children into German society, encouraging them to seek their Heimat (or "homeland") outside of Germany.[29] When the Federal Ministry of the Interior held a census in November 1950 to discuss "the problem" of the Black children, they concluded that international adoption was best, citing fears that the children's racial differences would be an insurmountable obstacle to their integration within German society. Many were adopted to African American homes in the United States.[30]

In 1959, the president of the Federal Labor Office (now the Federal Employment Agency) let employment offices know that the first six thousand Afro-German mixed children were set to begin to look for apprenticeships, noting that Section 1, Article 3 of the Basic Law in the constitution would be used to discourage any discrimination they might face.[31] In 1962, the German magazine *Stern* did a report on the experiences of Afro-German children in Hamburg, Frankfurt, and Munich. Students reported that they felt accepted within their immediate circles, but they were often the targets of racist hostilities at school, treated as foreign, and insulted by strangers.[32] Messaging from every direction seemed to convey that these children were not welcome in Germany, and that they came from morally dubious origins.[33]

This is the climate that May Ayim grew up in. The same year that Ayim was kicked out of her home, she graduated from the Episcopal school in Münster, where she had studied to become a nurse, and then enrolled at a teacher's college to study German and social studies. But after a trip to Israel and Egypt, she transferred to the University of Regensburg to study psychology and education. She later returned to Israel and traveled throughout sub-Saharan Africa—particularly Kenya and Ghana, where she reconnected with her father and, after several more visits, his extended Ghanaian family. This turned out to be very significant for Ayim, who appears to have struggled to reconcile her identity as an African woman who spoke German as her mother tongue.[34] Poems like "borderless and brazen: a poem against the German 'u-not-y'" articulate how she defied German racism that attempted to create a sense of estrangement from her Ghanaian heritage, asking what it means to be African, Black, and German—how these identities interact with and change one another.

This poem decenters the decisions and labels of German authority, positions her as the sole arbiter of what Germanness looks like for her—including her Ghanaian heritage and ancestry, which she was able to do after reconnecting with her father's family. For the first time, she was able to experience a feeling of communal acceptance in a West African country, and she adopted her father's surname as her pseudonym—becoming May Ayim.

In 1984, Ayim became a lecturer at the Free University of Berlin, where she settled permanently. That same year, she met a visiting African American scholar named Audre Lorde, who had been invited by Dagmar Schultz to teach a poetry workshop. The women Lorde met, taught, and mentored included Helga Emde, Ika Hügel-Marshall, Katharina Oguntoye—and May Ayim. The latter two went on to become founding members of Die Initiative Schwarzer Menschen in Deutschland, or the Initiative for Black People in Germany—one of the country's first organizations dedicated to supporting Black people and the disambiguation of Afro-German history. Since its inception as a grassroots organization, ISD has fought for the rights of Black people across Germany, taken up campaigns to address the racist practice of blackface, and pushed for a suitable German alternative to the English word *race*.[35] They have also worked with other organizations to lobby the Berlin government to change streets named for prominent German colonizers.

And their joint efforts succeeded. In 2020, it was announced that M-Straße would be renamed to Anton-Wilhelm-Amo-Straße, after a man who was born in Ghana in 1703, sold into slavery, and went on to become Germany's first Black scholar. Lüderitzstraße would be named after Cornelius Frederiks, a Namibian resistance fighter. Nachtigalplatz would be named after the Cameroonian king Rudolf Duala Manga Bell, and Petersallee would be divided and given two new names: Anna-Mungunda-Allee, for the Namibian independence fighter, and Maji-Maji-Allee after the Maji Maji Rebellion in German East Africa in the early twentieth century.[36]/* ISD remains one of the most significant and powerful coordinated efforts in the country and has been vocal in every major civil rights movement since its founding.

In 1986, Ayim, Oguntoye, and Schultz published *Farbe bekennen*—a seminal text that asserted the Afro-German experience firmly into the country's discourse. Though these essays center on the experiences of Afro-German people, including their extensive history, these pieces also highlighted anti-Blackness as a universal experience among the diaspora. They captured my own feelings of growing up in the United States and falling in and out of love in Australia. It's a project that emphasizes the importance of Black friendships, especially among Black women. It reminded me that the power stripped from me in white environments gets reclaimed the moment I—as Oguntoye and Ayim put it in *Farbe bekennen*—no longer felt the need to explain my existence.[37]

Farbe bekennen highlighted the ways in which Afro-German women have challenged and redefined what it means to be Black within their respective environments.[38] In the chapter

---

* Even though the local city councils announced these changes in 2020, local resistance from residents and bureaucracy have slowed them from actually being changed. The names were finally changed in 2023.

"Afro-Germans after 1945: The So-Called Occupation Babies,"
Ayim notes that the German government's approach toward Afro-
German children framed them as a problem or concern that needed
a resolution; Ayim turns the gaze outward, identifying Germany's
"intolerance" and discriminatory culture as the actual problem.
She noted that the success of Germany's racism stems from disem-
powering Afro-German people in order to prop up a richer, whiter
society, which she saw as symptomatic of a larger global phenomenon that behaves as a foundation for all other forms of discrimination: sexism, ableism, queerphobia. The white mothers of these
Black children also carried a burden of shame because women historically bear the burden of society's intolerances. Ayim also notes
that any white German woman labeled as immoral for having a relationship with a Black man could discard the label by discarding
the child, but it was inescapable for Afro-German women because
their shame became their skin color *and* their gender.[39] This essay,
on top of all the others, is a brilliant, insightful, thought-provoking
illumination that showcases the gaps in German social psychology. But it's her analysis of race language that is imprinted on me
forever.

Terms like *mulatto* and *half-breed*, made popular by eugeni-
cists like Sir Francis Galton, Madison Grant, and Eugen Fischer,
reveal how language informed the treatment of Afro-German
children when they entered German educational and working institutions. These words focused on and distorted the ethnic differences of Afro-Germans into curiosities that reinforced their
inferiority. These words remind me of other vernacular I've seen
in my travels: terms like *octoroon*, *quadroon*, and *hāfu*. All of them
reduce a person's ethnic identity to the blood quantum of their
differences, of their otherness, the amount of which becomes the
sole factor used to determine just how human they are, and just
how reasonable it is to treat them like people. The darker they are,

the Blacker they are, the easier they become to disenfranchise, to oppress, to exclude, and to kill. But we were never seen as whole, just as fractions of a white person: a half, a quarter, an eighth, or by Jim Crow standards—three-fifths. Even the way some people in Melbourne argued with me about being African American and not Black was about how *they* saw me rather than how I saw myself. All this achieves the same goals in the end—pushing people to the margins of a society where everyone else can pretend they don't exist. Language has *always* had that power.

Language has also always had ability to liberate.

Together, Ayim, Oguntoye, Emde, Hügel-Marshall, and Lorde created the vocabulary they wanted to describe how the Black German community saw itself—rather than how they felt seen by white Germans. They coined the term *Afro-Deutsch*, or "Afro-German," which first appeared in *Farbe bekennen*. Like the term *African American*, it's a phrase instilled with pride and identity that inserts itself firmly in the discourse of what it means to be German—an identity that had previously been restricted exclusively to people who were white. They knew then, just as I know now, how important it was to create language to define the experiences we embody, so that we can define ourselves for ourselves— rather than accepting the terms coined by others that are used to our detriment.

They did this by sticking together, by supporting one another, and by finding common ground in their shared experiences. In this way, they were able to be themselves. And this inspired me because when I realized I had the language, as well as an understanding of the history that made it deeply necessary, I stopped trying to distort myself so that *others* could be more comfortable with me. I stopped needing to find a context, or a country, in which I could fit. I laid my arsenal of identities to rest. And those skills of adaptability, language, code-switching, and reading the temperature of a room to within a single degree change became less relevant because I realized I was safe where I was—as long as I stayed authentic to myself. That consistency is something I best experience around other Black women and women of color—when we gather like a coven of witches to center our own joy, to worship at the altar of our own creativity, when we deploy radical self-expression to extract the most beautiful, vulnerable parts of one another that we nurture with unconditional love. That's what I found in Berlin. Maybe I could have found it in Melbourne, Kudamatsu, or Chicago—but I found it in Germany's capital. And it feels remarkably like what happened between Audre Lorde and Ayim, Oguntoye, and others.

Audre Lorde spoke lovingly about her time in Berlin, describing this period in her life as one of creation and empowerment. The years between 1984 and 1992 became one of the most significant periods of her life. She seemed particularly enamored with the city's green spaces and was a regular haunt at Berlin's scenic lakes, including Krumme Lanke and Schlachtensee. One photo of Lorde that pops up in queer, Black spaces shows her rowing in an inflatable boat in a red T-shirt with a quote by anarchist Emma Goldman that reads, IF I CAN'T DANCE, I DON'T WANT TO BE PART OF YOUR REVOLUTION.

Lorde loved to dance. Her favorite spots were in Schöneberg, the city's most prominent gay neighborhood, where she regularly frequented queer clubs like Die Zwei (Those Two) and Pour Elle (For Her).[40] Both of them are closed now, but there is no shortage of lesbian and queer bars in Berlin today that have taken their place. Anyone who wants to check out her favorite dance spots, as well as her former residences, can take the Audre Lorde tour using the website created and curated by her close friends Dagmar Schultz and Ika Hügel-Marshall (who passed away in 2022). The online map reaches north to Frannzclub in Prenzlauer Berg and as far south as Limonenstraße, where she shared a home with her partner Gloria Joseph, and Wannseeterrassen, where she enjoyed spending time with her loved ones. Lorde passed away on the Caribbean island of Saint Croix in 1992. In accordance with her wishes, one of the places her ashes were scattered was Krumme Lanke in Berlin.[41]

Maybe it's a coincidence. Maybe it's just something about the kind of people who are drawn to this place: the creative, dynamic, constantly evolving artists of color who have found their ways to the chronically gray Berlin, a metropolis that operates as the concrete avatar for the collective anxieties, fears, and mental illnesses of the people it attracts. This city is also an artist, constantly changing, inked by art and scarred by memory—and we're the ones drawn here. We're the sporophytes crawling out of its wet, dark dirt toward the sunlight so that we can find one another.

While I do have a natural soft spot for artistic postindustrial capitals built on the chronicles of gang violence, it's only Berlin where I have found a circle of kindred explorers. That simple validation in the shared experiences of others has been transformative, healing, and even transcendent. As we love one another, I feel that we are also continuing to expand the definition of what love can do. It can't rewrite history, but it can change the course of the future.

MAY AYIM TOOK her own life in 1996. In 2011, a street in Kreuzberg previously named Gröbenufer, after the German colonizer Otto Friedrich von der Gröben, was renamed to May-Ayim-Ufer. Von der Gröben was responsible for erecting the Groß Friedrichsburg fort in present-day Ghana, and I can now walk that street remembering one of the people who fought tirelessly for a public acknowledgment and reckoning for Germany's colonial atrocities. I still stop on occasion to look up at her name on the sign, including once with the person who introduced me to her work, our arms interlocked. We later sat on the riverbank soaking up the sun while watching people paddle in the Spree. We were quiet for a while. After a long German winter, there's absolutely nothing like the intoxicating effects of spring.

"It's enough to make you wanna dance," I said while looking around the river.

Susanna smiled at me.

"Well, you better dance your fucking tits off, bitch."

21.

My Pisces Heart

Do you think that you were the only person to have had this experience? Are you really surprised, as if it were something unprecedented, that so long a tour and such diversity of scene have not enabled you to throw off this melancholy and this feeling of depression? A change in character, not a change of air, is what you need. Though you cross the boundless ocean, though, to use the words of our poet Virgil, "Lands and towns are left astern," whatever your destination you will be followed by your failings. Here is what Socrates said to someone who was making the same complaint: "How can you wonder your travels do you no good, when you carry yourself around with you? You are saddled with the very thing that drove you away." How can novelty of surroundings abroad and becoming acquainted with foreign scenes or cities be of any help? All that dashing about turns out to be quite futile. And if you want to know why all this running away cannot help you, the answer is simply this: you are running away from your own company.

—SENECA, *LETTERS FROM A STOIC*

Y GRANDPA AND I WROTE OUR LAST LETTERS TO each other right before I began the ninth grade. If I had known they would be our last, I would have tried to be less absorbed in the social engineering of high school: the friendships, the gossip, the glittering distraction of romance, the stresses of an International Baccalaureate program, and the terror of a drastically changing body that attracted attention from grown adults both on and off the internet. I wrote about the anxiety I felt not knowing what I wanted to be when I grew up—adding how much I loved art only to then outline all the "practical reasons" that pursuing such interests was doomed to fail, as my parents and brother often reminded me. The letter he wrote in response, which was accompanied by two ten-dollar bills, assured me that it didn't matter what I did with my life, or who I wanted to be—that he would love me no matter what, and that the only thing *he* wanted was for me to be happy.

At the time, it felt like one of those platitudes that adults say because they can't actually engage, or have no interest in actually engaging, with a child's feelings. Many years later, after I grew up and he had passed away, I found that letter tucked in the back of an old dresser drawer and read it again. He wrote how important I was to him, and how important it was for him to know that my family was doing well. He didn't want me to worry about the future because life would sort it out for me. And in that last sentence, the one I had remembered through the years, he had underlined "be happy." If I had known how difficult that goal really is, it would have felt much more profound when I first read it.

I wonder what he would think about me living in places like Japan, Australia, and Germany—especially considering he went to war against two of those countries.

Would my travels have been his greatest dream come true, or his greatest nightmare realized?

I think he would have felt right at home in Yamaguchi's abrasive humidity, with the mikan oranges. He would have gotten himself a place in the middle of the woods, next to a small creek. He would have been annoyed that none of the traditional clothing fit him. He might have been amused when I taught my students the difference between Beyoncé and me, and my students would have gotten a kick out of his tall, robust frame, asking him to compare their feet to his, to arm wrestle with him. I think he would have eaten blowfish with me, if I didn't tell him what it was. I don't think he would have approved of me getting tattooed in Osaka, but he wouldn't have fought it either. He would have been devastated by a visit to the Hiroshima Peace Memorial Museum. In my heart, I believe he would have struggled to reconcile what he had fought against with what he would have seen there, and what he left behind in Georgia. I think about how sad he might have been seeing me passed out on a kitchen floor from a panic attack—how he would have worried for days about whether I would ever get control of my anxiety. He would have wondered if he could have done something to help. I think he would have shed a tear to see me in a yukata giving a farewell speech in Japanese to my students.

Grandpa would have laughed his ass off seeing me ferret around a "big city" like Chicago, trying to make sense of the geographical politics, navigating the Loop, and dropping eggs on drunken pedestrians below my window late at night. He would have been confused about my art, but I think he would have come to my graduation show anyway and watched me talk about my drawings and paintings with a curious mix of pride and bewilderment. I don't think he would have liked Chicago very much, but he would have visited me—and driven right back to Florida the moment I gave him leave to do so.

I can picture him being confused by Australia, but even more by Matteo. He would have struggled not to reprimand Emilia's two-year-old when he proudly declared he didn't like me because I was Black. My grandpa would have been able to admonish Matteo with a glare. He would have tried to drag me out of that situation. I would have fought him hard and told him to kick rocks because I'm just as stubborn as he was. He would have pulled back—begrudgingly—and waited for me to end the relationship on my terms. He might have snapped once or twice, demanding that I explain why I thought so little of myself. I would have asked him what was wrong with me—as I've done alone so many times. He would have bit his tongue because, even with me fully grown, he would know that any answer would be difficult to scrub from my internal monologue. We would have gone for a while without talking after that.

He would have taken those walks with me around the block and sat with me on a park bench while I cried. He would have waited until it was all out of my system and I returned to Matteo, pretending to be happy. He wouldn't speak, but I would feel his frustration in all the things he didn't say—mad that the problem couldn't be fixed with a ten-dollar bill. When I finally ended the relationship, Grandpa wouldn't have held it against me. He never would have even brought it up. He would have just been relieved it was over.

He would have been proud that I got my master's in Melbourne and both joked and bragged about all the "big words" I'd learned. Driving on the other side of the road would have terrified him, but not as much as hook turns, which I still don't do. He would have gotten a piece of land in the Outback and settled on a billabong and made friends with the local crocodiles. He would have cared for that piece of land like he would have a small child. Shotgun cocked on the porch, prepared for any bandits who attempted to steal any of his emu eggs. The interior would have been simple, with a small kitchen table big enough to seat two—and he would have prepared me kangaroo steak and set up the checkerboard, then sent me back into the city before it got too dark to drive. He would have loaded a cooler of fresh meat in my trunk and bragged about giving me the best cuts.

I think Germany would have been the most difficult place for him to live in. The bad weather, the culture of rules, the lectures from strangers—whom he surely would have cursed to kingdom come. He would have hated the noise, and he would have yelled at people who don't clean up after their dogs. He would have skull thumped that neo-Nazi on the train. He would have said, "I thought we killed all of you cunts," and kicked him off the platform. He would have enjoyed kebabs a lot—and asked for the Knoblauch ("garlic") and scharf ("spicy") sauces on his lamb. I can see him with a girlfriend in Schöneberg, someone classy and proper, but I think he would have lived in the industrial hub of Humboldthain, next to the park, where he would have eaten his lunch every day. He would have done something with his hands to feel useful, like drive a train. He *loved* to drive. He would have liked Susanna and probably been a bit confused by "the whole queer thing"—but I don't think he would have criticized it. I don't think he would have cared. I think he would have scratched his head, shrugged, and concluded that no man was ever good enough anyway.

He would have adopted a mutt from the Tierheim and trained her, feeding her bits of Currywurst as treats every time she mastered a new trick. I would have visited him once a week and brought him Streuselkuchen baked in my kitchen—the classic version with apples and cinnamon. We would have practiced German, and he'd have defaulted to English after five minutes. We would have sat on the balcony complaining about the myth of German efficiency in a city where half the train lines go out of commission every winter. He would have told me how much he missed the Florida heat and the citrus and the mud, and he would have told me the only reason he came was to make sure I was okay—asking me for silent permission to go back to the place where he felt most at home and leaving me to the place I had made into mine. Now that he saw how Berlin had given me a community of people who looked after me—he could leave in peace. He didn't have to worry because Berlin brought out the best in me, which also reflected the best parts of him. Of course I would have let him go. I wouldn't have needed an explanation. When you understand each other as well we did, when you were as alike as we obviously were, the rest would be said in letters anyway.

This is a fiction I've invented to bridge the time that's passed since he died, and since I've learned to really live. I like to picture him in this world, this place I've made for myself. I like knowing that in every place I've visited and lived, there could have also been a place for him—because I would have made one for him.

The world he came from never truly deserved him.

*

The first anxiety attack I described in Japan was not my last. They followed me around the world. They became the punctuation marks between different places, phases of relationships, and jobs along the way. I still remember shrinking in the grotty bathroom of a Muy Thai boxing ring on my first trip to Thailand. The crowded New Year's bash in Singapore that made me feel like I was suffocating. How the anxiety from my relationship with Matteo felt different from the anxiety I felt when I arrived in Germany. It all stemmed from the same place—the same fears of being unwanted, unloved, unnurtured, and unprotected. This is what makes me leave a place. This is why I've never stayed.

I once told a friend about this in Berlin. I was so vulnerable and open with her then, when I'm normally anything but. She's an esoteric person who loves tarot and astrology, so she looked up my birth chart. She scrolled through the placements, the glittery beauty mark piercing above her lip twirling in place.

"Aha!" she said when she landed on my Venus-in-Pisces placement. She began to explain the traits, saying that it was a "good one to have" but also made me more sensitive to changing environments and people. The symbol of Pisces is the dueling fish, which move around with the currents and tides of the ocean. They're curious, carry deep secrets, and love with the force of the rolling tide. Belonging to the element of water, Pisces is as creative as it is mercurial. They want to be absorbed in whatever they love, and a spiritual connection is needed to hold their interest, time, and energy.

Most noticeably, she said this: Just like fire needs air to breath, water needs earth to grow. "Otherwise," she added, "it can feel like drowning in your own emotional chaos."

I IGNORED HER at first. I ignored it all. But her words rang true the moment she said them. It was ground I needed in my life, and *grounding*, more specifically. I had spent a life on the run. What would happen if I just stayed still? How bad could it possibly be to build a life with and around people who had come to Berlin looking for the same things, finding them in one another?

One day, I looked up my grandpa's chart—or what I could of his chart, not knowing the time he was born. I was surprised to see that we shared an Aquarius sun, a Pisces heart, and a watery Piscean Mars. That, like me, he only has one earth placement. That he was mostly air, fire, and water. I thought of us like the hurricanes that ravage Florida every year, moving across the earth, unable to last in one spot.

I wonder if he was happy in Haines City when he decided to settle there. If I could write one more letter to him, I would ask that question first.

If my grandpa were still alive today and asked me if I was "happy," what would I say? Maybe this: That happiness speaks a different language every few hundred miles. That, for some people, it's found at opposing corners of the world. I would say that sometimes it's the perfect cherry blossom in a manicured garden at the edge of a Buddhist temple. I would say that it can be a drive along a southern coast to watch whales and hold koalas. I would say that sometimes, it can be a person, but that it never should be because people change—or worse, sometimes they stay exactly the same. I would tell him that it can be a community of Black and Brown women who fiercely nurture the most vulnerable, emotional, and marshmallowy-soft parts of one another. I would say that happiness is not just a state of *being*. Sometimes, it's a state of moving—but it can never replace the contentment I found in staying still. I would tell him that demons, like personal failings, know how to cross the boundless ocean—and that it's important to learn how to shed them. For now, it means standing still with the churning tide of my interior world.

And I only have to leave when I want to.

It's a letter than would go on for ages, maybe even run the length of one hundred thousand words, bound between two covers, divided into sections to describe its many different faces, languages, and histories that reach across four different continents and connect to one another.

I know that he would read it, from beginning to end, with a big smile on his face.

Epilogue

All Roads Lead to Georgia

When you see them Confederate flags you know what it is
Your folks pick cotton here that's why we call it the field
— "GEORGIA" BY LUDACRIS AND FIELD MOB
FT. JAMIE FOXX

M Y BLACK HISTORY CONNECTS ME TO A PART OF the world that I haven't even visited in eight years— the U.S. South. I never had a chance to meet my cousin Brenda, who passed away in 2012. The only time I had even spoken to her was on the phone in February of that year, when she encouraged me to consider making Atlanta my new home. I hadn't thought much about the construct of family for many years—not until becoming estranged from my older brother and, later on, both my parents. But I think about Brenda often. I met her son Joe and his fiancée, now wife, in November 2019 before the COVID pandemic shut down air travel. Kellie and I started following each other on Instagram. I saw she was a pilot and gushed to Joe about how cool she seemed, simultaneously demoting him on the cousin hierarchy. He didn't mind. Kellie mentioned that she had miles and that she could bring Joe to visit some time. I told her to pull up, and less than two weeks later, they were on a flight to Berlin.

I met Joe and Kellie at their hotel and took them for a schnitzel dinner in Mitte. Joe exuded big brother energy, even though he's a few years younger than me. He had dark, wavy hair that made him look like a divorced Kappa with kids who don't know about one another—and I told him so. It's difficult to describe the Georgia Southern accent. It sounds like stretched white singlets drying on a clothesline beneath the sun; people yelling directions at you from a front porch they have no intention of leaving; bad traffic in every direction; the distant plume of exhaust from someone's homemade smoker hidden deep in the longleaf pines; lemon-pepper hangovers; fireflies at late-night bonfires; makeshift shacks at major intersections selling boiled peanuts, fresh peaches, and candied pecans (emphasis on the second syllable). So you'll know what I mean when I describe the excitement in his Southern timbre as his food came out and he said: *"Shiiiiiiieeeet."*

Up until that moment, I had been cut off from my grandpa's side of the family, which I didn't even know existed until Brenda, Joe's mom, reached out to us on Facebook. But sitting next to Joe, I saw many of the things I remembered about my grandpa in my cousin. The thoughtful expressions and no-fucks-given attitude. If we disagreed on something, he hit me with a pensive lean into the back of his chair and a hand half covering his mouth to stop himself from saying what he really meant—something I realized we were both doing at the same time. In the same way. With the same curious expressions on our faces.

Shiiiiiiiieeet.

I was tempted to think that years of corresponding on social media had given me a false sense of familiarity, but that wasn't it at all. He was definitely family. It felt as if we had grown up together. As if his house had been one of the stops my dad made on the way to my grandparents', as if we had spent the visit sitting on his screened-in front porch while someone's mom whispered the dirty laundry of everyone who waved when they walked past. We spoke at that dinner table for six hours. Joe told me about his sisters, Karen and Angel, whom I had previously connected with on Facebook. We occasionally messaged about meeting, but life kept getting in the way. When jet lag began to catch up to Joe and Kellie both, I took them back to their hotel. Joe told me to consider coming to Atlanta for a visit, and I hugged them both—feeling jarred by a sudden, unmistakable attachment.

Four years later, I took him up on his offer. On Juneteenth weekend 2023, I flew down to Atlanta from New York. Joe picked me up in a massive pickup truck that looked like it could bulldoze through traffic, and Kellie sat with me in the back seat while we all caught up. The last time I was in Georgia's capital was 2003, when I was straight and *Speakerboxxx/The Love Below* was playing on heavy rotation in my boyfriend's car as we drove up I-75. Atlanta's traffic is still awful. Everyone still plays Outkast. But now I'm visiting family I didn't know I had. Their house is surrounded by woods, and Joe shows me the fence grating used to keep deer from eating his tomato plants. Inside, they have a dedicated corner to Outkast that looks more like a shrine, and Joe plays *ATLiens* while doing barbecue prep for the next day. Kellie tells me that one of Wesley Snipes's relatives lives somewhere around here. The humidity is familiar and unreal, and I'm reminded of why people always move slowly in the South.

I finally met Joe's sisters. Karen threw a Juneteenth barbecue at her home, where I met her husband, Carl, and their dog, Jackson. I was filming the barbecue spread when Karen popped up behind me. We swung back and forth in her kitchen, both squealing about the moment that had finally come. When I pulled back, I noticed how much she looked like her mom: her flipped-out bob, freckled cheeks, and expressive eyes that were definitely capable of judging even, and especially, if she politely held her tongue. She exuded that cool calm, letting anything that wasn't her business roll off her back and bother somebody else. Our meeting was brief, as she had more guests she started to greet, but Joe handed me a plate, and I knew what to do next.

I had salivated over Joe's shoulder as he smoked a rack of ribs and brisket all morning. Carl represented his home in Tennessee with classic Circle B hot link sausages, pork ribs heavy with paprika and garlic, and slow-cooked baked beans with ground beef. Everyone else brought mac and cheese, different types of salad, dump cakes, meringue pies, and chicken wings. I ate more food that afternoon than in the week prior. I was sweating liquid smoke and rethinking my choices when I sat down with everyone who had been defeated by their own gluttony. Small children ran around the house screaming.

Joe, Kellie, Karen, and I sat around the table and began to disentangle the stories of our family. Their grandpa Sam and my grandpa Warren Jr. were brothers—but we didn't know anything about the other. For every thing they told me about Sam, I shared something about Warren. Karen had done a deep dive into our family history around the same time I had, a little over ten years prior. She knew the names of their other siblings, whom I had never heard of before. They are all gone now. In that moment, the window to our Black history felt like it was closing shut. We all had a lot of unanswered questions—the biggest one was, why did my grandpa leave Woodland, Georgia? What compelled him to run away and never go back? And why hadn't he ever mentioned any brothers?

After pausing for a moment, Karen sighed, flipped her bob, and said: "Jennifer, the thing is—we don't know a lot about what happened back then because a lot of what may have happened wasn't good. Nobody talked about things the way they do now. Who knows what was going on?"

We all groaned in agreement, rubbing our distended bellies. It's true. If all the research I had done on Black histories around the world had taught me anything, it's that you're not always prepared to discover what you find. Every Black family from the South carries a part of that legacy, its wounds and sorrows, its triumphs and successes. Ours is no different.

"But you know…" Karen said, leaning in conspiratorially. "Cousin L might."

I was also connected to a Cousin L on Facebook but had never spoken to her.

"She was Mom's sister," Joe chimed in. They nodded.

"She knows *everybody's* business," Karen added. Her accent was similar to Joe's. It sounded like Rap Snacks and shiny Impala grilles, collard greens and red clay baked in the sun.

THE NEXT DAY, Joe and Kellie hosted a Juneteenth brunch at their house. Joe made rich grits with shrimp, crispy thick-cut bacon, French toast, and pan-fried salmon. Joe and Kellie's beagle, Cooper, planted himself in the middle of the kitchen, begging for scraps until his shrill howls announced the arrival of Joe's other sister, Angel; Karen; and Carl. For the first time ever, we were all together. Angel and Joe could have been twins. They had the same smile, the same crinkle in their eyes, the same brand of healthy skepticism that kept them from being swept up with popular opinion.

We sat around the table rehashing the conversation at Karen's the day before. Angel spoke about how interconnected everyone in Atlanta was, saying that somebody knew something. She spoke about going to school with some famous rappers and actors, knowing cousins who dated famous singers and dancers, having friends who were owed money by producers—knowing which celebrities were as cool as they seemed and which ones had kids they didn't take care of. It was just getting anybody to talk that was the issue. Kellie told a story about running into former U.S. congressman John Lewis at Kroger and giving him a kiss on the cheek.

"John Lewis tried to steal my girl!" Joe exclaimed.

I told Angel about the questions we had discussed the day before, and she also advised us to visit Cousin L.

Carl, who had been tinkering with his phone, put it down and cleared his throat.

"The question is, what happens if you never find out?"

Everyone paused and looked at me.

"Well, at least I have y'all."

JOE CALLED L as we cleaned up to head to a Juneteenth yoga class at Kellie's studio. L said we couldn't visit the next day because she had a revival planned—but told us to come the day after that. So, two days later, we were at Cousin L's house, sitting beneath a dozen framed Bible verses decorating her living room while poring through a stack of albums overflowing with discolored photos, faded birth certificates, funeral programs, and a few letters, heavily creased in their plastic covers. Kellie sat with me, and we passed photos back and forth, remarking on the unmistakable physical resemblance of the Neal genes. Looking at my grandpa's brothers and sisters was like looking into a prism. I saw bits and pieces of him in all of them, his face broken up and scattered among ten other people. His eyes above someone else's nose. His cheeks on either side of someone else's mouth.

Joe and Karen said that their dad's place wasn't too far away and that they would get some more photos and come back. L's son came by to say hello to the distant cousin visiting from Germany. Every time someone comes back to visit, it becomes an event. When Joe and Karen returned, we had about a dozen photo albums between us. On the dining table, in everyone's lap, sitting on the sofa cushions. I held up photo after photo, asking, "Who's this?" and, "Which relation are they?" Trying to make organized notes in my journal of a family tree that extended as far north as Detroit and as far as west as Los Angeles. Great-aunts and -uncles, cousins once and twice removed, people who had taken off and never looked back, moving in every single direction like the roots of a tree. I ended with a map of dozens of people, filled in with names I had never heard, doing things I had never known about before.

Then I came across a photo of someone that made my heart stop. A tall man standing in front of a stoop, in a trucker's cap with a pencil-thin mustache, staring into the camera with copper-toned eyes.

"That's Grandpa Sam," Joe said.

I didn't believe him at first, but he insisted. Karen and Cousin L all confirmed. He could have been my grandpa's doppelgänger—right down to the hat, which I could have sworn I'd seen him wear many times. But they were right.

"Were you close to him?" I asked L. She had been quiet for the most part, until I asked that question. She paused, smiled, and replied, "Yeah! I was his favorite."

"Well, why do you think he left?" I asked her.

She softened a bit behind the eyes, perhaps sensing that I really wanted to know. I was warned that she might be diplomatic with her answers because she was old-school and didn't believe in speaking ill of the dead. Putting family under a microscope attracts scrutiny, and that's felt by everyone still living.

"They were very cliquey, cousin. I think Sam and your grandpa butted heads quite a lot." I implored her to go on, but she didn't have much else to say except this: "The thing is, Jennifer, I just don't think they really liked each other that much."

JOE TOOK US to Brenda's grave. We stopped at the Dekalb Farmers Market on the way, where I collected a stack of spices that I knew

I couldn't find in Germany, and Kellie picked a couple of bouquets of flowers. We drove to a cemetery high up on a hill where you can see Atlanta's entire skyline. It was windy, and the rain clouds were rolling in. Brenda had a stone inlaid into the ground, and we laid the flowers on top before Kellie and I decided it would be better to crisscross them so that her name wasn't blocked by the leaves. We stood on the hill while Joe pointed out the familiar landmarks and buildings, telling stories of never-ending construction.

"This isn't how I wanted to meet her," I said.

"The point is that you came, cousin," Joe replied. "That's what matters."

While driving back home, we took a detour in downtown Atlanta to visit the King Center, a historically preserved museum that houses clothing items, books, and journals by Dr. Martin Luther King Jr. and his wife, Coretta Scott King. We walked to the house where Dr. King lived with his family, and Joe drove me to the house where he was born. Murals of Stacey Abrams and quotes by John Lewis, Shirley Franklin, and Ralph Abernathy were emblazoned on building facades. Atlanta is built upon U.S. Civil Rights history, which had reached to every corner of the world—from Hiroshima, to Melbourne, and finally Berlin. Everything I had seen felt connected in that moment, allowing me to appreciate—more deeply than ever—the global impact of Black activism. Because racism had a much longer head start. Returning to the South, I was in awe of how some of the most powerful forces come from such small places and ripple across time for generations. How ideas travel with the people who carry them and have the capacity to be revolutionary wherever they are planted.

I was thinking about my visit to the King Center early one morning before I left. Joe and I were eating banana muffins and sipping on mugs of tea with crystals attached to the strainers. We had been to a strip club the night before, and he wore a T-shirt

that said, I SAW YOUR MAMA DANCIN' AT THE CLERMONT
LOUNGE. He asked me if I felt like I had gotten the information I
needed, and I shrugged. I knew more than I had the week before,
and I was grateful for it—but maybe some answers just weren't
meant to be had. I trusted that my grandpa had his reasons for
leaving. He never did anything without one. The catalyst for me
leaving Florida was my own falling-out with my brother, one that
turned into an estrangement that has lasted for nearly twenty
years now. Our falling-out eventually led to my estrangement from
my parents as well. Those stories are too complicated to articulate.
I'll carry them with me forever, and I feel compelled to extend the
same ambiguity to my grandfather. Some stories can be excavated.
Some just stay buried.

The fact that we have similar stories, which led to similar es-
capes, is something I'll think about forever.

Who knows why he never said anything about having brothers,
or never spoke about Woodland. Who knows what kind of life that
town must have given people circa 1919. I have finally decided to
respect that silence, by accepting that the answers to my questions
are this: The past is rarely ever resolved. It lives with us, inside of
us, and it shapes us. It's important to understand because how we
make sense of it now is all that matters for the future. Thinking
about all the histories I've learned about in my travels, that seems
to be the discrepancy. An absence of the desire to understand. A
reluctance to connect the past with the present so that a better future can be made, even though one cannot be done without the
other. Both require a kind of courage that people only seem to possess when they need to, when their survival depends on having it.
Grandpa left his family in the past; now, they are part of my future.
My connection to him is made stronger by having them in my life.
I'd like to think that if he had known my cousins, he would have
also found a reason to come back.

Just like I did.

He also would have left again because he had his own life. Just like I did. That's what he would have wanted for me—to find my own happiness.

And I have. It's taken me far away.

And now, it's given me a reason to come back.

Sometimes.

Acknowledgments

Praise to the most high for my agent and personal cheerleader, Milly Reilly, who helped me shape this idea into a proposal of which she read countless drafts before submission. Andrea Joyce for operating tirelessly from the shadows to champion obscure authors like myself.

My editor, Alicia Kroell, whose edits helped me fashion this book into something of which I could not be prouder (for the second time!). To the entire team at Catapult for launching this project into every corner of Planet Earth: my publicist, Andrea Córdova; the VP of publicity, Megan Fishmann; Laura Berry for the gorgeous layout; Jordan Koluch for the extensive fact-checking and copyedit; and Farjana Yasmin, who designed this stunning cover.

Sincere thanks to my brilliant readers, for their attention to detail, invaluable perspectives, generosity, and wisdom: Angie Faye Martin, Elizabeth Schumacher, (Dr.) Malika Stürznickel,* and Dr. Cassandra Thiesen.*

To my blurbers: Dr. Jessica J. Lee,* Dina Nayeri, Fiona Williams, Monica Byrne, and Zinzi Clemmons, for jumping down the rabbit hole with me and reemerging with kind words.

To Natasha Lomboy—whose love and friendship have been an anchor across time and continents. Thank you for always being willing to travel—and eat. I'll conjure the dead with you any time.

---

* O.G.s who also sent me academic articles when my free JSTOR account, notes, editorial access, and rabid Googling just weren't cutting it.

To Pedram Baldari, my MacDowell bestie, who—at an early stage of this project—reminded me that this book would work only insofar as I was prepared to be courageous.

Kamimoto Shuji, for taking the time to talk to send me resources about the JBSA. The Japan Exchange Teaching Programme, for giving me the opportunity of a lifetime. All the teachers who patiently guided me through my time in the "ken."

Much of the historicization outlined in the Germany section came from articles I wrote for CNN, *Atlas Obscura*, and *Handelsblatt Today*. I'd like to thank the people I interviewed to bring those essays, and that portion of the book, into the world: Dr. Robby Aitken, Biplab Basu (Rest in Power), Tahir Della, Dr. Tiffany Florvil, Christian Kopp, Eben Louw, Sophia Schmitz from the Stolpersteine office, Anna Yeboah—and "Bill," wherever you are.

Thank you to my assistant, Karolina, for corralling unwanted email from my inboxes, a truly underrated talent.

The A'lan'a cousins: Joe, Kellie (cousin-in-love) Karen, Angel, for giving me the best Juneteenth ever, and growing my family. Nikki, for talking me through onslaughts of panic attacks for years and years.

Claire—always. Michael and Jude, forever. See you again someday soon.

Archana, there are no words to convey the depth of my gratitude. Thank you.

To all my pals at *DADDY Magazine*, Oyoun, *poco.lit.*, the Berlin Writer's Workshop, and the Reader, for being the beating heart of Berlin's intersectional and multilingual arts and writing scene.

This book was an absolute marathon of emotional and psychological athleticism that triggered a lot of difficult feelings and even worse memories. To the beautiful souls who held my hand and dragged me across the finish line when I wanted to faceplant on the pavement: Shannon Lewis, Carleen Coulter, Jessica Lee, Jen Bell, Danielle Smith, Annaïck Farrell, and Cassandra Thiesen. Whether

you took a distressed phone call from me while I was shivering in
Tiergarten, shared a piece of cake and a tight hug, drove two hours
last minute to meet me at an airport hotel, or extended a place for
me at a warm hearth in County Kerry during Christmas—you
were a safe haven during a very lonely and very arduous process.

The last time I wrote an acknowledgments section, I learned
that I also have a lot of friends who need written validation, otherwise they might doubt my (fierce, unabiding, bloodthirsty) love
for them. I've kept my thank-yous close to the experience of writing this book. Other names have been intentionally withheld to
protect their identities. But my village is massive and international.

So, if you feel left out, then feel free to write your name here:
_____.*

And just know that—whoever you are—I couldn't have done
this without you! That's the truth.

Now, Black by popular demand, the *My Pisces Heart* playlist in
no particular order:

She Reaches Out to She Reaches Out to She by Chelsea Wolfe
DNK by Aya Nakamura
 -!- and *Fission* by Dead Poet Society
The Boy Who Died Wolf by Highly Suspect
Gigi's Recovery by The Murder Capital
Black and Gold by Eagle Eye Williamson
Unreal Unearth by Hozier
Life of a Kid in the Ghetto by Ed O.G. & Da Bulldogs
Time by Mr.Kitty

---

* DO NOT DO THIS IF YOU ARE BORROWING THIS BOOK OR
CHECKED IT OUT FROM A LIBRARY. Unless you are someone
stocking this book in a library. Then write the name of your library here,
because the same is true for you too.

In Times New Roman . . . by Queens of the Stone Age

Goodnight, God Bless, I Love U, Delete by Crosses

The Land Is Inhospitable and So Are We by Mitski

New Blue Sun by André 3000

Prelude to Ecstasy by The Last Dinner Party

Igor by Tyler the Creator

Why Does the Earth Give Us People to Love? by Kara Jackson

I Inside the Old Year Dying by PJ Harvey

Blonde by Frank Ocean

The Lamb as Effigy by Sprain

Most Known Unknown by Three 6 Mafia

Scaring the Hoes by JPEGMAFIA & Danny Brown

Stereo Mind Game by Daughter

Jar by Superheaven

Larger than Life by Brent Faiyaz

Put Ya Boots On by Double X Posse

Fruits of Nature by The U.M.C.'s

Sundial by Noname

Red Moon in Venus by Kali Uchis

nadie sabe lo que va a pasar mañana by Bad Bunny

The Right Man by D.K. Harrell

Ain't That Good News by Sam Cooke

Pain in My Heart by Otis Redding

Endless Affair by Ailbhe Reddy

The Valley of Vision by Manchester Orchestra

Black Rainbows by Corinne Bailey Rae

Shout-out to the activists and the rabble-rousers, the word-smiths and the painters, the musicians and the liberators. Like my man Howard Zinn said, "They have the guns, we have the poets. Therefore, we will win."

See y'all in the streets.

Author's Note

I began writing my Blaxit column for *The Root* in 2017, shortly after the inauguration of President Trump. My agent and I pitched this book shortly after the election of President Biden at the end of 2020, and we sold it a few days before Russia invaded Ukraine. I joined the world in watching journalists, diplomats, and statesmen remove every ounce of red tape to make way for immigrants from "civilized" countries* with "blue eyes and blonde hair,"† while African residents in Kyiv were tossed off trains. As my editor prepared this round of edits, I watched Australia undergo another contentious referendum to give Aboriginals and Torres Strait Islanders a voice in federal parliament, which seemed like, to quote my mother, "the gutter beneath" the bare minimum. Then, a 2023 report by the European Union Agency for Fundamental Rights called anti-Black racism worse now than it was six years ago, with Germany leading the way among European countries. Of the Black participants polled, 64 percent cited discrimination based on race, nearly doubled from the 33 percent it was twelve months before.[1]

As I prepare to submit this final round of edits to my publisher,

---

* This was said by CBS News senior correspondent in Kyiv Charlie D'Agata, who went on to say that Ukraine wasn't like Iraq or Afghanistan, where conflict instigated by Western intervention has been "raging for decades."

† This was said by Ukraine's former deputy general prosecutor David Sakvarelidze.

Congo is being ravaged by a genocide fueled by Western exploitation of natural resources, while Sudan is in the midst of a horrific war. NATO is leading EU countries in military exercises while peacemakers call for an end to its proxy wars. Countless people around the world are demanding a ceasefire to stop the genocide in Palestine and urging a meaningful conversation on the history of Western-backed settler-colonial projects. I'm preparing for my fourth protest this weekend, but I'm choosing my path to the demonstration carefully because a neo-Nazi group known as Der Dritte Weg (The Third Way) has been flyering my neighborhood and hanging out at a local Kneipe, or "bar," to recruit new members. They're emboldened now because the AfD—once considered a fringe group—is now the second-most-popular political party in all of Germany. And Chancellor Scholz, who leads the SPD, was featured in a cover story for *Der Spiegel*, the country's leading news magazine, calling for mass deportations of refugees to compete with his far-right rivals. Both are on a race to the bottom, and we're all being taken along for the ride.

A book, any book, is a snapshot in time—but the global events reflecting the unhealed wounds of the past make this project feel like a chronicle. While every author wants their book to stand the test of time, I'm worried that mine actually will. And there's still so much left unsaid that I want to include. Obviously, I have kept the events discussed close to my experience, but at times, this can seem like an arbitrary selection process. After all, isn't it all connected? I'm trying to tell you a story about *my* life, but there are many other stories that deserve your time and attention. I include now a nonexhaustive list of suggested subjects for further reading for people who are so inclined to continue learning, as I will. They underscore the interconnectivity of these events and how they will in all likelihood be used to rewrite the existence of Black, Brown, and Asian voices, immigrant or otherwise, if *we* choose to forget them.

Suggested Reading

JAPAN

The National Socialist Japanese Workers' Party

A small neo-Nazi group in Japan led by Yamada Kazunari, a Holocaust denier who praised Adolf Hitler and the 2001 terrorist attacks on the World Trade Center. He vocally criticized Germany's ban of the Nazi salute, an action he compared to an act of North Korea's. He is also friends with former internal affairs minister Takaichi Sanae, who served under Abe Shinzo.[1]

Zainichi Tokken o Yurusanai Shimin no Kai, or Zaitokukai

An ultranationalist, far-right, extremist organization that wants to end social welfare programs for Korean immigrants and descendants of Korean workers who were brought over to work in mines and factories during the imperial era. Japan's National Police Agency has cited the group as responsible for a rise in xenophobic rhetoric and sentiment. The Zaitokukai have described Korean people as "cockroaches" and "criminals" and made calls for them to be killed.[2]

Japan First Party

A far-right political party founded by Sakurai Makoto in 2016. In 2021, Sakurai ran for a gubernatorial election in Tokyo but only won with 2.92 percent of the vote. But several of his campaign policies included the prohibition of foreigners from receiving welfare, making the emperor the head of state once again, and installing a military that turned service into a civic duty. For context, article 9 of Japan's postwar constitution currently forbids the country from having an army for waging war. Although, there have been calls and efforts to change this.

Solidarity in Reparations

A group of Japanese Americans who were once forcibly removed to concentration camps on U.S. soil are now fighting for reparations for African Americans. This movement is being led by survivors of Executive Order 9066, including Ochi Kay and Tamaki Don, who were both imprisoned. When questioned about this solidarity, Tamaki said, "There's a recognition among Asian Americans that if it wasn't for the civil rights movement, where would we be?"[3]

Camp Majestic

An 24th Infantry Regiment was an all-Black unit in the U.S. Army that moved from Okinawa to mainland Japan in 1947 to Camp Majestic in Gifu, 270 miles southwest of Tokyo. Placed in a position of "privilege" over an occupied people, they were nonetheless subjected to racism from Japanese and American people, where "trans-Pacific interaction" led to deeply racialized and gendered depictions of Black masculinity. And this led Black GIs to "grapple" with concepts of military occupation, national belonging, and gender norms.[4]

The Manila Massacre

In 1945, the Imperial Japanese army slaughtered tens of thousands of Filipino men, women, and children in what has been described as "one of the worst massacres of World War II." The assault lasted for twenty-nine days and included burning people alive, rape, and tossing infants in the air then skewering them on bayonets. One gruesome account includes blindfolded men being led into a Manila home and decapitated with swords. Two men died from this method.[5] At least 100,000 unarmed Filipinos were killed—or one in ten Manila residents.[6]

CHICAGO*

Charlotte "Lottie" Wilson Jackson

The first African American person to attend the School of the Art Institute of Chicago, who also oversaw an exhibit of African American artists at the Pan-American Exposition in 1901. As an oil painter, sculptor, curator, and suffragist, she might be best known for her portrait of Abraham Lincoln with women's rights activist Sojourner Truth—which was accepted into the White House's permanent collection by Theodore Roosevelt. She also painted a portrait of Booker T. Washington, which resides at the Tuskegee Institute.[7]

The Homan Square Facility

In 2015, Chicago became the first U.S. city to offer reparations for racially motivated police violence at the Homan Square facility. This location had been described in an article by American journalist Spencer Ackerman as an "off-the-books interrogation warehouse ... The domestic equivalent of a CIA blacksite" where seven thousand men (six thousand of whom were Black) were "disappeared" and tortured.[8] This package included education on police torture in public schools, a formal apology from the Chicago

---

* I'm sticking with people and events whom you may not have heard about. Apologies to Oprah.

City Council, free college education for survivors and their families, $5.5 million in financial compensation, free counseling, and a
public memorial to torture survivors.[9]

Vina Fields

A former slave who began her brothel business as one of Chicago's
most sought-after madams. Vina began with eight Black women
and one white servant in the 1870s. At her prime, she managed
sixty to seventy women. And when the Panic of 1893 hit Chicago,
she used a portion of her profits to feed and clothe people who
were out of work and homeless.

Mariane Ibrahim

Born in New Caledonia, raised in Somaliland and then France, this
prominent contemporary-art gallerist opened her first flagship gallery, M.I.A., or Missing in Art, in Seattle in 2012. Her focus is on
artists from the African diaspora who have traditionally been underrepresented in fine art spaces. In 2019, she moved her gallery to
Chicago, an American city with one of the country's strongest Black
legacies, as her base. Then, she expanded to Paris—where artists
from the former French colonies have little to no representation—
and Mexico City. She now represents, among others, Amoako
Boafo, Zohra Opoku, Ayana V. Jackson, and Peter Uka.[10]

AUSTRALIA

The Apology to the Stolen Generation

On February 13, 2008, then prime minister Kevin Rudd made a
formal acknowledgment and apology to Aboriginal and Torres
Strait Islander peoples on behalf of the nation at Australian Parliament House. This was a landmark moment, in no small part

because the previous government led by conservative prime minister John Howard had refused to make any such declaration.[11]

The Mabo High Court Decision

On June 3, 1992, the Australian High Court officially recognized the land rights of the Meriam people, Traditional Owners of the Murray Island Group (including the Mer, Dauer, and Waier islands) of the Torres Strait. This was a significant judicial moment for two major reasons: it directly contradicted the colonial claim that Australia was terra nullius, or "land belonging to no one," which had been used to justify the colonial invasion and occupation of the land, and it acknowledged that Aboriginal people had been living in Australia for thousands of years in accordance with their own customs, practices, and laws. The five Meriam people who brought the case forward were Eddie Koiki Mabo, Reverend David Passi, Sam Passi, James Rice, and Celuia Mapo Sale.[12]

The Royal Commission into Aboriginal Deaths in Custody

On August 10, 1987, prime minister Bob Hawke announced the formation of a royal commission to investigate the causes of deaths of Aboriginal people in police custody for the first time in response to heightened public concern that they took place too often and with no explanation. And this led to a wider discussion on what drove underlying issues like alcoholism, jailing, and low education—treating the deaths as symptomatic of other issues that underscored systemic inequality. The final report was signed on April 15, 1991, and concluded that First Nations people had a higher chance of dying in custody because they had a higher change of *being* in custody, and that the overrepresentation of Aboriginal people had "origins in structural, systemic injustice to a disadvantaged minority rather than in a propensity in this group [Aboriginal people] to increased criminality." A total of 339 recommendations were made to reduce deaths and increase accountability, including better collaboration with Aboriginal communities, a process of reconciliation between Aboriginal and non-Aboriginal communities, and comprehensive coroner inquiries for every death in police custody. Another outcome was the establishment of a National Deaths in Police Custody Program at the Australian Institute for Criminology. But, since the release of the RCIADIC report in 1991, more than 455 Aboriginal and Torres Strait Islander peoples have died in custody. And First Nations peoples "continue to be among the most incarcerated peoples in the world." In fact, between 1991 and 2018, Aboriginal people have been dying in police custody at a significantly higher rate of 15.1 deaths per year. Between 1980 and 1989, that rate was 10.5 deaths per year.[13]

A National Day of Mourning

The twenty-sixth of January, or Australia Day, commemorates the arrival of the First Fleet, which began the country's colonization. In 1938, on the 150th anniversary of the First Fleet's arrival, Aboriginal Australians declared a Day of Mourning. A group of Aboriginal men and women gathered at Australian Hall in Sydney to move a resolution that acknowledged the "callous treatment" they had endured since the white invasion had begun; they also appealed for new laws that looked after their educational and social well-being, demanding that they be granted "full citizen status."[14] That same month, Aboriginal activists Jack Patten and William Ferguson published a pamphlet titled *Aborigines Claim Citizen Rights!*, calling Australia Day a "day of mourning," that commemorated 150 years of misery, degradation, persecution, and white invasion.[15] Certain passages list land rights as central to these efforts, including this one: "You are the New Australians,

but we are the Old Australians. We have in our arteries the blood
of the Original Australians, who have lived in this land for many
thousands of years."[16]

That following week, on January 31, a group of twenty Aboriginal people met with prime minister Joseph Lyons and his wife, as
well as several prominent cabinet members, to propose a national
policy for Aboriginal people that demanded, among other things,
Commonwealth control of all Aboriginal issues and equality in
labor, education, worker compensation, pensions, wages, and
land ownership.[17] And in 1940, the Australian Aborigines League
(AAL) also convinced many religious denominations to recognize
the Sunday before Australia Day as Aboriginal Sunday, to remind
the wider white communities of the unjust treatment endured by
Indigenous Australians. This continued until 1955, and in 1957,
Indigenous organizations, alongside local churches, with the assistance of state and federal government support, formed the National Aborigines Day Observance Committee (NADOC), which
is still active and now operates under the name NAIDOC.[18] All
of this began in 1938, a year that paved the way for the broader
demonstrations on Black Power that are discussed in this book.

The South Sea Islander Slave Trade

Between 1863 and 1904, between 55,000 and 62,500 people were abducted from more than eighty Pacific islands and
brought to Australia and forced to work as slaves on sugar and
cotton farms in Queensland and northern New South Wales.
They came from countries like Vanuatu, the Solomon Islands,
Papua New Guinea, Kiribati, and Tuvalu. This process of kid-
napping was known as blackbirding, and *blackbird* became
synonymous with *slave*. In 1901, there were ten thousand enslaved Pacific Islanders working in Australian cane fields, but
most were deported between 1904 and 1908 under the guise of

racially purifying Australia, which was largely implemented under the Pacific Island Labourers Act of 1901.[19]

The Australian Indigenous Voice Referendum of 2023

In 2023, a constitutional referendum was held—largely led by
Aboriginal activists—to approve an amendment to the Australian constitution that recognized Indigenous Australians by pre-
scribing a body called the Aboriginal and Torres Strait Islander
Voice to federal parliament that would make representations on
matters concerning First Nations Australians. On October 14, it
was rejected by a majority in every Australian state and territory.
Nationally, only 39.9 percent of people voted for the Voice. The
rest voted no. Many Australians who voted for the Voice describe
the result as a new kind of national shame that underscored the
racism First Nations people in the country had endured since it
was first invaded. But some Aboriginal activists voted against it,
not because they were opposed to representation, but because Aboriginal people make up 3 percent of the total population, and the
referendum placed the fate of Aboriginal people in the hands of
the other 97 percent. Lidia Thorpe, an Independent and Victoria's
first Aboriginal senator, called the referendum a "shame," saying
that the real focus should be on truth telling and creating a treaty
before any amendment to the constitution:

"The Constitution should not have happened without a treaty
with first peoples in this country. This is not our Constitution. This
was developed in 1901 by a bunch of old white fellas who had no
regard for black fellas."[20]

Street-Name Changes in Queensland

In 2016, in Brisbane's West End, street names were being changed
from Boundary to Boundless Street by an unknown street artist—
perhaps calling attention to the racist segregation that once existed

in the city. In the 1840s, boundary posts were used to label exclusion zones for Aboriginal people, to enforce curfews and segregate them from European arrivals. According to Aboriginal elder Sam Watson, "mounted police would use bull whips to move Blacks out of the area."[21] After the street signs were changed, there was a subsequent push to officially rename the streets, but some Aboriginal people felt this would sanitize history. As of 2023, they have not changed.[22]

GERMANY

National Socialist Underground Murders
Between 2000 and 2007, the German neo-Nazi group the National Socialiwst Underground, or NSU, committed a series of right-wing attacks, including nail-bomb attacks, burglaries, and racist murders, across Germany against people who operated kebab stands and small grocers, most of whom were ethnic Turks. For years, police argued that the murders were the result of Turkish-gang activity, while the German media derogatorily described the murders as *Döner-Morde*, or "kebab murders." The families of the victims were also routinely harassed with accusations of criminal activity. Only when a German police officer was killed did anyone begin to question this ongoing narrative. Several high-ranking neo-Nazi figures received "large sums of money from the state," implying the involvement of German intelligence agencies who may have colluded with the NSU in these attacks. In 2018, five criminals and three accomplices were convicted and sentenced for the crimes. But the stain on German law enforcement and media remains.[23]

Day X
In 2018, a foiled 2017 plot by the Kommando Spezialkräfte, or Special Command Forces of the German Armed Forces

(Bundeswehr), targeting several left-learning politicians for assassination was revealed. The primary instigator for this plot was Franco A., a German soldier who planned to frame the attacks on asylum seekers.[24]

Eugenics and Ableism

The eugenics movement that swept across the West in the early twentieth century is considered to be the foundation of systemic ableism, which has impacted everything from immigration law to reproductive rights. While not specifically covered in this book, they are also interlocking systems of oppression. For that reason, I recommend several important sources that can be used to understand the connection between them: the 2021 paper "Confronting Eugenics Means Confronting Its Ableist Roots" by Robyn M. Powell (when last I checked, it's available to read for free online), the *You're Wrong About* podcast episode "Eugenics with Eric Michael Garcia" by Michael Hobbes and Sarah Marshall (also free), and the 2018 book *Unlearning Eugenics: Sexuality, Reproduction, and Disability in Post-Nazi Europe* by Dagmar Herzog. If you're unsure of where to begin, start there.

Stolpersteine for Afro-German Victims of National Socialism Laid in Berlin Sidewalks in 2023

Benedikt Gambé and Charlotte Rettig

Benedikt Gambé and Charlotte Rettig were artists who lived together in Berlin. Gambé was born in Cameroon in 1904, and a colonial officer brought him to Germany after the end of World War I. He was a musician and played drums in a band, performing under the stage name James Dixon during the Weimar Republic era. Charlotte Rettig was born in Strasburg in the Uckermark in 1913. When the Nazis rose to power, she was not allowed to complete her vocational training. Like Gambé, Rettig worked the Deutschen Afrika-Schau, or German Africa Show, a continuation of the original human zoos where Afro-Germans performed in stereotypical and exoticized roles that upheld German colonial propaganda. Neither were allowed to pursue other professions. In 1937, Benedikt Gambé was admitted to the Wittenau sanatoriums, then transferred to the Wahrendorff clinics in Lower Saxony. He died there in August 1940; the circumstances of his death remain unclear. Charlotte Rettig was able to flee to Copenhagen, and she survived National Socialism. Their Stolpersteine rest at Fuggerstraße 20 in the Berlin district of Tempelhof-Schöneberg.[25]

Josef and Stephanie Boholle (with their child Josefa Luise; her husband, Cornelis; and their son, Peter van der Want)
Josef Bohinge Boholle was born in Cameroon in 1880 and moved to Berlin in 1896 to participate in the first German Colonial Exhibition. Josef began an apprenticeship with an amber master in Gdańsk before moving to Berlin, where he worked as a carpenter. He and his partner, Stephanie, married in 1909. Stephanie came from Lodz and worked as a housekeeper. The couple had three children: Josefa Luise, born in 1907; Rudolf Bohinge, born in 1910; and Paul Artur, born in 1911. In 1928, the Boholle family received German citizenship—which rarely happened for Afro-German people. Rudolf and Paul grew up, got married, and started their own families. During the 1930s, the Bohollles' three children worked in show business but found their work opportunities increasingly restricted by National Socialism. In 1935, their citizenship status came under scrutiny. Due to what are likely extraordinary circumstances, the family was able to retain their status as German citizens. In 1939, Josefa had a child with Dutch vaudeville artist Cornelis van der Want, and they married

in August 1943, even though this violated certain provisions of the Nuremberg Laws.

In March 1943, their house was destroyed by an Allied bomb attack. Josefa, Cornelis, and their son, Peter, moved with Josefa's mother, Stephanie, to Bromberg (Bydgoszcz, Poland), where Cornelis worked as a stagehand. It doesn't appear that Josef went with them, and he might have already passed away by then. In 1944, Cornelis and Josefa were arrested in Bromberg by the Gestapo and were sent to Stutthof concentration camp. A few weeks later, Stephanie was also arrested. Her four-year-old grandson, Peter, was left alone in the family apartment, where neighbors looked after him.

Stephanie Boholle died, either in the Gestapo prison in Bromberg or in Stutthof concentration camp. Cornelis, Josefa, and their son, Peter, survived. Josefa died in 1955 from chronic illnesses caused by her time in Stutthof concentration camp. Her brothers, Paul and Rudolf Boholle, survived National Socialism. The Stolpersteine for Josef and Stephanie Boholle, along with the Stolpersteine for Josefa, Cornelis, and Peter van der Want rest at Alte Jakobstraße 134 in the Berlin district of Friedrichshain-Kreuzberg.[26]

Zoya Gertrud Aqua-Kaufman and her son Hans Joachim Aqua-Kaufman

Zoya Gertrud Aqua-Kaufmann was born in Berlin on November 28, 1918, to Antonie Kaufmann and Thomas Manga Akwa. When the Nazis took power, she had to leave school and was denied training as a pediatrician. She worked as a dancer but was no longer eligible for gainful employment after 1939. In 1941, Zoya went into hiding to avoid forced sterilization, moving first residences and then countries. In November 1944, she was reported in Prague and imprisoned in Pankrác prison with her three-year-old son, Hans Joachim. They were both released on May 13, 1945, after the end of World War II. Their Stolpersteine rest at Friedrich-Wilhelm-Straße 8 in the Berlin district of Tempelhof-Schöneberg.[27]/*

Ludwig M'Bebe Mpessa and Erika Emilie Mpessa née Diek
Erika Diek was the daughter of a Cameroonian immigrant named Mandenga Diek, who moved to Germany in 1891. At the end of the Second World War, she lived with her first husband, Ludwig M'bebe Mpessa, a political activist and a successful actor who performed under the stage name Louis Brody. Ludwig performed in more than twenty colonial-propaganda and antisemitic films, where his roles were to affirm the inferiority of Black people. From 1946, Erika Diek lived in Tempelhof, where she coordinated with her sister to create a space for Black people to meet and network. Their Stolpersteine rest at Gaudystraße 5 in the Berlin district of Tempelhof-Schöneberg.[28]

Oury Jalloh
In 2005, an asylum seeker from Sierra Leone named Oury Jalloh burned to death under what was described as "mysterious circumstances." Police claimed Jalloh set fire to his own mattress. But his hands were tied to either side of the mattress, and no lighter was found on him when he was initially searched. A report by an arson investigator from Ireland was released in 2013 stating that the presence of accelerants suggested that Jalloh was murdered.[29]

---

* After being released, Zoya wrote a handwritten Lebenslauf (like a CV or personal data sheet) of her experiences, which included the following statement: "In 1934 I was thrown out of my apartment because it was needed by the Nazis. In 1936 I was thrown out of school because, as a non-Aryan, I was no longer worthy of attending a German secondary school. In 1936 I was made stateless because I was not worthy of being German ... My son was born in 1941. We had to live illegally to avoid being prosecuted for racial defilement [Rassenschande]."

Years of legal proceedings followed. One officer was acquitted in 2008 but later convicted of involuntary manslaughter in 2012, for which he was fined €10,800. A 2019 medical report requested by Jalloh's family found he may have been tortured before his death, citing broken ribs and fractures to his septum, as well as the base of his skull.[30]

Notes

Preface

1. Nicholas Lemann, *The Promised Land: The Great Black Migration and How It Changed America* (New York: Vintage Books, 1992).
2. Joe William Trotter Jr., "The Great Migration," *OAH Magazine of History* 17, no. 1 (October 2002): 31–33; James N. Gregory, *The Southern Diaspora: How the Great Migrations of Black and White Southerners Transformed America* (Chapel Hill: The University of North Carolina Press, 2006).
3. Frederick Douglass, "Frederick Douglass in Ireland," *The Journal of Negro History* 8, no. 1 (1923): 102–107.
4. Frederick Douglass, "The Rights of Women," *The North Star* (Rochester, New York), July 28, 1848.
5. Yasser K. R. Aman, "A Reading in the Poetry of the Afro-German May Ayim from Dual Inheritance Theory Perspective: The Impact of Audre Lorde on May Ayim," *International Journal of Arts and Sciences* 9, no. 3 (January 25, 2016): 27.
6. Paul Finkelman, "Dred Scott v. Sandford," in *The Public Debate over Controversial Supreme Court Decisions*, ed. Melvin I. Urofsky (Washington, D.C.: CQ Press, 2005), 24–33.
7. Fatima El-Tayeb, "Blackness and Its (Queer) Discontents," in *Remapping Black Germany: New Perspectives on Afro-German History, Politics, and Culture*, ed. Sara Lennox (Amherst: University of Massachusetts Press, 2016), 243–58.

1. Stick with the Devil You Know

1. Carole Marks, "Black Workers and the Great Migration North," *Phylon* 46, no. 2 (1985): 148–161.

2. Trevor M. Kollmann and Price V. Fishback, "The New Deal, Race, and Home Ownership in the 1920s and 1930s," *American Economic Review* 101, no. 3 (May 2011): 366–370.

3. The Myth of Homogeneity and the Ballad of Yasuke

1. Tsujiuchi Makoto, "Historical Context of Black Studies in Japan," *Hitotsubashi Journal of Social Studies* 30, no. 2 (December 1998): 95–100.
2. Tsujiuchi, "Historical Context of Black Studies in Japan."
3. David Wright, "The Use of Race and Racial Perceptions Among Asians and Blacks: The Case of the Japanese and African Americans," *Hitotsubashi Journal of Social Studies* 30, no. 2 (December 1998): 135–52.
4. Tsujiuchi, "Historical Context of Black Studies in Japan."
5. Ōta Gyūichi, *The Chronicle of Lord Nobunaga* (Leiden: Brill, 2011); Tsujiuchi, "Historical Context of Black Studies in Japan."
6. Jacquelyne Germain, "Who Was Yasuke, Japan's First Black Samurai?" *Smithsonian Magazine*, January 10, 2023, www.smith sonianmag.com/history/who-was-yasuke-japans-first-black-samurai -180981416.
7. Ibid.
8. Ibid.
9. Thomas Lockley and Geoffrey Girard, *African Samurai: The True Story of Yasuke, a Legendary Black Warrior in Feudal Japan* (New York: Hanover Square Press, 2019), 64–65.
10. Morikawa Suzuko, "*Nihonjin to Afurikakei Amerikajin* (Japanese and African Americans: Historical Aspects of Their Relations)," *The Journal of African American History* 91, no. 3 (Summer 2006): 339–41.
11. John Russell, "Race and Reflexivity: The Black Other in Contemporary Japanese Mass Culture," *Cultural Anthropology* 6, no. 1 (February 1991): 3–25.
12. Endō Shūsaku, *Kuronbō* (Nigger) (Tokyo: Kadokawa Bunko, 1973), 20–21.
13. Wagatsuma Hiroshi, "The Social Perception of Skin Color in Japan," *Daedalus* 96, no. 2 (Spring 1967): 407–43.
14. Murasaki Shikibu, *The Tale of Genji* (North Clarendon, VT: Tuttle Publishing, 2018); Wagatsuma, "Social Perception."

15. Murasaki, *Nikki* (Tokyo, 1957), 182–84; Wagatsuma, "Social Perception."
16. Ibid.
17. Ibid.
18. The Editors of Encyclopaedia Britannica, "burakumin," Encyclopedia Britannica, accessed November 29, 2023, www.britannica.com/topic/burakumin.
19. Ibid; Russell, "Race and Reflexivity."
20. Wagatsuma, "Social Perception."
21. Wright, "Use of Race and Racial Perceptions."
22. Wagatsuma, "Social Perception."
23. Ibid.
24. Ibid.
25. Ibid.
26. Russell, "Race and Reflexivity."
27. Ibid.
28. Ibid.
29. Roger Pineau, ed., *The Japan Expedition, 1852–1854: The Personal Journal of Commodore Matthew C. Perry* (Washington, D.C.: Smithsonian Institution Press, 1968), xix, 241.
30. Wright, "Use of Race and Racial Perceptions."
31. Russell, "Race and Reflexivity."
32. Wagatsuma Hiroshi and Yoneyama Toshinao, *Henken no Kozo* (The Structure of Prejudice) (Tokyo: NHK Books, 1980).
33. Russell, "Race and Reflexivity"; The Editors of Encyclopaedia Britannica, "burakumin."
34. Tsujiuchi, "Historical Context."
35. Ibid.
36. Charles Darwin, *The Descent of Man, and Selection in Relation to Sex* (London: William Clowes and Sons, 1871).
37. Ishibashi Mari, "Review: The Myth of Japaneseness," *The Review of Politics* 63, no. 4 (Autumn 2001): 831–34, www.jstor.org/stable/1408869.
38. Ayelet Zohar, "Introduction: Race and Empire in Meiji Japan," *The Asia-Pacific Journal: Japan Focus* 18, no. 20 (October 15, 2020): 1–12.
39. Kato Tsunehiko, "The History of Black Studies in Japan: Origin and Development," *Journal of Black Studies* 44, no. 8 (November 2013): 829–45.
40. Zohar, "Introduction."

41. Fukurai Hiroshi and Alice Yang, "The History of Japanese Racism, Japanese American Redress, and the Dangers Associated with Government Regulation of Hate Speech," *Hastings Constitutional Law Quarterly* 45, no. 3 (2018): 533.
42. Ibid
43. Ibid.
44. Ibid.
45. Chatani Sayaka, "How to Address the Racism at the Heart of Japan-South Korea Tensions," United States Institute of Peace, January 17, 2023, www.usip.org/publications/2023/01/how-address-racism -heart-japan-south-korea-tensions.
46. Fukurai and Yang, "History of Japanese Racism."
47. Chatani, "How to Address the Racism."
48. Kate E. Taylor, "Japan: Colonization and Settlement," in *The Encyclopedia of Global Human Migration*, ed. Immanuel Ness (Hoboken: Blackwell Publishing, Ltd., 2013).
49. Ogawa Shuko, "The Difficulty of Apology: Japan's Struggle with Memory and Guilt," *Harvard International Review* 22, no. 3 (Fall 2000): 42–46, www.jstor.org/stable/42762634.
50. Yōko Hayashi, "Issues Surrounding the Wartime 'Comfort Women,'" *Review of Japanese Culture and Society* 11/12 (December 1999–2000): 54–65, www.jstor.org/stable/42800182.
51. Beverly Milner (Lee) Bisland, Jimin Kim, and Sunghee Shin, "Teaching about the Comfort Women during World War II and the Use of Personal Stories of the Victims," *Education About Asia* 24, no. 3 (Winter 2019).
52. Yōko, "Issues Surrounding the Wartime 'Comfort Women.'"
53. Julie McCarthy, "PHOTOS: Why These World War II Sex Slaves Are Still Demanding Justice," NPR, December 4, 2020, www.npr.org /sections/goatsandsoda/2020/12/04/940819094/photos-there -still-is-no-comfort-for-the-comfort-women-of-the-philippines.
54. David Brudnoy, "Japan's Experiment in Korea," *Monumenta Nipponica* 25, no. 1/2 (1970): 155–95.
55. Taylor, "Japan: Colonization and Settlement."
56. Report of the Special Rapporteur on Contemporary Forms of Racism, Racial Discrimination, Xenophobia and Related Intolerance, Doudou Diène, on his mission to Japan (3-11 July 2005).
57. Ibid.
58. Yamamoto Kana, "The Myth of 'Nihonjinron,' Homogeneity of Ja-

pan and Its Influence on the Society" (working paper, Centre for Ethnicity and Racism Studies, University of Leeds, Leeds, 2015).

59. S. Asano, "Structure and Change of 'Mono Ethnicity Myth' in Japan" (working paper, Kobe University, Kobe, 1993).

60. Yamamoto, "Myth of 'Nihonjinron.'"

61. Amnesty International, *Japan: Submission to the United Nations Human Rights Committee: 111th Session of the Human Rights Committee (7–25 July 2014)* (London: Amnesty International Publications, 2014).

62. David McNeil, "The Senior Political Adviser Who Advocates Racial Segregation in the 21st Century," *indy100*, February 14, 2015, www.indy100.com/news/the-senior-political-adviser-who-advocates-racial-segregation-in-the-21st-century-7259456.

63. "Bad Timing," *The Economist*, February 20, 2015, www.economist.com/asia/2015/02/20/bad-timing.

64. McNeil, "Senior Political Adviser."

65. Jake Adelstein, "South Africa Scolds Japanese Author for Endorsing Apartheid," *The Daily Beast*, last updated April 14, 2017, www.thedailybeast.com/south-africa-scolds-japanese-author-for-endorsing-apartheid.

66. "Japan: UN Rights Expert Warns of Serious Threats to the Independence of the Press," United Nations Human Rights Office of the High Commissioner, www.ohchr.org/en/press-releases/2016/04/japan-un-rights-expert-warns-serious-threats-independence-press.

67. Osaki Tomohiro, "Diet Passes Japan's First Law to Curb Hate Speech," *The Japan Times*, May 24, 2016, www.japantimes.co.jp/news/2016/05/24/national/social-issues/diet-passes-japans-first-law-curb-hate-speech.

68. Japan NGO Network for the Elimination of Racial Discrimination (ERD Net), *Follow-up Information from Civil Society—Japan*, April 2020, imadr.org/wordpress/wp-content/uploads/2020/06/ERD-Net_Joint-Civil-Society-Follow-up-Report_CERD_2020.pdf.

7. Problematizing the "Meaning" of Japan

1. Stephanie Shaw, "An Alternative View of Du Bois's Talented Tenth," *Black Perspectives*, February 19, 2018, www.aaihs.org/an-alternative-view-of-du-boiss-talented-tenth.

2. Juan Battle and Earl Wright II, "W.E.B. Du Bois's Talented Tenth:

A Quantitative Assessment," *Journal of Black Studies* 32, no. 6 (July 2002): 654–72, www.jstor.org/stable/3180968.

3. William Edward Burghardt Du Bois, *The Souls of Black Folk: Essays and Sketches* (Chicago: A. C. McClurg & Company, 1903).

4. Du Bois, *The Souls of Black Folk.*

5. Battle and Wright, "W.E.B. Du Bois's Talented Tenth."

6. Reginald Kearney, "The Pro-Japanese Utterances of W.E.B. Du Bois," *Contributions in Black Studies* 13, no. 1 (1995).

7. Mark Phelan, "'Keep California White'—James D. Phelan and the 'Yellow Peril' race controversy," *History Ireland* 26, no. 4 (July/August 2018): 34–35.

8. Kato, "History of Black Studies in Japan."

9. Kearney, "Pro-Japanese Utterances."

10. Ibid.

11. Ibid.

12. W. E. Burghardt Du Bois, "The Meaning of Japan (1937)," *CR: The New Centennial Review* 12, no. 1 (Spring 2012): 233–55, www.jstor .org/stable/41949774.

13. Kearney, "Pro-Japanese Utterances."

14. Ibid.

15. Du Bois, "Meaning of Japan."

16. Kenneth C. Barnes, "Inspiration from the East: Black Arkansans Look to Japan," *The Arkansas Historical Quarterly* 69, no. 3 (Autumn 2010): 201–19, www.jstor.org/stable/23046112.

17. Kearney, "The Pro-Japanese Utterances."

18. Rachel Pawlowicz and Walter E. Grunden, "Teaching Atrocities: The Holocaust and Unit 731 in the Secondary School Curriculum," *The History Teacher* 48, no. 2 (February 2015): 271–94, www.jstor .org/stable/43264405.

19. Kearney, "Pro-Japanese Utterances."

20. Ibid.

21. Ibid.

22. Pawlowicz and Grunden, "Teaching Atrocities"; Keiichi Tsuneishi, "Unit 731 and the Japanese Imperial Army's biological warfare program," *The Asia-Pacific Journal: Japan Focus* 3, no. 11 (November 24, 2005), apjjf.org/-Tsuneishi-Keiichi/2194/article.html.

23. Pawlowicz and Grunden, "Teaching Atrocities"; William H. Cunliffe, *Select Documents on Japanese War Crimes and Japanese Biological Warfare, 1934-2006,* National Archives, 2007.

24. Gerhard Baader, Susan E. Lederer, Morris Low, Florian Schmaltz,

and Alexander V. Schwerin, "Pathways to Human Experimentation, 1933–1945: Germany, Japan, and the United States," *Osiris* 20, no. 2 (2005): 205–31, www.jstor.org/stable/3655257; Jonathan Watts, "Japan 'bombed city with plague,'" *The Guardian*, January 24, 2001, www.theguardian.com/world/2001/jan/25/jonathanwatts.

25. Baader, et al., "Pathways to Human Experimentation."
26. Pawlowicz and Grunden, "Teaching Atrocities."
27. Kearney, "Pro-Japanese Utterances."
28. Ibid.
29. Reginald Kearney, "Langston Hughes in Japanese Translation," *The Langston Hughes Review* 4, no. 2 (Fall 1985): 27–9, www.jstor.org/stable/26432726.
30. Kato, "The History of Black Studies in Japan"; Kearney, "Langston Hughes in Japanese Translation."
31. Kato, "History of Black Studies in Japan."
32. Kearney, "Pro-Japanese Utterances."
33. Ibid.
34. Ibid.
35. Du Bois, "Meaning of Japan."
36. Ibid.
37. Kato, "History of Black Studies in Japan."
38. Tsujiuchi, "Historical Context of Black Studies in Japan."
39. Barnes, "Inspiration from the East."
40. Tsujiuchi, "Historical Context of Black Studies in Japan."
41. Barnes, "Inspiration from the East."
42. Ibid.
43. Tsujiuchi, "Historical Context of Black Studies in Japan."
44. Ibid.
45. Ibid.
46. Mitsukawa Kametarō, *Kokujin Mondai* (1925); Tsujiuchi, "Historical Context of Black Studies in Japan."
47. Barnes, "Inspiration from the East."
48. Mohammed Elnaiem, "Black Radicalism's Complex Relationship with Japanese Empire," *JSTOR Daily*, July 18, 2018, daily.jstor.org/black-radicalisms-complex-relationship-with-japanese-empire.
49. Barnes, "Inspiration from the East."
50. Ernest Allen Jr., "When Japan Was 'Champion of the Darker Races': Satokata Takahashi and the Flowering of Black Messianic Nationalism," *The Black Scholar* 24, no. 1 (Winter 1994): 23–46.
51. Elnaiem, "Black Radicalism's Complex Relationship."

52. Allen, "When Japan Was 'Champion.'"
53. Elnaiem, "Black Radicalism's Complex Relationship."
54. Barnes, "Inspiration from the East"; Allen, "When Japan Was 'Champion.'"
55. Ibid.
56. Ibid.
57. James Weldon Johnson, *Along This Way: The Autobiography of James Weldon Johnson* (New York: The Viking Press, 1933).
58. Amy Sommers, "Ready, Willing and Able: James Weldon Johnson at the Institute of Pacific Relations' 1929 Conference in Kyoto, Japan," *BlackPast*, January 29, 2022, www.blackpast.org /global-african-history/perspectives-global-african-history/ready -willing-and-able-james-weldon-johnson-at-the-institute-of-pacific -relations-1929-conference-in-kyoto-japan.
59. Kearney, "Pro-Japanese Utterances."
60. *Pittsburgh Courier*, March 27,1937; W. E. B. Du Bois, "A Chronicle of Race Relations," *Phylon* 1 (4th Quarter, 1940): 378; W. E. B. Du Bois, "A Chronicle of Race Relations," *Phylon* 2 (2nd Quarter, 1941): 183; *Chicago Defender*, September 26, 1942.
61. Connie Y. Chiang, "Imprisoned Nature: Toward an Environmental History of the World War II Japanese American Incarceration," *Environmental History* 15, no. 2 (April 2010): 236–67, www.jstor.org /stable/20749671.
62. "Behind the Wire," Library of Congress, accessed October 2, 2023, www.loc.gov/classroom-materials/immigration/japanese/behind -the-wire.
63. History.com Editors, "Japanese Internment Camps," History.com, October 29, 2009, www.history.com/topics/world-war-ii/japanese -american-relocation.
64. Elnaiem, "Black Radicalism's Complex Relationship."
65. Ibid.
66. Allen, "When Japan Was 'Champion.'"
67. Elnaiem, "Black Radicalism's Complex Relationship."
68. Allen, "When Japan Was 'Champion.'"
69. Ibid.
70. Ann Lyon Ritchie, "Historian Examines Japan's Unexpected Alliance with Nazi Germany," Carnegie Mellon University, November 1, 2019, www.cmu.edu/dietrich/history/news/2019/law-book.html.
71. Marc Gallicchio, *The African American Encounter with Japan and*

China: Black Internationalism in Asia, 1895–1945 (Chapel Hill: The University of North Carolina Press, 2003).
72. Ibid.
73. Ibid.
74. Ibid.

8. Problematizing the "Meaning" of Solidarity

1. Becky Little, "The Atomic Bomb's First Victims Were in New Mexico," History.com, last updated July 28, 2023, www.history.com /news/atomic-bomb-test-victims-new-mexico-downwinders.
2. Little, "Atomic Bomb's First Victims."
3. Little, "Atomic Bomb's First Victims."
4. Wada Kayomi, "Black Studies Association *(Kokujin Kenkyu no Kai)* of Japan," *BlackPast*, December 29, 2008, www.blackpast.org /global-african-history/black-studies-association-kokujin-kenkyu -no-kai-japan.
5. Kato, "History of Black Studies in Japan."
6. Wada, "Black Studies Association."
7. Ibid.
8. Kato, "History of Black Studies in Japan."
9. Ibid.
10. Ibid.
11. Ibid.
12. Kim Kyung Hoon, "Black Lives Matter protesters march through Tokyo," *Reuters*, June 14, 2020, www.reuters.com/article/idUSK BN23L0FY.
13. Kim, "Black Lives Matter protesters march through Tokyo."
14. Cara Giaimo, "Why MLK Day Is a Big Deal in Hiroshima," *Atlas Obscura*, January 18, 2016, www.atlasobscura.com/articles/mlk -day-hiroshima-japan.

9. That Inescapable Delicious Feeling

1. Kalervo Oberg, *Culture Shock* (Indianapolis: The Bobbs-Merrill Company, 1954); Deirdre A. Meintel, "Strangers, Homecomers and Ordinary Men," *Anthropological Quarterly* 46, no. 1 (January 1973): 47–58.
2. Meintel, "Strangers, Homecomers and Ordinary Men."

3. Alfred Schuetz, "The Homecomer," *American Journal of Sociology* 50, no. 5 (March 1945): 369–76.
4. Meintel, "Strangers, Homecomers and Ordinary Men."
5. Jessica B. Harris, "A Way With Words and a Spice Rack," *The New York Times*, June 2, 2014, www.nytimes.com/2014/06/04/dining /recalling-maya-angelous-love-of-cooking.html.

11. An Australian Werewolf in America

1. Erica Chito Childs, "Looking Behind the Stereotypes of the 'Angry Black Woman': An Exploration of Black Women's Responses to Interracial Relationships," *Gender & Society* 19, no. 4 (August 2005): 544–61.
2. Gretchen Livingston and Anna Brown, "Trends and Patterns in Intermarriage," Pew Research Center, May 18, 2017, www.pew research.org/social-trends/2017/05/18/1-trends-and-patterns-in -intermarriage.
3. Sharon Sassler and Kara Joyner, "Social Exchange and the Progression of Sexual Relationships in Emerging Adulthood," *Social Forces* 90, no. 1 (September 2011): 223–45.

12. The Blackface, the Minstrel, and the Golliwog

1. "Blackface: The Birth of an American Stereotype," National Museum of African American History & Culture, accessed July 11, 2023, nmaahc.si.edu/explore/stries/blackface-birth-american -stereotype.
2. Richard L. Hughes, "Minstrel Music: The Sounds and Images of Race in Antebellum America," *The History Teacher* 40, no. 1 (November 2006): 27–43, www.jstor.org/stable/30036937.
3. Hughes, "Minstrel Music."
4. Richard Waterhouse, "The Internationalisation of American Popular Culture in the Nineteenth Century: The Case of the Minstrel Show," *Australasian Journal of American Studies* 4, no. 1 (July 1985): 1–11, www.jstor.org/stable/41053377.
5. Waterhouse, "Internationalisation of American Popular Culture."
6. Tracy C. Davis, "Acting Black, 1824: Charles Mathews's *Trip to America*," *Theatre Journal* (May 2011): 163–89.
7. Ibid.
8. Ibid.

9. Waterhouse, "Internationalisation of American Popular Culture."

10. Ibid.

11. Jack Latimore, "Blak, Black, Blackfulla: Language is important, but it can be tricky," *The Sydney Morning Herald*, August 30, 2021, www.smh.com.au/national/blak-black-blackfulla-language-is-important-but-it-can-be-tricky-20210826-p58lzg.html.

12. Peter M. Sales, "White Australia, Black Americans: A Melbourne Incident, 1928," *The Australian Quarterly* 46, no. 4 (December 1974): 74–81.

13. Donna Leslie, "Loved and Despised: Imaging the Golliwog Doll in the Australian Context," *Journal of Australian Indigenous Issues* 21, no. 1–2 (June 2018): 61–79.

14. Fiona Probyn, "The White Father: Denial, Paternalism and Community," *Cultural Studies Review* 9, no. 1 (September 13, 2003): 60–76.

15. Clemence Due, "'Aussie Humour' or Racism? *Hey Hey It's Saturday* and the Denial of Racism in Online Responses to News Media Articles," *PLATFORM: Journal of Media and Communication* 3, no. 1 (March 2011): 36–53.

16. Ibid.

17. Ibid.

18. Ibid.

19. Jens Korff, "Blackface & Minstrel Shows," Creative Spirits, last updated March 22, 2022, www.creativespirits.info/aboriginalculture/arts/black-face-minstrel-shows; Benjamin Miller, "'Come Be Off with You': White Spatial Control in the Representation of Aboriginality in Early Australian Drama," *The Journal of Commonwealth Literature* 52, no. 2 (October 14, 2015): 365–81.

20. Miller, "'Come be off with you.'"

21. Margaret Williams, *Australia on the Popular Stage, 1829–1929: An Historical Entertainment in Six Acts* (Oxford: Oxford University Press, 1983).

22. Jirra Lulla Harvey, "Blackface Not Funny," *Koori Mail*, October 21, 2009.

23. Jens Korff, "Trooper O'Brien," Creative Spirits, last updated December 21, 2018, www.creativespirits.info/resources/movies/trooper-obrien.

24. Korff, "Blackface & Minstrel Shows."

25. "Australia: Aboriginal and Torres Strait Islander Population Summary," Australian Bureau of Statistics, July 1, 2022, www.abs.gov.au/articles/australia-aboriginal-and-torres-strait-islander-population-summary; "Prisoners in Australia," Australian Bureau of Statistics,

January 25, 2024, www.abs.gov.au/statistics/people/crime-and-jus tice/prisoners-australia/latest-release.

26. Ryan Broderick, "Meltdown On Facebook Over Whether Or Not It Was Racist For Two Men To Wear Blackface," *BuzzFeed*, February 1, 2016, www.buzzfeed.com/ryanhatesthis/outrage-after-a -photo-leaks-of-two-men-in-full-blackface-at.

27. Miller, "'Come be off with you.'"

28. Dr. David Pilgrim, "The Golliwog Caricature," Jim Crow Museum, November 2000, jimcrowmuseum.ferris.edu/golliwog/home page.htm.

29. Robin Bernstein, *Racial Innocence: Performing American Childhood from Slavery to Civil Rights* (New York: NYU Press, 2011).

30. Bernstein, *Racial Innocence*.

31. Robert M. MacGregor, "The Golliwog: Innocent Doll to Symbol of Racism," in *Advertising & Popular Culture: Studies in Variety and Versatility*, ed. Sammy R. Danna (Madison: Popular Press, 1992), 124–32; Pilgrim, "Golliwog Caricature."

32. Ibid.

33. Ibid.

34. Enid Blyton, *The Three Golliwogs* (Sydney: Angus and Robertson, 1950), 51; Pilgrim, "Golliwog Caricature."

35. Erik Lords, "Keeping Jim Crow Alive: A Ferris State University museum aims to use the pain of racist and offensive materials to educate and foster racial healing," *Black Issues in Higher Education* 19, no. 8 (2002): 28, jimcrowmuseum.ferris.edu/links/newslist /pdfs-docs/issues.pdf.

36. Franklin Green, *Ten Little Nigger Boys went out to dine; One choked his little self, and then there were Nine.*, 1869, jstor.org/stable/com munity.32019337.

37. Enid Blyton, *Five Go to Smuggler's Top* (London: Hodder & Stoughton, 1945).

38. Brenda Haas, "Enid Blyton Fans React to 'Racist' Label," *DW*, June 18, 2021, www.dw.com/en/enid-blyton-fans-react-to-racist-label/a-5795 4638.

39. Nur Ibrahim, "The History of Golliwogs and Why They're Considered Racist," *Snopes*, April 20, 2023, www.snopes.com/articles /464628/golliwog-racist-history.

40. David Wilton, *Word Myths: Debunking Linguistic Urban Legends* (New York: Oxford University Press, 2004).

41. M. W. Daly, "The British Occupation, 1882–1922," in *The Cambridge*

History of Egypt, ed. M. W. Daly (Cambridge: Cambridge University Press, 1998), 239–51.

42. Donna Varga and Rhoda Zuk, "Golliwogs and Teddy Bears: Embodied Racism in Children's Popular Culture," *The Journal of Popular Culture* 46, no. 3 (June 13, 2013): 647–71.

43. Varga and Zuk, "Golliwogs and Teddy Bears."

44. B&T Magazine, "'Golliwog' Retail Display Has Toowoomba Slammed As 'Most Racist City In Australia,'" B&T, December 2, 2016, www.bandt.com.au/golliwog-retail-display-toowoomba-slammed-racist-city-australia.

45. Anna Hartley, "'Ashamed to be Australian': Tourist's outrage sparks Golliwog doll debate," ABC News, last updated February 2, 2018, www.abc.net.au/news/2018-02-03/should-golliwog-dolls-exist-in-australia-in-2018/9391188.

46. Ibid.

47. Ibid.

13. Always Was, Always Will Be

1. "Congress of Racial Equality Organizes Journey of Reconciliation," SNCC Digital Gateway, accessed July 14, 2023, snccdigital.org/events/cores-journey-of-reconciliation.

2. "Congress of Racial Equality."

3. "Congress of Racial Equality."

4. History.com Editors, "Freedom Riders," History.com, last updated January 20, 2022, www.history.com/topics/black-history/freedom-rides.

5. History.com Editors, "Freedom Riders."

6. Gary Foley, "Black Power in Redfern 1968–1972" (Victoria University, 2001), vuir.vu.edu.au/27009/1/Black%20power%20in%20Redfern%201968-1972.pdf.

7. Foley, "Black Power in Redfern."

8. "Students Lead 'Freedom Ride' Through NSW Towns," Deadly Story, deadlystory.com/page/culture/history/Students_lead_%E2%80%98Freedom_Rides%E2%80%99_through_segregated_NSW_towns. Accessed: 20 September 2023.

9. "Students Lead 'Freedom Ride.'"

10. "Race Tour Bus Driver Walks Out," *The Australian*, February 22, 1965; Foley, "Black Power in Redfern."

11. Tillman Durdin, "Sydney Students on Freedom Ride to Aid

Natives," *The New York Times*, February 26, 1965, www.nytimes
.com/1965/02/26/archives/sydney-students-on-freedom-ride-to
-aid-natives.html.

12. "The 1967 Referendum," AIATSIS, last updated November 4, 2021,
aiatsis.gov.au/explore/1967-referendum.

13. Kathy Lothian, "Seizing the Time: Australian Aborigines and
the Influence of the Black Panther Party, 1969–1972," *Journal of
Black Studies* 35, no. 4 (March 2005): 179–200, www.jstor.org
/stable/40027217.

14. Ibid.

15. Ibid.

16. Kathy Lothian, "Moving Blackwards: Black Power and the Aboriginal Embassy," *Transgressions* 16 (2007): 19–34.

17. Lothian, "Seizing the Time."

18. Foley, "Black Power in Redfern"; Heather Goodall, *Invasion to Embassy: Land in Aboriginal Politics in New South Wales, 1770–1972* (Sydney: Sydney University Press, 2008)

19. Bain Attwood, *Rights for Aborigines* (New York: Routledge, 2020).

20. Foley, "Black Power in Redfern."

21. Lothian, "Seizing the Time."

22. "Federal Bureau of Investigation (FBI)," The Martin Luther King,
Jr. Research and Education Institute, accessed September 15, 2023,
kinginstitute.stanford.edu/federal-bureau-investigation-fbi.

23. "Malcolm and the Civil Rights Movement," American Experience,
June 22, 2018, www.pbs.org/wgbh/americanexperience/features
/malcolmx-and-civil-rights-movement.

24. "Malcolm X Backs House Rights Bill," *The New York Times*, March
27, 1964, www.nytimes.com/1964/03/27/archives/malcolm-x-backs
-house-rights-bill.html.

25. Lothian, "Seizing the Time."

26. Bruce McGuinness, "Review of the Book *Black Power* by S. Carmichael and C. V. Hamilton," *The Koorier* 1, no. 7 (1969), 12.

27. McGuinness, "Review of the Book *Black Power*"; Lothian, "Seizing
the Time."

28. Lothian, "Seizing the Time."

29. Lothian, "Seizing the Time."

30. Bruce McGuinness, "Will the Real Honky Please Stand Up?" *Origin*
3, no. 1 (1970), 6.

31. Lothian, "Moving Blackwards."

32. "Meagher Hits Back at Black Power Leader," *The Ballarat Courier*, August 30, 1969, www.kooriweb.org/foley/images/history/1960s /aalbp/rbdx.html.
33. Lothian, "Seizing the Time."
34. Ibid.
35. Ibid.
36. Ibid.; Black Panther Party of Australia, *Manifesto number three*, 1972.
37. Gary Foley, "One Black Life," *Rolling Stone Yearbook* (1988), 107–11.
38. Lothian, "Seizing the Time."
39. John Halden Wootten, *The New South Wales Aboriginal Legal Service*, 1974; Lothian, "Seizing the Time."
40. J. Norelle Lickiss, "Aboriginal Children in Sydney: The Socio-Economic Environment," *Oceania* 41, no. 3 (March 1971): 201–28.
41. Victoria M. Massie, "The Most Radical Thing the Black Panthers Did Was Give Kids Free Breakfast," *Vox*, October 15, 2016. www .vox.com/2016/2/14/10981986/black-panthers-breakfast-beyonce.
42. "'One of the Biggest, Baddest Things We Did': Black Panthers' Free Breakfasts, 50 Years On," *The Guardian*, October 18, 2019, www .theguardian.com/us-news/2019/oct/17/black-panther-party-oak land-free-breakfast-50th-anniversary.
43. Lothian, "Moving Blackwards."
44. Ibid.
45. Ibid.
46. Ibid.
47. Ibid; S. Robinson, "The Aboriginal Embassy: An Account of the Protests of 1972," *Aboriginal History* 18, no. 1/2 (1994): 49–63, www .jstor.org/stable/24046088.
48. Lothian, "Moving Blackwards."

14. Fear of a Brown Continent

1. Geoff Thompson, "Oceanic Viking Refugees Begin Resettlement," ABC News, last updated December 18, 2009, www.abc.net .au/news/2009-12-19oceanic-viking-refugees-begin-resettlement /1184716.
2. ABCLibrarySales, *Voice of the People: The White Australia Policy (1962)*, YouTube, January 22, 2018, video, 2:53, www.youtube.com /watch?v=6zb8yLammA0.

3. Ibid.
4. Ibid.
5. Ibid.
6. Ibid.
7. Jeremy Martens, "A Transnational History of Immigration Restriction: Natal and New South Wales, 1896–97," *The Journal of Imperial and Commonwealth History* 34, no. 3 (2006): 323–44.
8. Willard, *History of the White Australia Policy to 1920.*
9. Peter Richardson, "The Natal Sugar Industry, 1849–1905: An Interpretative Essay," *The Journal of African History* 23, no. 4 (1982): 515–27.
10. Richardson, "Natal Sugar Industry."
11. Martens, "Transnational History."
12. Ibid.
13. Ibid.
14. Ibid.
15. Jeremy Martens, "Pioneering the Dictation Test? The Creation and Administration of Western Australia's Immigration Restriction Act, 1897–1901," *Studies in Western Australian History* 28 (2013): 47–67.
16. Ibid.
17. Ibid.
18. Farrell Evans, "How Jim Crow–Era Laws Suppressed the African American Vote for Generations," History.com, last updated August 8, 2023, www.history.com/news/jim-crow-laws-black-vote.
19. Marilyn Lake, "White Man's Country: The Trans-National History of a National Project," *Australian Historical Studies* 34, no. 122 (October 2003): 346–63.
20. Ibid.; Martens, "A Transnational History."
21. Alan Lester, "Imperial Networks: Creating Identities in Nineteenth-Century South Africa and Britain," in *The New Imperial Histories Reader*, ed. Stephen Howe (London: Routledge, 2020), 139–46; Martens, "A Transnational History."
22. World Health Organization, *Global Tuberculosis Report 2022*, October 27, 2022, www.who.int/teams/global-tuberculosis-programme/tb-reports/global-tuberculosis-report-2022.

16. Mythologizing the Mixed Baby

1. Homi Bhabha, "Of Mimicry and Man: The Ambivalence of Colonial Discourse," *October* 28 (Spring 1984): 125–33.

2. Katherine Ellinghaus, "Absorbing the 'Aboriginal Problem': Controlling Interracial Marriage in Australia in the Late 19th and Early 20th Centuries," *Aboriginal History* 27 (2003): 183–207.

3. Ibid.

4. Ibid.

5. Ibid.

6. A. O. Neville, *Australia's Coloured Minority: Its Place in the Community* (Sydney: Currawong Publishing Co., 1947); Ellinghaus, "Absorbing the 'Aboriginal problem.'"

7. Christine B. Hickman, "The Devil and the One Drop Rule: Racial Categories, African Americans, and the U.S. Census," *Michigan Law Review* 95, no. 5 (1997): 1161.

8. Ibid.

9. F. James Davis, *Who Is Black?: One Nation's Definition* (University Park, PA: The Pennsylvania State University Press, 2001); Hickman, "Devil and the One Drop Rule."

10. J. C. Furnas, *Goodbye to Uncle Tom* (New York: W. Sloane Associates, 1956).

11. Carol Thomas, *Sexual Assault: Issues for Aboriginal Women* (Australian Institute of Criminology, 1993).

12. Ellinghaus, "Absorbing the 'Aboriginal Problem.'"

13. Ibid.

14. Thomas, *Sexual Assault*; Amanda Kane Rooks, "Sexual Violation and the 'Amoral' Woman in Aboriginal Verse," *Antipodes* 26, no. 1 (June 2012): 49–54.

15. Rooks, "Sexual Violation and the 'Amoral' Woman."

16. Boni Robertson, Catherine Demosthenous, and Hellene Demosthenous, "Stories from the Aboriginal Women of the Yarning Circle: When Cultures Collide," *Hecate* 31, no. 2 (2005): 34–44.

17. Rooks, "Sexual Violation and the 'Amoral' Woman."

18. David Margan, "Department's 'Flawed Culture' Led to Aurukun Rape: Former Staffer," ABC News, last updated December 19, 2007, www.abc.net.au/news/2007-12-20/departments-flawed-culture-led-to-aurukun-rape/2600226.

19. Barbara McMahon, "Nine Who Gang Raped Girl, 10, Escape Jail," *The Guardian*, December 11, 2007, www.theguardian.com/world/2007/dec/11/australia.barbaramcmahon; Rob Taylor, "Aust. police rule out sweep after child rape horror," *Reuters*, December 13, 2007, www.reuters.com/article/us-australia-aborigines-idUSSYD21441020071213.

20. Rooks, "Sexual Violation and the 'Amoral' Woman."
21. Ibid.
22. Ibid.
23. Martens, "A Transnational History."
24. John Harris, "Hiding the Bodies: The Myth of the Humane Colonisation of Aboriginal Australia," *Aboriginal History* 27 (2003): 79–104.
25. Ibid.
26. Ibid.
27. Ibid.
28. "Creation of the Reserve System," Deadly Story, accessed November 11, 2023, deadlystory.com/page/culture/history/Creation_of_reserve_system.

17. Problematizing Patriotism

1. "Why We Look to America," *The Mercury* (Hobart), March 16, 1942.
2. Ibid.
3. Sean Brawley and Chris Dixon, "Jim Crow Downunder? African American Encounters with White Australia, 1942–1945," *Pacific Historical Review* 71, no. 4 (November 2002): 607–32.
4. Kay Saunders and Helen Taylor, "The Reception of Black American Servicemen in Australia During World War II: The Resilience of 'White Australia,'" *Journal of Black Studies* 25, no. 3 (January 1995): 331–48, www.jstor.org/stable/2784641.
5. Ibid.
6. Ibid.
7. Brawley and Dixon, "Jim Crow Downunder?"
8. Ibid.
9. Saunders and Taylor, "Reception of Black American Servicemen."
10. Ibid.
11. Ibid.
12. Ibid.
13. Brawley and Dixon, "Jim Crow Downunder?"
14. Kay Saunders, "Racial Conflict in Brisbane in World War II: The Imposition of Patterns of Segregation upon Black American Servicemen," *Brisbane at War. Brisbane History Group Papers* 4 (1986): 29–34; Saunders and Taylor, "Reception of Black American Servicemen."
15. Saunders, "Racial Conflict in Brisbane."

16. Pelzeman to Walker, February 12, 1943, in Records of U.S. Army Operational, Tactical, and Support Organizations (World War II and Thereafter), T-1419, RG 338, National Archives; Schooley to Corrigan, February 20, 1943, in Records of U.S. Army Operational, Tactical, and Support Organizations (World War II and Thereafter), T-1419, RG 338, National Archives; John F. Line to Mrs. J. F. Line, undated, in Records of U.S. Army Operational, Tactical, and Support Organizations (World War II and Thereafter), T-1419, RG 338, National Archives; Barnwell, "Investigation of Racial Clashes," *Baltimore Afro-American*, September 4, 1943; Brawley and Dixon, "Jim Crow Downunder?"

17. Annette Potts and Lucinda Strauss, *For the Love of a Soldier: Australian War-brides and Their GIs* (Crows Nest, New South Wales, 1987), 63. (Australian Broadcasting Corporation, 1987), 63; Brawley and Dixon, "Jim Crow Downunder?"

18. Victoria Grieves, "Interracial Marriage, Children and a Family Forged in World War II Australia: Mum Dot's Heartbreak Marriage to an African American Sailor," *Vida!*, Australian Women's History Network, December 13, 2017, www.auswhn.com.au/blog/interracial-marriage-wwii.

19. Grieves, "Interracial Marriage, Children and a Family Forged in World War II Australia."

20. Saunders, "Conflict between the American and Australian Governments."

21. Paul Gilroy, "Nationalism, History and Ethnic Absolutism," *History Workshop*, no. 30 (Autumn 1990): 114–20.

18. A Graveyard of Streets

1. Paul H. D. Kaplan, "The Calenberg Altarpiece: Black African Christians in Renaissance Germany," in *Germany and the Black Diaspora: Points of Contact, 1250–1914*, ed. Mischa Honeck, Martin Klimke, and Anne Kuhlmann (Brooklyn: Berghahn Books, 2013), 21–37.

2. Paul H. D. Kaplan, "Black Africans in Hohenstaufen Iconography," *Gesta* 26, no. 1 (1987): 29–36.

3. Ibid.

4. Ibid.

5. Ibid.

6. Jennifer Neal, "How Berlin Is Reckoning With Germany's Colonial

Past," *Atlas Obscura*, November 19, 2020, www.atlasobscura.com /articles/renaming-racist-berlin-streets.

7. Balthazar Becker, "Rothberg, Michael. *Multidirectional Memory: Remembering the Holocaust in the Age of Decolonization* (Stanford: Stanford UP, 2010), 379." *Kritikon Litterarum* 43, no. 3–4 (2016): 308–13.

8. Neal, "How Berlin Is Reckoning With Germany's Colonial Past."

9. Philip Oltermann, "Germany agrees to pay Namibia €1.1bn over historical Herero-Nama genocide," *The Guardian*, May 28, 2021, www .theguardian.com/world/2021/may/28/germany-agrees-to-pay -namibia-11bn-over-historical-herero-nama-genocide.

10. Katharina Oguntoye, May Opitz, and Dagmar Schultz, *Farbe bekennen. Afro-deutsche Frauen auf den Spuren ihrer Geschichte.* (Berlin: Orlanda, 1986).

11. Neal, "How Berlin Is Reckoning With Germany's Colonial Past."

12. "Martha Ndumbe," Stolpersteine Berlin, accessed December 1, 2023, www.stolpersteine-berlin.de/de/max-beer-str/24/martha -ndumbe.

13. "Martha Ndumbe," Stolpersteine Berlin.

14. Benji Haughton, "Bonnie's Ranch: Berlin's notorious psychiatric hospital," *Exberliner*, March 11, 2021, www.exberliner.com/politics /bonnies-ranch.

15. "Martha Ndumbe," Stolpersteine Berlin.

16. Jennifer Neal, "The Overlooked History of Berlin's Black Community," *Atlas Obscura*, December 1, 2021, www.atlasobscura.com /articles/history-black-community-germany.

17. Julia Roos, "Schwarze Schmach," 1914 1918 Online, last updated May 28, 2015, encyclopedia.1914-1918-online.net/article /schwarze_schmach.

18. Timothy Scott Brown, "The SA in the Radical Imagination of the Long Weimar Republic," *Central European History* 46, no. 2 (June 2013): 238–74.

19. "Martha Ndumbe," Stolpersteine Berlin.

20. "Martha Ndumbe," Stolpersteine Berlin.

21. James Q. Whitman, *Hitler's American Model: The United States and the Making of Nazi Race Law* (Princeton: Princeton University Press, 2017).

22. Ibid.

23. Ibid.

24. Ibid.

25. Ibid.

26. "Mahjub bin Adam Mohamed," Stolpersteine Berlin, accessed December 1, 2023, www.stolpersteine-berlin.de/de/brunnenstr/193/mahjub-bayume-mohamed-bin-adam-mohamed-husen.

27. Harrison Mwilima, "The Swahili Teacher Killed in a Concentration Camp," *DW*, December 11, 2020, www.dw.com/en/the-swahili-teacher-killed-in-a-nazi-concentration-camp/a-55821458.

28. Mwilima, "Swahili Teacher Killed in a Concentration Camp."

29. Ibid.

30. Neal, "How Berlin Is Reckoning With Germany's Colonial Past."

31. Kenneth M. Ludmerer, "Genetics, Eugenics, and the Immigration Restriction Act of 1924," *Bulletin of the History of Medicine* 46, no. 1 (1972): 59–81.

32. Ludmerer, "Genetics, Eugenics, and the Immigration Restriction Act of 1924."

33. Whitman, *Hitler's American Model*.

34. "Ferdinand James Allen," Stolpersteine Berlin, accessed September 9, 2023, www.stolpersteine-berlin.de/de/torstr/174/ferdinand-james-allen.

35. Ibid.

36. Ibid.

37. Ibid.

19. Nazis on the Train

1. Katrin Bennhold, "Chemnitz Protests Show New Strength of Germany's Far Right." *The New York Times*, August 31, 2018. www.nytimes.com/2018/08/30/world/europe/germany-neo-nazi-protests-chemnitz.html.

2. Reuters in Berlin, "AfD Co-Founder Says Germans Should Be Proud of Its Second World War Soldiers." *The Guardian*, September 14, 2017, www.theguardian.com/world/2017/sep/14/afd-co-founder-alexander-gauland-says-germany-needs-to-reclaim-its-history.

3. Rebecca Staudenmaier, "Gay in the AfD: 'We're Not Seeking Equality,'" *DW*, March 19, 2017, www.dw.com/en/gay-in-the-afd-talking-with-lgbt-supporters-of-germanys-populist-party/a-38002368.

4. Loveday Morris and Kate Brady, "Germany's Far-Right Party Is More Popular Than Ever—and More Extreme," *The Washington*

Post, last updated August 21, 2023, www.washingtonpost.com
/world/2023/08/18/germany-afd-polls-krah.

5. Morris and Brady, "Germany's Far-Right Party Is More Popular
   Than Ever."

6. Gabriel Rinaldi, "3 Ways Germany's Migration Crisis Is Different
   This Time Around," *Politico*, www.politico.eu/article/germany-mig
   ration-crisis-refugees-asylum-seekers-ukraine-2022.

7. Josie Le Bond, "The Germans Welcoming Refugees into Their
   Homes," UNHCR, www.unhcr.org/news/stories/germans-wel
   coming-refugees-their-homes.

8. Christoph Hasselbach, "Syrian Refugees Find a Safe Haven in Germany," *DW*, www.dw.com/en/syrian-refugees-find-a-safe-haven-in
   -germany/a-56872099.

9. Philip Oltermann, "Syrian Refugee Drops Out of German Parliament Election After Threats," *The Guardian*, March 31, 2021,
   www.theguardian.com/world/2021/mar/31/syrian-refugee-drops
   -out-of-german-parliament-election-after-threats.

10. Philip Oltermann, "Crowd Cheer Fire at Hotel Being Converted
    into Refugee Shelter in Saxony," *The Guardian*, February 12, 2016,
    www.theguardian.com/world/2016/feb/21/crowd-cheers-fire
    -hotel-refugee-shelter-saxony-germany.

11. Amnesty International, *Living in Insecurity: How Germany is Failing
    Victims of Racist Violence* (London: Amnesty International Publica-
    tions, 2016).

12. "Germany hate crime: Nearly 10 attacks a day on migrants in
    2016," BBC News, February 26, 2017, www.bbc.com/news/world
    -europe-39096833.

13. Martha Gellhorn, *The Face of War* (New York: Simon and Schuster,
    1959).

14. AP, "Far-Right Protesters March in Berlin, Demand Merkel Ouster,"
    The Times of Israel, November 6, 2016, www.timesofisrael.com
    /far-right-protesters-march-in-berlin-demand-merkel-ouster.

15. Agence France-Presse, "Pig's Head Found Outside German Chan-
    cellor Angela Merkel's Office," *The Guardian*, May 15, 2016, www
    .theguardian.com/world/2016/may/15/pigs-head-found-out
    side-german-chancellor-angela-merkels-office.

16. Philip Oltermann, "Angela Merkel's Party Beaten by Rightwing
    Populists in German Elections," *The Guardian*, September 6, 2016,
    www.theguardian.com/world/2016/sep/04/mecklenburg-vorpom

mern-german-anti-immigrant-party-strong-regional-election-exit
-polls-merkel.

17. Oltermann, "Angela Merkel's Party Beaten."

20. Dance Your Fucking Tits Off, Bitch

1. "Race ≠ Rasse: 10 terms Related to Race That Require Sensitivity in Translation," *poco.lit.*, April 9, 2021, pocolit.com/en/2021/04/09/race-%E2%89%A0-rasse-10-terms-related-to-race-that-require-sensitivity-in-translation.

2. Johanna Rothe, "Fatima El-Tayeb. *European Others: Queering Ethnicity in Postnational Europe,*" *International Feminist Journal of Politics* 15, no. 4 (2013): 572–74.

3. Basic Law for the Federal Republic of Germany in the revised version published in the Federal Law Gazette Part III, classification number 100-1, as last amended by the Act of 19 December 2022, www.gesetze-im-internet.de/englisch_gg/englisch_gg.html.

4. "Race ≠ Rasse."

5. Anna von Rath and Lucy Gasser, "10 Terms Related to Gender and Sexuality That Require Sensitivity in Translation," Goethe Institut, February 2021, www.goethe.de/ins/gb/en/kul/lue/art/art/22105931.html.

6. Von Rath and Gasser, "10 Terms Related to Gender and Sexuality."

7. Volker Witting, "Germany's Heated Debate over 'Race' in the Constitution," *DW*, June 13, 2020, www.dw.com/en/race-has-no-place-in-the-german-constitution-or-does-it/a-53790056.

8. Aminata Touré and Robert Habeck, "Diskriminierung in Deutschland: Verlernen wir Rassismus!" *taz*, June 9, 2020, taz.de/Diskriminierung-in-Deutschland/!5687742.

9. Witting, "Germany's Heated Debate over 'Race' in the Constitution."

10. Cengiz Barskanmaz and Nahed Samour, "Das Diskriminierungsverbot aufgrund der Rasse," *Verfassungsblog on Matters Constitutional*, June 16, 2020, verfassungsblog.dedas-diskriminierungsverbot-aufgrund-der-rasse.

11. Ibid.

12. Ibid.; El-Tayeb, "Blackness and Its (Queer) Discontents."

13. Ibid.

14. Ibid.

15. Ibid.

16. Oguntoye, Opitz, and Schultz, *Farbe bekennen*.

17. Margaret MacCarroll, "May Ayim: A Woman in the Margin of German Society" (master's thesis, Florida State University, 2005), digi nole.lib.fsu.edu/islandora/object/fsu:181057/datastream/PDF.

18. Silke Mertins, "Blues in Black and White: May Ayim (1960–1996)," in *Blues in Black and White: A Collection of Essays, Poetry, and Conversations*, trans. Anne V. Adams (Trenton: Africa World Press, Inc., 2003), 141–67.

19. May Ayim, "mama," in *Blues in Black and White: Essays, Poetry, and Conversations*, trans. Anne V. Adams (Trenton: Africa World Press, Inc., 2003), 24.

20. Mertins, "Blues in Black and White."

21. MacCarroll, "May Ayim."

22. Julia Roos, "Die 'farbigen Besatzungskinder' der zwei Weltkriege," BPB, March 18, 2022, www.bpb.de/shop/zeitschriften/apuz/schwarz-und-deutsch-2022/506170die-farbigen-besatzungskinder-der-zwei-weltkriege.

23. MacCarroll, "May Ayim."

24. Eva Simonsen, "Into the Open—or Hidden Away? The Construction of War Children as a Social Category in Post-War Norway and Germany," *NordEuropaforum* 2 (2006): 25–49.

25. Rosemarie K. Lester, "Blacks in Germany and German Blacks: A Little-Known Aspect of Black History," in *Blacks in German Culture: Essays*, ed. Reinhold Grimm and Jost Hermand (Madison: University of Wisconsin Press, 1986), 113–34.

26. Oguntoye, Opitz, and Schultz, *Farbe bekennen*.

27. Lester, "Blacks in Germany and German Blacks."

28. Simonsen, "Into the Open—or Hidden Away?"

29. Ibid.

30. Roos, "Die 'farbigen Besatzungskinder' der zwei Weltkriege."

31. Ibid.

32. Ibid.

33. Simonsen, "Into the Open—or Hidden Away?"

34. Aman, "A Reading in the Poetry of the Afro-German May Ayim."

35. "Über uns," Die Initiative Schwarzer Menschen in Deutschland, accessed September 10, 2023, isdonline.de/ueber-uns/#geschichte.

36. Neal, "How Berlin Is Reckoning With Germany's Colonial Past."

37. Oguntoye, Opitz, and Schultz, *Farbe bekennen*.

38. Tina M. Campt, "Reading the Black German Experience: An Introduction," *Callaloo* 26, no. 2 (Spring 2003): 288–94.

39. Oguntoye, Opitz, and Schultz, *Farbe bekennen*.
40. Charly Wilder, "Audre Lorde's Berlin," *The New York Times*, July 19, 2019, www.nytimes.com/2019/07/19/travel/berlin-audre-lorde .html.
41. Wilder, "Audre Lorde's Berlin."

Author's Note

1. *Being Black in the EU—Experiences of People of African Descent* (Vienna: European Union Agency for Fundamental Rights, 2023), fra .europa.eu/en/publication/2023/being-black-eu.

Suggested Reading

1. Justin McCurry, "Neo-Nazi Photos Pose Headache for Shinzo Abe," *The Guardian*, September 9, 2014, www.theguardian.com/world /2014/sep/09/neo-nazi-photos-pose-headache-for-shinzo-abe.
2. Justin McCurry, "Police in Japan Place Anti-Korean Extremist Group Zaitokukai on Watchlist," *The Guardian*, December 4, 2014, www .theguardian.com/world/2014/dec/04/police-japan-rightwing-anti -korean-extremist-group-zaitokukai-watchlist.
3. Caitlin Yoshiko Kandil, "Think Reparations Are Impossible? The Story of Japanese Americans Proves Otherwise," *The Guardian*, September 4, 2023, www.theguardian.com/us-news/2023/sep/04 /japanese-americans-incarceration-reparations-slavery.
4. Okada Yasuhiro, "Race, Masculinity, and Military Occupation: African American Soldiers' Encounters with the Japanese at Camp Gifu, 1947–1951," *The Journal of African American History* 96, no. 2 (Spring 2011): 179–203.
5. James M. Scott, "'An Orgy of Mass Murder': In a New Book, James M. Scott, NF '07, Investigates World War II Atrocities in the Philippines," *NiemanReports*, October 30, 2018, niemanreports.org /articles/an-orgy-of-mass-murder-in-a-new-book-james-m-scott -nf-07-investigates-world-war-ii-atrocities-in-the-philippines.
6. Bob Drogin, "This City Was Ravaged in WWII. Why Do Few Remember the Suffering and Sacrifice?" *Los Angeles Times*, May 29, 2023, www.latimes.com/world-nation/story/2023-05-29/manila-was -ravaged-in-wwii-why-does-no-one-remember-this.
7. Michelle Sibilla, Fiana Arbab, Afaf Humayun, Narmeen Shammami, and Alex Kaniaris, "Biographical Sketch of Charlotte 'Lottie'

Wilson Jackson,1854–1914," Alexander Street, accessed December 1, 2023, documents.alexanderstreet.com/d/1007600749.

8. Spencer Ackerman, "The Disappeared: Chicago Police Detain Americans at Abuse-Laden 'Black Site,'" *The Guardian*, February 24, 2015, www.theguardian.com/us-news/2015/feb/24/chicago-police -detain-americans-black-site.

9. Spencer Ackerman, "Homan Square Revealed: How Chicago Police 'Disappeared' 7,000 People," *The Guardian*, October 19, 2015, www .theguardian.com/us-news/2015/oct/19/homan-square-chicago -police-disappeared-thousands.

10. Jacqui Palumbo, "The Somali-French Art Dealer Bringing Black Perspectives to Paris' Gallery Scene," CNN, May 5, 2022, edition.cnn .com/style/article/mariane-ibrahim-paris-gallery-nomad/index .html.

11. "Apology to Australias Indigenous Peoples," Parliament of Australia, accessed December 1, 2023, www.aph.gov.au/Visit_Parliament /Art/Icons/Apology_to_Australias_Indigenous_Peoples.

12. "The Mabo Case," AIATSIS, accessed December 1, 2023, aiatsis .gov.au/explore/mabo-case.

13. "Deaths in Custody," ANTAR, last updated December 12, 2023, antar.org.au/issues/justice/deaths-custody.

14. "The 1938 Day of Mourning," AIATSIS, accessed December 1, 2023, aiatsis.gov.au/explore/day-of-mourning.

15. "The 1938 Day of Mourning."

16. J. T. Patten and W. Ferguson, *Aborigines Claim Citizen Rights!: A Statement of the Case for the Aborigines Progressive Association* (Sydney: The Publicist, 1938).

17. "The 1938 Day of Mourning."

18. Ibid.

19. Tracey Flanagan, Meredith Wilkie, and Susanna Iuliano, "Australian South Sea Islanders: A Century of Race Discrimination Under Australian Law," Australian Human Rights Commission, January 1, 2003, humanrights.gov.au/our-work/race-discrimination/publications /australian-south-sea-islanders-century-race.

20. Ally Foster, Alex Turner-Cohen, Clare Sibthorpe, and Samantha Maiden, "Indigenous Voice to Parliament: Lidia Thorpe Slams Voice to Parliament Referendum as 'Waste of Money,'" news.co.au, October 14, 2023, www.news.com.au/national/politics/indigenous -voice-to-parliament/news-story/09e16ebc27cf92c30570adcc8596 bab4.

21. Jessica Hinchliffe, "Boundary Street Signs Changed to 'Boundless' in Brisbane's West End in Anonymous Nod to Dark Past," ABC News, last updated January 27, 2016, www.abc.net.au/news/2016 -01-27/streets-signs-changed-from-boundary-to-boundless-street /7117038.

22. Nick Whigham, "The Dark History Behind Brisbane Street Name," *Yahoo! News,* last updated June 14, 2020, au.news.yahoo.com/the-dark-history-behind-brisbane-street-names-085139596.html.

23. Marc Saha, "NSU: Germany's Infamous Neo-Nazi Terror Cell," *DW,* November 3, 2021, www.dw.com/en/nsu-germany/a-39777036.

24. Lauren Jackson, Tara Godvin, Katrin Bennhold, Melissa Eddy, Christopher F. Schuetze, and Peter Robins, "On the Path to Day X: The Return of Germany's Far Right," *The New York Times,* last updated July 6, 2021, www.nytimes.com/2021/06/25/world/europe /germany-nazi-far-right.html.

25. Sigrid Kneist, "Zwei neue Stolpersteine in Schöneberg: Gedenken an die Opfer des NS-Rassenwahns," *Tagesspiegel,* August 23, 2023, www.tagesspiegel.de/zwei-neue-stolpersteine-in-schoneberg-ged enken-an-die-opfer-des-ns-rassenwahns-10348882.html.

26. "Verlegung von neun Stolpersteinen in Kreuzberg," Berlin.de, October 2, 2023, www.berlin.de/ba-friedrichshain-kreuzberg/aktuelles /pressemitteilungen/2023/pressemitteilung.1371518.php.

27. "Stolpersteinverlegung für Zoya Aqua-Kaufmann und ihren Sohn Hans Joachim," Museumsportal Berlin, accessed December 2, 2023, www.museumsportal-berlin.de/de/veranstaltungen/stol persteinverlegung-fuer-zoya-aqua-kaufmann-und-ihren-sohn -hans-joachim; grid Kneist, "Der lange Weg zur Erinnerung: Wie schwarze Menschen der Verfolgung durch die Nazis ausgesetzt waren," *Tagesspiegel,* March 7, 2023, www.tagesspiegel.de/berlin /bezirke/der-lange-weg-zur-erinnerung-wie-schwarze-menschen -der-verfolgung-durch-die-nazis-ausgesetzt-waren-9466727.html.

28. Kneist, "Der lange Weg zur Erinnerung."

29. Philip Oltermann, "German Police Urged to Re-Investigate Asylum Seeker's Death in Custody," *The Guardian,* November 12, 2013, www.theguardian.com/world/2013/nov/12/german-police -asylum-seeker-death-in-custody.

30. Elliot Douglas, "Oury Jalloh: Police, Courts and Politicians Made Mistakes," *DW,* August 28, 2020, www.dw.com/en/germany-asylum -seeker-dessau-oury-jalloh/a-54727651.